Life for Life's Sake

A BOOK OF REMINISCENCES

RICHARD ALDINGTON

LIFE FOR
LIFE'S SAKE

A Book of Reminiscences

CASSELL · LONDON

CASSELL & COMPANY LTD
35 Red Lion Square, London W C 1
Melbourne, Sydney, Toronto,
Johannesburg, Auckland

S.B.N. 304 93255 8

Printed in Great Britain
by Unwin Brothers Limited
Woking and London
F.768

Dedication

To Leonard Bacon and Howard Lowry:

I asked permission to put your names at the head of this book, because you are responsible for it to the extent that without your (quite independent) suggestions and encouragements it would not have been written.

An autobiography is a license to be egotistical. It is tacitly agreed between author and reader that the former is to be allowed to expatiate on the delightful (to him) subject of himself. I have enjoyed many autobiographies, particularly of travellers and writers, but I had no intention of adding to them; not, at any rate, until I was seventy, and lapses of memory might excusably have been fortified by a little romance. I felt that an autobiography, if written at all, should be positively a last appearance.

For more than ten years I had been engaged on a series of more or less satirical novels, giving my views of the period which was called "post-war" but was in fact merely a long armistice. After listening to Mr. Chamberlain's speech over the radio on the morning of 3 September 1939, I threw the novel I was writing into the waste basket. It would be absurd to denounce calamity; ignoble to satirise people fighting for their existence.

For some months I felt that my occupation in life had gone, and that I had better find something else to do. I was so much haunted by forebodings of the disasters which must inevitably afflict our unfortunate epoch that what little I did write was lifeless. But as the war dragged on, I saw clearly that the Europe I had known and the kind of life I had led there would soon be as much a matter of the past as the 18th century before the French Revolution. Whatever sort of world results from these convulsions will be different from what I have known, and, I suspect, far less pleasant for people like myself, who will doubtless be eliminated. But the mere fact of this sudden and artificial remoteness has enabled me to write of myself and that period of my life with a certain detachment, as if I were treating a historical theme. It would be presumption to think that such a record might interest a future generation, but I can at least hope that it may amuse a few people in still intact America, if only because of its remoteness from the familiar scene.

One last point. Certain reticences in this book may excite comment. Yeats used to say of George Moore: "Other men kiss and don't tell; George Moore tells and doesn't kiss." I would give a great deal to write as well as George Moore, but in this respect I prefer to be like other men.

Richard Aldington wrote these memoirs as the Second World War brought the collapse of the life he had known. In 1939 he moved to New York with his wife and daughter and there the book was written. It was published by the Viking Press, New York, in 1940 and received critical acclaim, one reviewer saying that it was "as great as his *Death of a Hero, All Men are Enemies* and *The Colonel's Daughter*".

Mr. Cyril Connolly recently remarked in the *Sunday Times* that he could not understand why this excellent book of memoirs had never appeared in Britain. There were no doubt good reasons at the time. 1940 was a highly critical year. The advent of paper rationing made publishers very wary. And there was undoubtedly a chauvinistic feeling about those who had made their home overseas when the country was at war.

But these events are now more than a quarter of a century behind us, while the book seems an important one for the light which it casts upon the literary scene in the twenties and early thirties. It is therefore at last being published in Britain in the expectation that it will take its place among the valuable literary memoirs of its period.

Aldington remained in the United States, where he died on 27 July 1962.

D.F.
35 Red Lion Square, WC1.

"To talk in public, to think in solitude, to read and to hear, to inquire and answer inquiries, is the business of a scholar. He wanders about the world without pomp or terror, and is neither known nor valued but by men like himself." —RASSELAS.

Chapter I

"IT'S long past your bedtime. See! The mist is rising," she said, holding me up to the window. There was a blood-red streak on the horizon, and the wheat stooks were dark in the twilight. I didn't know what mist was, and hopefully expected the piled wheat sheaves would levitate, perhaps fly up into the sky and disappear.

"There, you see?" she said. "Now off to bed we go."

But my voice filled the air with wails of protest. The ruthless logic of children and savages was outraged. The mist (i.e., the piled wheat) was not rising; therefore it was not late; therefore I should be allowed to stay up longer. But how to put that into words, how even to formulate it as anything approaching an idea, I didn't know. All that was manifest and indisputable was the evil nature of my nursemaid. So early do we discover with astonishment and indignation that our view of the universe differs from that of others. So early those who disagree with us are the wicked.

There was a strange narrow little room, with windows at each end and a high green seat along each side. The order of the incomprehensible but all-knowing ones was to sit still, when plainly the sensible thing was to profit by the high seat, and slide off and climb back as often as possible. Presently something or somebody uttered a loud shriek, and puffed ferociously, and the little room began to move. It moved fast, fast, fast, and the flat green earth went circling backwards. Sometimes it slowed and stopped, and you saw the tops of men go

A*

by the window. What had they done with their legs? Then on and on, with more stops, until all the green earth had gone in blackness, and you got tired of the little room, and the all-powerful ones refused to produce a glass of milk, and refused to let you get out of the little room, and were annoyed by your protests. And then, O magic! O wonder! the little room glided gently into a high palace of great glittering lights, lovely sharp-edged lights, so good, so dazzling after the long blackness. And you were released from the horrid little room and carried half asleep through a jam of people, looking up, up at the sharp magic lights.

So for a time I became a town child. There was no wheat field behind the new house, no trees and flower garden in front. From the bedroom windows I saw a large asphalt yard with a row of dust bins and the backs of houses. From the other windows I saw the High Street, full of umbrellas and horses; and opposite, the fronts of houses with shops. Whenever I looked at the yard it was wet with rain; whenever I looked at the street there were bobbing black umbrellas glistening with rain. Waking in the morning I would hear dimly the "clop, clop" of horses' hoofs on the stones, and because of the queer hollow echoing sound I knew there was still rain. Yet even here was magic. On the floor of the two attics lay little coloured pictures, heads of men and women, ships, a parrot. If the angels had shed peacock feathers on the floor they could not have seemed more supernatural and delightful. . . .

"How did you get hold of those stamps?" said my father severely.

The first time I saw one of the old brownstone houses in New York I stopped to look at it with surprise, and that tenderness we feel at the unexpected revival of childish memories. There in Manhattan was a near cousin to the house I lived in after leaving the one which rained down a manna of postage stamps. True, the English version was in yellow brick and perhaps a little smaller. Everything else was there, even the awkward flight of stone steps leading to the front door, steps which in those days had to be whitened daily by sad housemaids. There were the same area steps and semi-basement, providing the servants with a plentiful lack of air and sunlight. Was the style imported into England by some wandering jerry-builder? Had there been an international competition in ugliness?

In other respects this move was a gain, because in front of the house stood a fine avenue of old trees, and at the back was a longish but narrow garden; behind that, a large market garden of vegetables, flowers and fruit trees. So that when I looked from the windows I again saw a green world. From there I went to a small private school, and at an incredibly tender age was set to learning the less important exceptions in the rules of French and Latin grammar. Some of these I still remember. For instance, the French words ending in *"al"* which form the plural by adding *"s,"* instead of changing to *"aux"*:

"Bal, cal, carnaval, chacal, régal, nopal, pal."

Now in the course of my life I have written some hundreds of letters in French, chiefly to authors, without ever having had a chance to display this valuable knowledge. For some reason we never discussed balls, calluses, carnivals, jackals, treats, nopals, or instruments for impalement. So I have had to be content with knowing for knowing's sake.

The obvious way of going to school was out the front door and down the street, but for reasons I have forgotten this seemed too tedious or too complicated. Certainly I left by the front door, but then immediately made my way by the tradesmen's entrance to the garden, and over the end wall into the florist's "horticultural establishment." Here were long rows of interesting vegetables and rare flowers, worth being a little late for French grammar. Occasionally a hoarse and distant

"Oi!"—the garden-god sharp after thieves?—would send me scampering past the greenhouses to the entrance and the safety of the streets.

Directly opposite the school was another of those New York houses, larger than ours, with more white steps, and far gloomier within because every window was bunged up with unhealthy trees. The inhabitants of this perpetual night should have gone about with lights on their heads, like coal miners. Here dwelt a small boy who honoured me with his friendship, the only child of a moderately wealthy widow. Demented either with grief or joy at the death of her husband, this lady formed a large collection of ailing cats who made her heavily furnished house stink like a zoo. She also had a fair-sized aquarium, with a dribbling fountain in the centre, full of diseased goldfish, weeds, fresh-water snails, and slime, which gave an added touch of dampness to this dank and fetid abode.

Fortunately, there was a large garden to which we hurriedly escaped as soon as the lady paused in her narrative of her husband's last illness, which she judged most likely to entertain a young gentleman of five or six. She lived in a constant panic that God would snatch her one ewe lamb, and then where would she be? Consequently her son was not only pallid and over-clothed, but timid and unmuscular, and though two years my senior quite unable to resist my assaults when I chose to invade him. No doubt he had been selected as my companion with the idea that his gentle nature would restrain my mischief; with entirely opposite results. Shrieks of horror and indignation arose when we were discovered some twenty feet up a large mulberry tree stained and smeared with its luscious fruit; for, as I had pointed out, we had only been forbidden to eat the squashed fallen fruits on the earth, and there could be no possible objection to eating the fresh ones high up in the air.

My friend took a gloomy view of his life; and, again at my suggestion, began digging a hole through the centre of the earth to Australia, in order to escape to more genial surroundings. Each evening we concealed this pit with sticks and newspaper sprinkled with earth. Unluckily, when we had got down about three feet, and, according to our calculations, well on the way to Australia, the gardener discovered our plan of escape by falling into it and nearly impaling himself on a five-pronged fork.

There was one unpleasant aspect of my own house. It was full of ghosts. Of course, I had put them there, but they had been put into me by the illustrated Christmas annuals which were supposed to foster the spirit of Christmas and to uplift the young. It seems to me that they were full of pictures of ghosts, each more horrible than the one before. There was a whole series of coloured pictures about the wicked Sir Something de Somebody, who even in limbo wore Elizabethan clothes and a ruff the size of a cartwheel. All of him was spectral white, except for his blood-shot eyes which darted rays of horrid light like a deep-sea fish.

According to my information, this loathly old reprobate from the other world spent the hours of darkness in jumping out on people in dark passages, lurking behind curtains to wave a bony hand, kneeling on their chests when they were asleep, and detaching his head from his body to frighten his victims into fits. Unluckily I was not told that all this was only a combination of healthy humour and Christmas goodwill to men. I took it to be a branch of religious instruction, and calculated with dismay the poor chances of surviving in a world infested with such malignant apparitions. From this it was but a step to seeing Sir Something de Somebody flitting along a passage in the shadows thrown by a moving candle, or hiding

13

with felonious intent under the bed. It was nerve-shattering, and I would as soon go over the top again as brave the terrors of going to bed with Sir Something de Somebody around.

In that house, also, I first became dimly aware of those public events which are supposed to embody the collective wisdom of nations, but in fact seem devised by crafty monsters to prevent any of us living a decent and agreeable life. At breakfast, my father rustled the newspaper and spoke anxiously of a certain Lady Smith, who seemed to be in great trouble somewhere or other. The errand boys began to whistle a new set of tunes of a martial kind. The Queen gave my father a sword and a lovely set of soldier's clothes, which, however, he had to pay through the nose for; and in the evenings a sergeant came and played games with him with matches. At school there was a fashion for collecting celluloid buttons with coloured heads of generals, who possessed odd names such as Gatacre, Buller, Wauchope (who was, I believe, always getting himself and his men "cut up" in some inexplicable way), Baden-Powell.

Patriotic pictures appeared on the nursery wall. One represented a British officer with a cluster of Arrow-collar Tommies waving his revolver at a line of unkempt and ugly Boers, with the caption: "There's no surrender here!" evidently spoken by the heroic English commander. I then blindly admired his courage and determination, but I now think he ought to have been court-martialled for endangering his men and position by allowing the enemy to come so close without opening fire. Some of these pictures were so downright and defiant about British superiority over everything and everyone that with a little alteration and change of caption they might have later come in handy for Dr. Goebbels.

One night I was suddenly awakened from sleep, hurriedly dressed in my sailor suit, and hoisted into a large cart with a number of other children dressed as soldiers and sailors. We paraded about for a very long time in a torch-light procession, with the populace shouting and singing like a pack of maniacs. I didn't know what it was all about. I was cold and sleepy, and the boy next me had a real soldier's suit instead of my commonplace everyday sailor things. All I wanted was to get back to bed, and all I remembered of this strange patriotic orgy was the word "Mafeking."

And as if this were not enough, later on the Queen died. A black band was put on my arm, and I was told to go and play nicely and quietly. As if you can play nicely and quietly! You might just as well not play at all.

But before the Queen's death and before Mafeking, an event happened of more importance to me. I went to live in the country.

Chapter II

I WAS by no means free of the town. For a couple of years we were away only during the summer. Even when we lived entirely in the country I was drawn back to Dover, and spent the larger part of several years at school there. Yet the shorter periods in the country seem the more important. I think one reason is that in the town I was being manufactured into the sort of human product a not too intelligent provincial society thought I should be; whereas, in the country, I was busily but unconsciously developing into something on my own.

Houses and streets are a poor environment for children, even when, as in this case, the town abuts on the sea. Instead of a real shore there was a tame and genteel marine parade, with a pier, a row of slightly decayed Victorian residences, and a yacht club built in the peculiar style affected by yacht clubs, with a great deal of window space showing bald heads and newspapers, and balconies supported by slender iron columns which seemed inadequate to the weight of so many ponderous amateur sailors.

The docks offered more rational entertainment, but they were forbidden to well-guarded children. I don't know why, unless it was suspected that we might be kidnapped as cabin boys by skippers, who doubtless had children of their own and no wish to add to their troubles. But just as it was impossible to refrain wholly from buying hokey-pokey, which was said to be kept under the bed at night and hence to swarm with disagreeable bacilli, so it was impossible not to dodge off occasionally to the docks. There one could stroll along and see the bowsprits and figureheads of sailing ships projecting over the muddy quays, battered-looking tramps noisily swinging derricks, a bustle of bales and casks and cases and sacks, informally clad men messing about in a leisurely way with paint and putty, and enjoy a pungent composite smell of coal, timber, mud, ropes, tar, malt, horse dung, and sea water.

But at most times we were dragooned into walking sedately about the streets, tipping our caps to schoolmasters, old ladies, clergymen, and other enemies. We lived in a world made almost wholly by men, and very dull men too, cut off from earthy verities by bricks and decorum. Nature we touched only at its tamest and most banal, in public parks rich in suburban flora and that odd plant "Keep off the Grass," or in little walled gardens.

It was no earthly paradise I inherited by this change, but a bleak, nearly treeless upland of chalk downs, the South Foreland of England. The roll of these great chalk waves starts inland and grows steeper and steeper as they approach the sea, until the last suddenly breaks into the white English cliffs. Memories of calamities haunted that coast. Tradition and history still remembered a night of terror and destruction, far back in the 11th century, when the rich lands of Earl Godwin, with their villages and churches and cattle, were overwhelmed by the sea. The Earl's vanished property rights were still commemorated in the Goodwin Sands.

They were real enough. Not many big winter storms passed without our hearing the cry: "Ship on the Goodwin Sands!" Out we would rush with field glasses and telescope, and there sure enough the doomed and battered ship weltered in the waves on the verge of that death trap. Faintly but with appalling solemnity the boom of her distress guns came over the wind-torn sea. Next day we would read a curt notice that the coastal lifeboats had or had not saved the crew. No spectacle in towns could approach the terror and grandeur of the lifeboat being launched into seas so tremendous that involuntarily one shrank back from the roar and tumult of waters. For interminable minutes the boat and the men in their shiny oilskins and cork lifebelts waited on the slips for that briefest lull which would make the hazard of launching not wholly desperate. Suddenly there would be a shout, a rush, the mad water swirling round the knees and waists of the launchers, the last man flinging himself aboard, a dizzy lurch and pitch as the light boat hit the first white comber, a curious gasping cheer from the crowd. Women hid their faces in their hands and aprons. Cold and breathless, your eyes smarting with spray, you watched the steady rhythm of the oars, the wild tossing of the boat, until it was only a brave speck occasionally visible on the crest of a wave. Then slowly, reluctantly you would go away, leaving the women to their long sea-drenched wait.

There was nothing to break the force of these gales on the uplands. Most of the houses were so much exposed to the driving rains that double windows were essential. The icy north-easters were fortunately rare. The usual gales were sou'-westers off the Atlantic which came roaring up the bottle-neck of the Channel and forced even the biggest ships to anchor in the Deal Roads. At night during such gales I would peer from the warm lighted room into the darkness, and if it were low tide see dimly far below a great belt of raving foam on the rocks. Later I lay awake in bed with the wind screaming and howling outside, the rain rattling against the outer window like buckets full of dried peas flung against the glass, and the flash of the Foreland lighthouse winking through a gap in the curtain.

You cannot experience the force of such elemental powers in a town. In a town gale there is a certain amount of comic drama, such as everted umbrellas and falling chimney pots, but nothing like the power and beauty of a great wind lashing the sea and sweeping over the downs.

Naturally life on the South Foreland was not merely a succession of storms and shipwrecks. They come first to mind because they were exceptional. Incredible as it may seem, my recollection is that the summers were sunny and warm. How otherwise could I have spent so many days in and out of the sea?

There were three ways down the cliffs, of which I naturally chose the shortest, steepest, and least safe. The advantages of going straight up or down the face of the cliff instead of doodling along a path will be obvious. The cliffs themselves were not wholly reliable. Great cracks formed near the brink, and from time to time a slice broke off like the front of a glacier, walloping down thousands of tons of chalk boulders. I never saw one of these avalanches, but I heard them, a muffled and majestic roar in the distance. It strikes me now that I was a little careless in crossing these cracks to stand on the last verge of the cliff. I knew they portended a fall, but I failed to see that even the slightest extra strain might destroy the precarious balance of weight, and that I might have been the sufficient cause of a cliff avalanche and my own spectacular disappearance.

In the course of ages these falls had formed a band of rocks all along the coast, covered with seaweed, and at low tide full of valuable pools. Exploring these for sea creatures was a timeless pleasure. You wandered on and on in a wilderness of green and brown rocks, into pure solitude out of sight of people and houses. At the tide-edge a light blue sea surged gently. The dazzling white cliffs reflected the sunlight and made the blue sky bluer. Hundreds of gulls and kittiwakes soared or perched in crevices, filling the air with sharp plaintive calls. In the transparent rock pools every frond and shell and darting sea creature was exquisitely clear. How unreasonable were complaints and sanctions on account of being late for meals.

A more serious and admissible pleasure than mere wandering was prawning. The outfit for this barbarous and plebeian sport consisted of half a dozen small drop nets with cork floats, a long pole with a cleft end to lift and lower them at a distance, sharp wooden skewers, a blunt knife, and a fishmonger's straw bag.

The professional began by baiting his net with a bit of spoiled meat. I never reached that distinction. However tactfully I approached cook for a supply of this valuable commodity I was always driven off with insults. How dared I imagine such a disgrace to her larder? What next! I could only suppose that my more fortunate rivals must have buried their dinners, like prudent terriers, and dug them up again at the right moment.

The only alternative was limpets, flat-footed conical shellfish which glue themselves on rocks by creating a partial vacuum. You forced some of these off with the blunt knife, cut them from the shells, and skewered them into the nets. They soon attracted plenty of green and red crabs. You had to handle these nimble and pugnacious beasts with caution, for their claws can nip hard. Then, I regret to say, the crabs were torn in half and skewered, even as the horrid Polyphemus dismembered and skewered the dear companions of Odysseus. With these you fished for prawns.

Unlike most creatures captured by small boys, prawns were considered delicacies, and after a good catch I had the proud satisfaction of seeing them sent off to gastronomic friends in London. There was one old and extremely gastronomic friend of the family, whom I will call Sir Patrick, a successful Scottish barrister at the English bar, who became a judge and was knighted. Legend had it that he was so fond of crustacea that every day for years he lunched at the Junior Carlton Club on lobster and a bottle of champagne, until doctors and his own intestinal troubles forbade. But prawns were still allowed, and the best of my catch went to him.

I don't recollect any tangible expression of gratitude from other beneficiaries, but Sir Patrick did the right thing. Each Christmas, with true Scottish generosity, he sent me a large box of shortbread and a five-shilling piece. Only later and by accident did I learn that parental perfidy deprived me of an annual gold sovereign, under pretext that it was too much money for me. I never heard such nonsense. Nobody needs a sovereign so much as a schoolboy. It would have raised my prestige enormously with my friends. Nor would it have been wasted. This pledge of Sir Patrick's gastronomic gratitude would have been gastronomically expended—on chocolate cream frogs, Cupid's Whispers, and tuppenny-mixed ice-creams.

There was a tragedy connected with prawning and one of the village boys, known as Bunny, who was my chief rival in the art. A Saturday afternoon in March happened to coincide with the lowest spring tide, the ideal moment for prawning. Unluckily there was also a bitter north-east wind. When I announced my intention of going for prawns, it was at once vetoed under the absurd pretext that I should catch my death of cold. At last, after a lot of argument, I gave my word not to go prawning, and went out in a sulky mood which was not in the least improved by seeing Bunny in full prawning array jog-trotting down to the shore. For a moment I was tempted to disobey, but—see the power of the old school tie!—it was impossible to break one's word of honour. Sulkily and gloomily I watched Bunny in the distance from a sheltered nook of the cliffs, and was still there when he returned. The sight of him made me rather glad I hadn't gone. He was blue with cold, and his teeth were chattering so much I couldn't catch what he said as he went by. A week later I was even more glad I hadn't gone prawning that day, for poor Bunny lay dead of pneumonia.

It was a straggling community. Between the beach and the cliff were some old coastguard cottages, a hotel, and a desiccated bun-shop run by a religious lady who didn't believe in pleasure and kept even her buns austere and flavourless. There were also some small residences with wave-eaten lawns in front, and the Green Man which had a bowling lawn. On top of the cliff were two long lines of detached houses with big gardens, and, about a mile inland, the village.

The only buildings of any distinction were a Georgian farmhouse and a Norman church, built of flints, which are the only stones available in chalk countries. This church was massively constructed and set on a knoll, so that like a good many others it probably served as a refuge from pirates and robber barons in Mr. Chesterton's Merrie England. Inside the church was a fine satirical Norman string course of grotesque animals and faces, which I studied during many a cold sermon and unwelcome litany. I was nearly roped into this establishment as a choir boy, but when we were perfidiously told that the vicar was coming to hear us sing and we were to show him what the school could do, I was suspicious and sang even more out of tune than my natural capacity in that direction. Those boys drafted as sacred songsters were very much pitied by the others.

The land near the sea, except for a few nooks, was either waste or unenclosed sheep walks. Then came the familiar English checker board of hedged pastures, with farms huddled in the valleys behind wind screens of ancient trees. But six miles or so inland the country was rich with wheat and barley fields, lush pasture, orchards, hop gardens. After our white shadeless roads it was wonderful to cycle through the sunken lanes with their flowery banks and spreading elms and oaks.

It was a land drenched in history. The arms of the county were the Saxon white horse, with the motto "Invicta," because (so it was claimed) the ancestors had never submitted to

Norman William. Saxon place names were common, Worths and Wolds and Hams. There was a Wodensborough with earthworks, said to mark the shrine of Woden. There was Roman Richborough with its indestructible walls built on a low cliff from which the sea had long ago receded. There was once wealthy Sandwich (also deserted by the sea) with its mediæval Fisher Gate and Barbican, its old churches and houses, its narrow twisting streets which then were cobbled and grass-grown. There were Canterbury with its cathedral; Dover and its great castle which included a Roman watch tower and where they show some of the actual jousting lances used at the Field of the Cloth of Gold; there was Minster with the church William Morris praised so highly and the monument out in the marshes to the missionary, Augustine.

There was scarcely a village which had not preserved some venerable relic of its ancient past. The utterly peaceful landscape seemed brooding in an ancient primitive dream, as if unchanged for ages. And indeed to a large extent that was so. By a wonderful stroke of luck I had glimpses of an England, a nook of it, which had changed little since Shakespeare or even since Chaucer. There were no motor cars and the railways had a splendid inefficiency all their own. Communication was by horse-bus and carrier's cart. There was no gas and no electricity. Among those inland cottagers a telegram was dreaded—only urgent bad news was ever sent that way. The Bible was still God's infallible word, except that for purposes of immediate prophecy Old Moore's Almanac was consulted. Peddlers, descendants of Autolycus, came round selling gewgaws to the women. On holidays and Sundays many of the girls still wore their purple plush mourning for the great and good Queen. The men were heavy, bread-beef-and-beer Saxons, slow-witted, incredibly opposed to all innovation, respectful of the gentry except in matters of religion, and so moral that the few policemen seldom had anything to do.

Our own policeman was a ponderous yokel named Saunders, who was seldom visible and never needed. Coming home from church one morning, my father and I were astonished to see Saunders striding along at about three times his usual policeman's stroll, and beaming with smiles. As he saluted, my father stopped him.

"Good morning, Saunders. You're looking very cheerful."

"I've got a body, sir," said Saunders, beaming, and oozing with self-importance.

"A body!" said my father in astonishment. "What do you mean?"

"One of them foreigners over to Ringwold 'as cut 'is throat something 'orrid, sir."

The foreigners in question came from another county.

"Have you any idea why he did it?"

"That'll come out at the inquest, sir. I've got me clue, sir, I've got me clue."

And off he went, still beaming.

"Now, to my certain knowledge," said my father, "that's the first job Saunders has had in two years. He thinks he'll be promoted for his 'clue.' No wonder he looks so happy."

Such was the country and such the people of that little pocket of ancient England, an anachronism in the first decade of the 20th century. Yet before that decade ended the change began. One or two noisy motor cars, forerunners of the coming hordes, began crashing through the narrow lanes, frightening horses and expectant mothers. In 1909 the conservative inhabitants suffered the unbearable affront of having Blériot land his airplane on their cliffs. Since then two coal mines have been opened up, with "model" mining villages of red brick. The roads and lanes are no longer white but black with asphalt. The widening and straightening has swept away the flowery banks and the old trees. There are garages and petrol pumps instead of smithies ringing with the clink of hammers on anvils and full of the acrid smell of burning hoofs. The old dialect talk has almost disappeared before the classy cockney talked in school. The blunt good-natured manners have become wretchedly genteel. Farming is no longer a way of life, following the rhythm of the seasons, but a hard way of earning a poor living. Olde Tea Shoppes lurk round beauty spots, which because they are spots are no longer beautiful. Dear old ladies in thatched cottages will sell you at high prices the centuries-old family heirlooms planted there last week by London antique dealers. The windmills are in ruins; the oast houses turned into music rooms or cocktail bars by artistic Londoners who come down for week-ends. There are new suburban houses and new suburban people, who go to the movies and shop by telephone. The old mansions are often golf clubs, and the tweeded heroes of the links have frightened away the fallow deer for ever.

All gone, as children say.

Chapter III

WHEN the Union Jack over the white ensign fluttered up the mast at the coastguard station I ran for my telescope. That meant part of the Channel Fleet was in sight. There they were! Usually half a dozen light cruisers and as many torpedo destroyers, with the leading ship also carrying the same two flags. A line of little coloured signal flags would go up at the station, and be answered by another far out at sea. Some of H.M.'s ships on their lawful occasions.

It is a known fact that grown-ups have little observation and no sense of fun. It was always necessary to point out to visitors the flags and the warships, but they took no intelligent interest in the event. The men would pretend to take a squint through the telescope, but you could see by the way they waggled it about that they couldn't pick up the squadron even after you'd pointed out exactly where it was. The women would say what a dreadful waste of money it was in our modern world where war between civilised nations had become unthinkable. And then off they'd all go, gabble, gabble, gabble, about the income tax and those dreadful radicals and how coal had gone up from nineteen shillings to a pound a ton. Yes, the men would agree, and just imagine, with all these taxes, whisky was now a guinea a gallon. Horrible, dreadful, we shall all be ruined. Won't Mrs. Aldington cheer us up with a song? And then my mother would go indoors and sing some awful rot about the (long "i") winds of summer blowing soft across the dark blue sea, instead of looking at the blue sea and the fighting Navy.

"Thank you. Thank you very much. Charming. Delightful. Such exquisite feeling. Lord Henry Somerset's, isn't it? Why does he never come to England?"

Those drawing-room ballads! Mr. Noel Coward has pointed out very justly the power of old popular songs in evoking their period. The songs popular with the middle class in my childhood have dropped out of favour, and I am glad to say I now very seldom hear them. But I have only to think of them to evoke their epoch. The most obvious fault of the music was the sentimentality which haunts all middle-class art. But the words were almost always by poets or people supposed to be poets, and never dropped down to the sheer imbecility of contemporary song. There was a complete lack of critical sense, another middle-class trait. Shakespeare's "O mistress mine," Jonson's "Drink to me only," Davenant's "The lark now leaves," were confounded with such sentimental trash as "Pale hands I loved," "O my Dolores," and "Little brown seed."

What the people who sang and listened to those songs wanted was a luscious but respectable emotionalism, a little less vulgar but no less stimulating than the carefully measured kiss on the contemporary film. Among the innumerable clues to an understanding of the English which Henry James entirely overlooked are these very songs. After the hymns at Evensong on a summer evening they were the most potent of panders. The mood of twaddling sentimentality, religious or erotic, which they engendered, plus the physiological stimulus of singing, seemed to be about the only means of breaking down the terrific sex inhibitions of the time. Watchful mammas knew it, and acted accordingly. Only under the stimulus of "Pale hands I loved beside the Shalimar" and a full moon could the eligible but hideously bashful young man be brought to the point of uttering those almost obscene words: "Darling, will you marry me?"

But I am forgetting my telescope, which unluckily was not strong enough for my purposes. Somebody must have told me about Galileo or I read about him. At any rate I burned to see

27

Jupiter's moons, and harped on the subject of telescopes to such an extent that for the sake of peace I was given one. Alas, it was too low in power to pick up Jupiter's moons. But I made other discoveries in fields of science remote from astronomy. One Sunday afternoon, when everybody else was sleeping off the effects of beef and Yorkshire, I turned my telescope landwards and looked idly into a distant valley. And what did I see? Nothing less than one of my schoolmasters kissing the elder sister of one of my friends in the erroneous belief that they were invisible to human eyes. The importance of taking really effective cover on such occasions cannot be over-stressed; there may always be a small boy or a lewd old mariner with a telescope. I'm glad to say that some happy instinct inspired me to keep the discovery entirely to myself. Such was the impossible standard of behaviour then exacted of junior masters that, if I hadn't, this poor young man would certainly have lost his job.

So narrow is the Channel at this point that on clear summer afternoons the cliffs of France are visible to the naked eye, and with my telescope I could pick out the lighthouse and roofs of Calais. It will surprise nobody to learn that I wanted to visit Calais even more than I wanted to see Jupiter's moons. But how get there? A Cook's poster of those days advertised: "A Week in Lovely Lucerne, Five Guineas." But I hadn't got five guineas, and I didn't want to go on a conducted tour to lovely Lucerne. I wanted to go to Calais, and the only way to achieve that was to persuade somebody to take me. Hints and requests were met by that gentle ambiguous evasion of parents which is so familiar and so exasperating.

And then, just as I was despairing, the whole problem was solved in an instant by Sir Patrick. When his duties as Recorder brought him to the district, he often spent the week-end in our house. It was an anxious time. Sir Patrick was not only an exacting gourmet, but the most restless of men, unable to sit still for half an hour and demanding a succession of entertainments throughout the day.

Sunday morning was the crucial time. Like other Scots, Sir Patrick was apt to be morose before breakfast. He was also unpunctual. The word was therefore "hold everything" until his tread on the stairs released the porridge—a special porridge imported from Scotland, which took about eight hours to cook and *would* form lumps. This was absorbed in a funereal silence which did honour to any Calvinist Sunday. This was followed by fish. "Every nation," says Peacock, "has some eximious virtue, and that of the Scots is peculiarly fish for breakfast." Then came boiled eggs, probably timed with a stop-watch. A tense moment followed, while Sir Patrick decapitated one and through judicial glasses examined its criminal record. When a faint smile on the rubicund face indicated acquittal, you could almost hear us relax. Invariably at that moment he would turn to my father with the same brisk invariable remark:

"Well, Aldington, what are we going to do today?"

Glancing anxiously at my mother, my father would detail his programme. Generally it was approved, but sometimes captious criticism would force distracting re-arrangements. In summer a great stand-by was: "A run over to Calais for lunch, tea at the Lord Warden, and drive back for dinner." The great advantage of this was that it filled the whole day.

Sir Patrick was a friend of mine, albeit a somewhat awesome friend. There were those little amenities of prawns and shortbread. And then I would sometimes accompany him to his local club, where he stuffed my pockets and his own with headed stationery and lavatory paper. As Sir Patrick pointed out, he went to this club so seldom that this was the only way he could get some of his money back. So, one brilliant summer morning when that "run over to Calais" had been proposed and accepted, I found the fearful courage to pipe up and say that I would like to go. Before my parents could refuse, Sir Patrick intervened:

"Certainly. Why not? Do the boy good, and help to keep us amused."

That settled it. There was, however, a certain atmosphere of indirect disapproval. I was ordered to go and wash my ears, although I vainly pointed out that I had done so scarcely an hour before, and that anyway I was going to see the Calaisiens, not they me. Moreover, there were warnings and forebodings on the topics of gastronomic excess and the unfortunate effects of a rolling ship. Luckily, Sir Patrick was impatient to be off; and there I was, in my Eton jacket and school cap, sitting on the box of the landau beside my old friend Bill, the groom, rolling in the direction of the port. And at one o'clock we were sitting down to lunch in the Calais buffet.

The Calais buffet was totally unlike the gloomy torture chambers which fancifully call themselves "Refreshment Rooms" in English railway stations. It was an excellent provincial French restaurant, one of the best in Calais. It was spacious and sunny and decorated with potted plants and flowers. Nearly every table was occupied by well-dressed people, chattering and laughing. Waiters went to and fro swiftly and silently. There were a clatter of knives and forks, a popping of corks, an air of abundance and gaiety and good cheer. I dare say many of those people had their troubles (I myself was due to return to school shortly) but the whole feeling of the people was unhurried, untroubled, buoyant, carefree, as they have never been in Europe since August 1914.

Above all, there was none of that feverish effort after pleasure so characteristic of the post-war epoch even at its best; and no heavy drinking, such as became regrettably fashionable in the same epoch. My father and Sir Patrick shared a pint of champagne, and Sir Patrick's conversation was evidently very lively, as they laughed a great deal. The point of his anecdotes missed me because he so often whispered behind his hand. I attached myself warmly to a *poulet en casserole* with mushrooms, which did credit to the establishment. Hitherto I had known only the over-sized British fowls, plain roast or plain boiled, and I decided that French chickens must be a totally different species of animal.

After the coffee my father slipped off to pay the bill. Sir Patrick lighted a cigar and surveyed the room. Presently he called my attention to a lavishly dressed lady two or three tables away, and said abruptly:

"How old do you think that woman is?"

I had no theories, nor could I imagine why her age should interest my venerable friend. I said:

"I don't know, sir. She might be any age."

"Quite right, quite right," he said approvingly. "You never can tell with these damned Frenchwomen. Might be anything from fourteen to forty."

At that moment my father returned, and interrupted this instructive conversation.

We then took a stroll through the town, where I was delighted by the Sunday animation of the streets, by the sight of policemen sporting cocked hats and swords, by workmen who wore beards and pegtop corduroy trousers and red cummerbunds, and by the bright costumes of the fisher girls with their beautifully goffered white caps and large gold earrings. I approved of France without reserve, in spite of Sir Patrick's pungent remarks about the state of the drains.

I continued to approve. As I halted to look in a confectioner's window, Sir Patrick jovially offered to pay for chocolates if I could order them in French without any help. Having studied the shop notices carefully I went in and asked for *"Un kilo de chocolats mélangés,"* and was understood. Sir Patrick looked crestfallen; his little joke at my expense hadn't been so good. Hastily my father tried to reduce the damage to one-quarter. But Sir Patrick was a just and honourable judge. He had promised to pay, and he did pay.

Contrary to all misgivings and warnings, there were no gastric troubles on the return voyage. I felt fine. It was one of those very rare days when the Channel is blue and perfectly smooth. In some scores of later passages I don't think I've ever seen it so calm as that day. While Sir Patrick relentlessly marched himself and my father up and down the crowded decks, I sat philosophically eating chocolates, watching the marbled foam and thinking. I was thinking what a nice man Sir Patrick was, and how I wanted to go to France again, and go often. I reflected that the French must be nice, too; and that it was a gross slander to say that they lived on frogs and soup when I had such tangible evidence to the contrary. Dimly and vaguely I began to feel a suspicion that perhaps everything good and virtuous and pleasant was not confined to England.

Chapter IV

ALONG the bare cliffs there were, as I have said, a few fertile nooks where a deep fold in the chalk had gathered soil and gave protection from the winds and yet was open to the sun. In some of these bright red sainfoin came up every year with a profusion of wild flowers so that the early summer air was sweet with their scent. I was always sorry when I saw the scythes at work destroying this coloured flower pattern.

As boys do, I began collecting the butterflies which hovered over these flowers, sticking them clumsily on pins and trying to make out their names from one or two popular handbooks. And there the matter would have rested but for the Reverend Francis Austin.

Mr. Austin was a burly man with thick eyebrows and Henry VIII legs. He was unlucky enough to offend a very popular lady novelist who satirised him most unjustly with much ribaldry about his "grand pianoforte legs." But Mr. Austin was a scholar, and added to his small income by writing books on such pleasant but unremunerative topics as English mediæval seals and the flowers of Shakespeare. He was also a skilful and tireless field naturalist.

George Moore has told how stunned he felt when he read an article by Zola destroying all Moore's belief in the dramatic methods of M. Scribe. That was how I felt when Mr. Austin showed me his collections, all beautifully arranged in tall cabinets, with every specimen neatly labelled. Having no standard of comparison I had modestly thought I was doing pretty well, and in a flash I stood self-convicted as an incompetent and ignorant bungler.

B

This was all the more painful because my favourite book at that time was Bates's *The Naturalist on the Amazons,* and I had made up my mind to emulate and probably surpass him. I believe Bates's theory of mimicry has been severely handled by later biologists, for like certain cannibal tribes scientists enjoy devouring their ancestors as a sacred rite. But nothing can destroy his work as a field naturalist. The number of species "new to Science" he sent back from Brazil is stupendous. I spent so many hours with Bates on the Amazon (when I should have been asleep or doing my homework) that I began to feel I had been there myself. How often I hunted insects near Pará or Obidos, felt homesick for England when I heard a tropical bird with a note like a wren, had fever in Pará, grew disgusted with a turtle diet and so yearned for flesh that I ate the roasted arm of a monkey in spite of its dreadful resemblance to humanity.

Possibly—I throw this out as a mere suggestion—part of the lure of the Amazon lay in the fact that there seemed to be no school there, while Bates earned fame and money by doing things I could only do on half-holidays. At any rate, what with Bates and Mr. Austin, I plugged away at natural history in my spare time for years, preparing for the great day when I too should set forth to discover those magical creatures, species new to Science. I have never been to the Amazon, though of recent years I have been tempted to go, and once got as far as looking up shipping lines and rates. But on reflection I thought it better to keep one dreamland intact.

But if I couldn't go humping off to the Amazon, I began to see a little more of England on summer holidays. Those who have only seen Stratford-on-Avon in a bustle of tourists would find some difficulty in imagining the peace and remoteness of the place in pre-motor days. Except on market days it was so still that footsteps echoed in the silent streets, boys fished from Clopton bridge, and one policeman dozed in solitude by the town hall. Miss Marie Corelli scandalised the natives by driving about in a victoria drawn by six piebald Shetland ponies and by importing a Venetian gondola which wafted her, a best-selling Cleopatra, up and down the affronted Avon. People agreed that something ought to be done about these insults to Shakespeare, but nothing was done. Apart from this unseemly intrusion, Stratford with its water meadows and willows and Holy Trinity and "the birthplace" slept on in a peace which had been scarcely broken since the Great Rebellion. The last time I was there I could hardly find space to park my car.

A great contrast to this was north Devon, which had not then become the stamping ground for innumerable trippers in motor coaches. The high barren moor there suddenly falls to the sea in high rocky cliffs. The sheltered rainy combes are filled with trees and ferns and mosses, and there are clear rocky trout streams. We saw stags and half-wild ponies on Exmoor, and the wild-looking farmers who rode in to Lynton and Lynmouth on their shaggy horses spoke a dialect we could scarcely understand. We ate the Exmoor mutton and cream and brook trout, and there was a pleasant smell of burning peat and wood. Like every other visitor to those parts I read *Lorna Doone* and was greatly disappointed by the Doone valley; which only goes to show that sentimental fiction is no reliable guide to landscape.

In those days I began to form the habit of reading. Whether you consider that a virtue or a vice is apt to depend on whether you are or are not interested in the book and education trades. It is a habit I have no intention of trying to break. Even if all new books become political and economic propaganda, I shall go on reading old ones, which are more interesting anyway in most cases. I think it was fortunate that my schools paid no attention to "cultural interests," so that reading was pure fun.

I also think I was lucky in having the run of a large general library.

For some time my attention never strayed much beyond a shelf of adventure stories which my father had collected in his boyhood. Christmas and birthdays provided me with more recent versions of the gory yarns which for some strange reason are thought suitable for youthful minds.

These I read with great attention and popping eyes, but at last criticism reared its viperous head. Among these blood-thirsty panegyrics of violence was a story about the Wars of the Roses. The name of the author escapes me, but the hero bore the tremendous title of Sir Oswald Athelney. At a certain point in the book Sir Oswald vaulted lightly from his charger at the door of an inn, threw the reins to one of the lower classes conveniently located by the author for that purpose, and strode in with his customary "Ho! varlets!" That was all right with me, but then Sir Oswald went on to order a beef-steak from the bowing host, adding: "Let it be brown without and red when I apply mine knife." I paused. Did the scions of chivalry worry about the cooking of steaks? Did they have steaks in those days? A venison pasty or a baron of beef, yes. But a steak! By the simple process of reading the last page first I had learned that Sir Oswald eventually became an earl. I couldn't believe so noble a personage would disgrace himself and fiction by ordering a common beefsteak. Moreover, "mine knife" didn't sound right either.

I was so much worried about this that I put the whole prob-lem to my father, who was most unsympathetic. Without looking up from his own book he said if I didn't like what I was reading I'd better try Scott. That was no good, because I'd already tried Scott and didn't like him. Well, said my father impatiently, try Harrison Ainsworth.

The choice was not altogether happy, and I should have done better to persevere with the far more sensible Scotchman. For months my slumbers were haunted with the Satanic horrors of *The Lancashire Witches,* the revolting descriptions of the great plague in *Old St. Paul's,* the frightful tortures in *Guy Fawkes* and *The Tower of London,* and the supernatural terrors of *Auriol.*

Moreover, Ainsworth was a shade too zealous in recording the swearing habits of historical England. Henry VIII strode into his pages, exclaiming: "God's death, my lords!" Toying with Nell Gwyn and half a dozen spaniels, Charles II was never tired of swearing: "Odd's fish." Lesser personages peppered the books with " 'Sblood," " 'Sdeath," " 'Swounds," and "Zooks." There was one who swore "by the gallipots of Galen." I got into trouble at school for repeating the words of the ancient nobility and royalty. The worst moment was on the cricket field when I was overheard calling somebody a "lascivious varlet."

No doubt I should eventually have got free from this childish bugaboo on my own, but I was suddenly diverted from it by the merest chance. Coming into the library one afternoon I found on the table a dozen or more handsomely bound white books. I knew at once that they were the new limited edition of Oscar Wilde and one of my father's economies, about which there had been some discussion. I had never heard of Mr. Wilde until this purchase, but from one or two remarks in the discussion about it, I judged there was something mysterious to be learned.

One of the volumes lay open on the table with a heavy ruler across it. Curiosity made me read a paragraph. A sudden and violent interest made me read on. The book, I saw, was called *Intentions,* and the paragraph I had started on was about a poet called Keats. Presently I went over to the bookcase and found the Moxon edition of Keats. I turned up "Endymion" and began to read it. I despair of finding words to express the effect of these two books without seeming inadequate to myself or exaggerated to other people. It was like a combination of falling in love at first sight and finding Ali Baba's treasure cave. But lovers have their woes and Ali Baba had his perils; I had neither. There simply was no fly in that ointment. By the merest chance I had stumbled into a world of enchantment, of siren voices

"For ever piping songs for ever new."

Now that was really a stroke of good luck. From the obsolete sensationalism of Ainsworth I might have passed to more recent brands, and have ended up as one of those unhappy people who take their intellectual pleasures so sadly with newspapers, horror stories, jig-saw puzzles, and detective novels.

Observe, too, the good fortune of coming on those two authors. Suppose it had been Matthew Arnold or, which would have been infinitely worse, one of our own dreary critics who are always labouring to prove something irrelevant, mainly their own superiority. Obviously I should have been repelled. But with all his faults and affectations, Oscar Wilde's attitude was one of yea-saying to life and art. In his ornate fanciful way he was telling me why Keats should be admired, and not where he fails to please a super-highbrow taste. And then what poem was fitter to charm an immature mind than the lovely but still immature imaginings of "Endymion"?

Only one thing was required to feed this burning enthusiasm—books. And here again my luck held good. I hadn't to haunt public libraries or second-hand book shops. Everything I needed was at hand in my own home—all the major English poets from Chaucer to Browning, dozens of minor poets, the twenty volumes of Chalmers's *British Poets,* and a complete collection of Elizabethan dramatists. Here was matter for a lifetime of study. I went through them in two years, reading literally nothing but poetry in all my spare time; and owing to an operation and other reasons I had practically a whole year to myself. When I went to the university I found to my surprise that I had read every poet in the required English course, and scored about 98 out of 100 in a special test paper set for me by an incredulous faculty.

So much spontaneous ardour and persistence without the slightest outside pressure seems to show some innate disposition for literature. That may not be good psychology or philosophy, but it is a fact. Nobody had suggested to me that poetry may be an absorbing passion or even a proper study. All we did in that line at school was to parse, analyse, and (heaven help us!) paraphrase Shakespeare's *King John*. Moreover, in those days the very word "poet" (usually preceded by the Homeric adjective "long-'aired") was a term of abuse among the robust commonalty. In spite of the conditioned-reflexers, I must continue to believe that the love of poetry was there in me and was not induced by my spiritual pastors and masters.

It is even more improbable that anyone on this earth would attempt to condition a fifteen-year-old bourgeois schoolboy into writing poetry. Towards the end of that same summer when I discovered Keats through the kind offices of Mr. Wilde, I was out on the cliffs insect-hunting. I was tired and hot from chasing a very active fritillary up and down a steep slope, and sat down to rest. By accident I had there a very fine view of the cliffs and Channel, floodlit by the late afternoon sun. I wasn't thinking of poetry or conscious of anything in particular except a feeling of passive contentment, when a line of iambic pentameter suddenly presented itself, followed by another which continued the sense and rhymed with the first.

In my pocket I had a pencil and what I pompously called my "field note-book." Mr. Austin had gravely urged this course, bidding me note "all scientific phenomena" I happened to bump into on my walks. (I wish I had that book now to find what "scientific phenomena" I noted.) Turning this book upside down (symbolical gesture) I wrote down the two lines. Immediately others presented themselves, and very soon I had written thirty or forty. In fact, as I perceived with astonishment, I had written a poem.

The experience of writing a poem was entirely delightful, far more satisfactory even than reading poetry. But, how right Lucretius was! "From the midst of the fountain of bliss ever rises up something of bitterness." On re-reading my poem I discovered that it was a ramshackle affair. From the fountain of creative bliss rose up that horrid spectre of self-criticism which haunts the artist all his life. Dimly and reluctantly I began to see that genius is not enough; one must also work. And yet I believe that I had already doomed myself to what is jestingly called a literary career.

Who shall say what strange hidden motives, what curious aptitudes determined our job in life? We can never sufficiently remind ourselves how different are the ideals of different men. In the year 1918 I was much impressed by an example of this truth. I was then temporarily in command of an infantry company in France, and my sanitary man was wounded. A sanitary man fulfills a useful and hygienic function, but one devoid of glory—the efficient hiding of human ordure.

My sanitary man had worked with silent fidelity, and his loss was embarrassing. Time and tide would not wait. What was to be done? My second in command suggested realistically that I should order somebody to take over the vacant rank, but I did not care to use my undoubted power in so tyrannous a manner. Every soldier is potentially a hero. I didn't want to wound heroic susceptibilities by an appointment which might be considered insulting.

In this perplexity I consulted my sergeant-major, who bade me be of good cheer, and soon brought me a small, dark, rather dirty soldier whom I had more than once been compelled to reprove. The sergeant-major was a good and conscientious officer, but, like too many who are entrusted with great power, apt to be a bit arbitrary. It occurred to my suspicious mind that he might want to humiliate the deplorable soldier who stood before me so patiently and so humbly.

Therefore I sent the sergeant-major away and in private questioned the man closely to find out if any pressure had been put on him. If I had trodden on Vergil's snake I could not have been more startled than I was by his statements. He yearned to be a sanitary man, he said; he had long cherished an ambition for that fetid post; he felt it was his vocation in life. As I signed and handed him the necessary order, he thanked me warmly, as if it were I and not he doing the service.

It seems to me that I too had an inexplicable vocation.

The nature of youth turns to hero-worship as unconsciously as plants grow towards the light. By their heroes you shall know them. Instead of prize-fighters or political dictators, I admired poets. Indeed, anyone connected however distantly with writing, even a literary agent who sometimes stayed with us, seemed to me aureoled with prestige. I made two mistakes here. A man who has written great and attractive books is not necessarily a great and attractive person. Moreover, I had in the library the very best of centuries, without the bores and the failures and the false successes. I ought to have seen that in any one generation they were likely to be in the majority, especially since writing has become a trade.

As if by way of warning, I very early ran into one or two specimens of literary fauna. There was, for instance, Mr. Guy Thorne, a novelist, a pale plump man who thought very highly of his abilities. He had been a Fleet Street journalist, but faced with the alternatives of dipsomania or Cornwall, chose Cornwall. He was an industrious writer, so industrious that half the products of his literary factory were issued under his real name of Ranger Gull. At that time Guy Thorne had topped all other best-sellers with a novel called *When It Was Dark,* a sensational account of the disasters which happened to the world when it was proved by "Science" that Jesus did not rise from the dead. The British public fairly lapped it up, especially a prudish-prurient chapter headed: "Mary, Pity Women!" Of course, in the end "Science" was defeated, and the book ended on a Note of Hope. The idea of the book was said to have been suggested by the author's parson father, and it was skilfully exploited by an amiable cynic and practised journalist.

Even our village had heard of Mr. Thorne, and there was much excitement when the news went round that he had rented a large farmhouse in the district. There was an orgy of tea-fights to discuss what ought to be done about it. Should one call or should one not? Although his book was a snappy piece of Christian propaganda, and owed its initial success to a gratuitous pulpit advertisement from the Bishop of London, the general opinion was that it was blasphemous and that one definitely should not call. Hovering in the background of these debates, I failed to see that the real reason for not calling was the agonising suspicion, amounting almost to certainty, that the calls would not be returned.

My mother, ever ardent in generous opposition, decided that she would call, and thus I frequently had the privilege of seeing and listening to Mr. Thorne. I confess that at first his appearance was a shock. From the strong moral line he took in print, I had expected somebody rather austere and Dantesque, instead of a tubby little *bon vivant* who never refused a double whisky. Glass in hand, he invariably stood in front of the fireplace and discoursed. My awe at this eminent personage was tempered by the fact that his conversation was very worldly, not to say mundane, and apt to run on the theme of his superiority to all other living authors. He had a Morton's fork line of argument which is still popular with his tribe. Those writers who might have claimed superior literary merit were dismissed because they hadn't his sales; and the few who had his sales were easily disposed of for having no literary merit.

Through this modest genius I met my first minor poet, Cotsford Dick. He was known to the middle classes as a writer of drawing-room ballads, but I have since come across one or two of his poems in late Victorian anthologies. Mr. Dick was a slim, dapper, bright-eyed little man, frothing with verbal witticisms and looking rather like an intelligent groom. And did you once see Shelley plain? The last thing in the world Mr. Dick wanted to talk about was poetry. He affected a fine indifference for his own talents, but would have been greatly offended by anyone who shared it. With his affected Oxford accent, his "witty" chatter, his artless familiarity with titles, he was the prototype of the literary lounger with a small income, the social hanger-on, the bachelor who can be depended on to fill a seat at dinner on a moment's notice and pay for it by gossip and jokes filched from the green room and the bohemian club. *Non sic itur ad astra.*

But I was not easily cured of this literary hero-worship. Evidently it was still with me three or four years later when I was living in London and spent part of an afternoon at The Pines, Putney Hill. At that time I had a great admiration for Swinburne, which I am glad to say I have not altogether lost even now. Unluckily, Mr. Swinburne had recently died, but his friend or keeper Watts-Dunton still lived.

Admirers of Swinburne will always look on the relations of these two with mixed feelings. It is well known that young Swinburne drank. The pious old admiral Swinburne used to say: "God who has given my son the gift of genius has denied him that of self-control." Watts-Dunton undertook to be the control. It was rumoured that he diverted Swinburne from brandy to port because that was the drink of the Laureate, Tennyson; from port to claret because the three musketeers

43

drank it; and from claret to beer because beer should be the drink of an English patriot. He even induced the sedentary bard to take exercise by making him walk (some said, sprint) across Putney Common to a pub for his morning bottle of Bass.

Unhappily, as Algernon Charles became more and more sober, Swinburne became duller and duller, until the author of *Atalanta* and *Poems and Ballads* vanished in clouds of meaningless words and walloping rhythms. Swinburne survived his genius nearly forty years. Thus, owing to Watts-Dunton, England gained a respectable citizen (of whom she already had far too many) and lost one of the last of her great poets.

Nevertheless, I had my own reason for wanting to visit The Pines. I sent Watts-Dunton some of my poems, and he invited me to tea. The door of The Pines opened into a hall hung with Pre-Raphaelite pictures, and the servant led me to an over-furnished parlour with more pictures of the same school. After a formal and funereal pause I was shown into a large gloomy library, where a shrivelled old man was reading *David Copperfield*. We talked a little about Dickens, a lot about Swinburne and the Victorians, a little about my poems. He showed me Swinburne's writing table and chair and some of his books, and then I was once more on Putney Hill, feeling rather like a tourist who has been conducted round the historic mansion by the old family retainer.

My reason for intruding on the old man was a sentimental one. Swinburne had known Landor; Landor, Southey; and at one time Southey was very friendly with Shelley. The chain was a short one, and I was never likely to get humanly so near to Shelley again. He was only five hand-clasps away. In my enthusiasm I didn't even stop there, but somehow made the link back to Pope, and through Wycherley and Davenant to Shakespeare. An absurd fancy, but my own.

44

A far different character was Mr. Dudley Grey, who was for some time my closest friend. A second father would perhaps more accurately define the relation of a man of fifty·to a schoolboy of sixteen. In the language of his own generation Mr. Grey was a gentleman and a scholar. In Marxian terms I suppose he would be called a blood-sucking rentier permeated with bourgeois ideology. He was a Christian and a patriot, owner of a historic castle, yet a travelled cosmopolitan, widely read in several languages, an amateur poet, and an indefatigable art collector. He was an accomplished man of the world, well bred with charmingly easy manners, dressed with a careless elegance, a good shot, a good horseman. Though not so picturesque or so big a swell as Wilfrid Blunt and Cunninghame Graham, he belonged to their type, the embodiment of the words of Euphues: "It is virtue, yea virtue, gentlemen, that maketh gentlemen." "Virtue" here being meant in the Italian sense of *"virtù,"* all-round worth and accomplishment.

I never saw Mr. Grey in his castle. When I knew him he lived in a medium-sized house rather crowded with old furniture, works of art, books and a valuable collection of old jewellery. These were only a fraction of his collections which I saw years later, after the castle had been sold, in a large mansion Mr. Grey had bought in Buckinghamshire.

Now why had the owner of a castle come to live in a small house in an undistinguished community? His explanation was that the low-lying situation of his home and the worry of a staff of servants had made Mrs. Grey ill; that she no longer cared to travel out of England; and that the doctor had recommended our high, dry windy downs as healthy. A reasonable and simple explanation, but far too simple for our middle-class gossips, who resented Mr. Grey because simply by being himself he made them feel inferior. They said he was a degenerate (i.e., a homosexual) hiding from the police, because he once casually mentioned dining with Oscar Wilde. They said he had been forced out of "decent society" because he had married his cook; and this was founded on the fact that he was a good amateur cook and enjoyed preparing a good French meal. They also insinuated that he was a second-hand furniture dealer, only too willing to sell his Sheraton chairs and Renaissance cabinets.

Under pretext of playing chess (the only quasi-intellectual activity tolerated in our village) I visited Mr. Grey regularly. But we soon abandoned chess for better things. In his young days Mr. Grey had been a poet. At the age of nineteen, he said, he had gone about Venice in a cloak and a gondola, imagining himself another Byron. He appointed himself my poetic guardian, and each week read and criticised what I had written. Stimulated by this, his own Muse awoke from a long and frozen sleep. Mr. Grey read his verses in a strange droning chant which is said to derive from Tennyson. Afterwards it took me some time to get rid of the habit.

Mr. Grey was a most valuable ally. In spite of the twaddling gossips, he had considerable prestige, if only because he paid his bills so promptly. His whole-hearted encouragement of my writing was a shield against opposition. Even more to the point was the privilege of intimacy with a good European. Mr. Grey had lived in London, Paris, and Berlin, and could talk amusingly of life there. He talked of the theatre and grand opera, of symphonic and chamber music, when the best I knew were the Stratford performances of Shakespeare and my mother's playing of Chopin and Schumann. The classics, which had been a dreary school task, he brought alive. He made me see that Homer and Horace were as much living poetry as Keats and Shakespeare. Under his urging I made a strenuous effort and taught myself to read French. He introduced me to French poetry, and it was charming to see his enthusiasm for Ronsard and André Chénier. He started me off on Italian. He made me learn to ride a horse, and implored me not to marry my landlady's daughter. He was exacting and worked a willing pupil relentlessly, for after all during much of this time I had to cope with a full school programme; and I am very grateful to him.

But Mr. Grey's deepest enthusiasm was for Italy, for Italian art and literature. He was impatient for me to learn Italian, and would read and translate passages from Dante and Petrarch to goad me on. In the leisurely Victorian way Mr. Grey had travelled through Italy in his own carriage. Everywhere he went he bought or took photographs of cities, landscape, architecture, sculpture, pictures, gardens, fountains. I forget how many large albums of these photographs he had, but they seemed endless. With one of them open before us Mr. Grey was willing to talk for hours and I was as willing to listen. No doubt he saw these things through the eyes of Ruskin, Pater, and Addington Symonds, but that is vastly better than not seeing them at all or seeing them through the hard-boiled optics of the New Yorker. Certainly Mr. Grey was a *dilettante*, but the meaning of the word is "one who takes delight"; and what is art for if not to delight us?

"You must go to Italy," Mr. Grey would end up.

I didn't need any urging. I was already more than impatient to be off. But distances were longer in those days and Italy seemed a very long way off. Having pushed me on too far, Mr. Grey now tried to restrain me. I must prepare myself first by learning Italian and something of its complicated history. I must see first the collections in London and Paris, and learn to recognise styles and schools. Certainly I should not attempt to visit Italy until I had finished with the university. And then, seeing me still unconsoled, he added:

"If you want to go to Italy badly enough, you'll get there somehow."

I didn't believe him, but he was right.

Chapter V

DOES it sound absurd to list "learning to walk" among the pleasures and discoveries of those days? As I grew up I accepted without question the walking habits of a sedentary class. I thought walking a slow tedious method of covering distances and that four miles was about the limit of human capacity. If you had to go any further you naturally took a carriage or a train. Walking for pleasure was limited to golf and the constitutional.

I was freed from this error by an old friend, who is now one of His Majesty's judges but was then merely a barrister's devil. The experience made such an impression that I remember the exact date, 2nd of June. After breakfast Malcolm suggested a walk. It was a brilliantly sunny day; the fields were rich with daisies and buttercups; the young green leaves glittered; birds sang, and we talked and sang. I dare say Malcolm talked of his literary heroes, Henley, Pater, and Louis Stevenson. But after two or three miles I fell silent. I began to consider the distance back and was convinced that I already felt tired. I suggested we should turn back, or we might be late for lunch.

From his six feet three Malcolm looked upon me with scorn. Did I really propose to waste such a glorious day mugging indoors? Was I such a confounded weakling that I quailed at a mere fifteen- or twenty-mile stroll? I gasped. Why, Malcolm continued, he and George Somebody often did twenty-five to thirty a day. But lunch? I protested, imagining a picturesque vignette of my disabled body lying huddled on the dusty road far from human succour. But there is no getting past legal acumen. Pooh! We had some money in our pockets, hadn't we? Wasn't there a pub in nearly every village? *"Allons, en route!* Afoot and light-hearted we take to the open road."

Even a quotation from Whitman was no comfort, for at that moment I didn't feel at all light-hearted; but I was ashamed to give in tamely. Bracing muscles which I firmly believed could not carry me much longer, I plodded on. But as we went on I seemed to get a second walking wind. I recollected that I had once run seven miles in a paper-chase, and began to enjoy the rhythmic movement and exploring new country.

Some time after noon we came to the then remote and picturesque village of Barfreston, and went in to an old thatched pub (I believe it was called The Oak) with cool stone floors and scrubbed wooden tables and benches. There we ate bread and cheese, and I drank my first half-pint of ale. Later we looked at the remarkable Norman carvings on the church, and sat in the sunshine on a low tomb facing the sculptured porch. A butterfly settled on a lichened gravestone, and we remembered that for the Greeks it was a symbol of the soul, and discoursed of Plato and the myth of immortality.

A memorable day. My legs got me home all right, though I was stiff next morning. What did that matter? Malcolm had given me the freedom of the road. There was one amusing aspect of that expedition which his present lordship might consider. If the contemporary restrictions on the sale of drinks in England had been in force then, my friend, who now condemns people for such trifles as murder and robbery with violence, might himself have been indicted of a horrid crime; to wit, that he did procure a minor to be supplied with half a pint of ale which the said minor consumed on licensed premises in contempt of our Sovereign Lord the King his crown and dignity.

We got our walking done just in time. Within ten years the roads of England changed entirely and lost that empty, leisurely quality which had been theirs since the railways had taken over all long-distance travel. Thousands and eventually millions of people came to possess the equivalent of a private train with access to all roads. And many of them were not exactly the sort of persons who seek green haunts and loneliness; and if they did, their presence in such numbers destroyed the very things they sought. England is a small country with a wonderful network of roads, so that three decades have already been long enough for the motor car to suburbanise most of the areas which industrialism had not touched. It isn't much fun to walk there now.

Well, I've had a car myself for many years and know what fun it is, and yet the losses are serious. The long raw gash of a new motor road changes a whole landscape, especially when there is a ribbon development of new houses. What was yesterday still a stretch of 18th-century England looks like a dreary suburb.

The highways and the main streets of old towns in summer are as crowded as Piccadilly and far noisier. Moreover, everything supposedly beautiful or interesting is exploited for admission charges. Stonehenge has a barbed-wire fence round it and a turnstile. At the Devil's Bridge notices read: "One shilling to see the landscape immortalised by Wordsworth." It isn't the shilling one minds, especially since that is probably the only way of protection from complete wrecking. The trouble is the banality of it all. When such places lose their remoteness and wildness they lose most of their charm. The *genius loci* evaporates, and what is left is a mere curiosity. As Lawrence says, everything has been seen to death.

When it comes to a choice between the fun of motoring and the fun of walking, I think walking has it.

Consider. With a car 150 to 250 miles are easily covered in a day, and at the end you crawl away from the wheel, unexercised yet stiff and tired, having had innumerable hurried glimpses of things you immediately forgot. In a day or two your nerves are on edge with the strain of speed, and if you were asked to describe the country and places you have been through, you couldn't do it.

On foot 15 to 25 miles are about the limits to a reasonable day's march. In the morning when you start off you need a silent mile to get into stride and shake the rucksack into place. But as oxygenation livens up the blood, there is a gradual but quite irresistible trend towards exhilaration, not to say hilarity. You begin to talk to your companion, and find him responsive. After three or four miles mere talking is not enough; you shout, you sing, you bring out such good jokes that you both halt, doubled up with laughter. Your companion seems the wittiest and most delightful fellow in the world.

You proceed in this way for a length of time which seems twice as long and ten times as pleasant as a whole day in a car, when you observe an inn sign. This reminds you that you are hungry and you innocently suggest lunch, only to discover with astonishment that your watches and the church clock agree that the day is young—a few minutes past eleven in fact. Congratulating each other on this unexpected gift of time, you march on.

Meanwhile there isn't much in the slowly moving landscape that you have missed. As you look back you can still see the spire over last night's village, and the hill which was in front of you for the better part of a day. The names of villages and hamlets on the map become realities. You potter about them, looking at the big elms on the green and at old cottages. Or you drop in at the parish church, where you are rewarded by a Crusader's tomb, a 16th-century brass, or a fine window which luckily escaped the Reformers' philistine zeal. You come to the bridge over a stream and peer down at the green waving weeds and the shadowy fishes flitting about their watery shrubberies like dim subaqueous birds. For half an hour you have a succession of views of an old mansion in a park; you fit it up with a library and other necessities and live there for the rest of your life. And no sooner is it out of sight than you come to the crest of a hill, and look over a wide valley to blue hills.

How much better are bread and cheese and beer in a cheerful tap-room than a ghastly English hotel lunch in a prunes-and-prisms atmosphere of gentility and a doddering waiter with grease-spotted clothes! After a pipe or two comes the afternoon walk. This is a more sober intoxication of air and sun than the morning's. The world and yourself seem bathed in a warm golden glow, you linger more frequently on the way, and wonder how anyone can be a pessimist. You are filled with a placid satisfaction, and not even dismayed by the certainty that at your night's lodging you will get nothing to eat but ham and eggs. You are carefree, and yet as virtuously tired as if you had done a hard day's work.

Such at any rate is my recollection of a fortnight's walk through the West of England in 1910 and many another since. That was part of the good life.

Meanwhile other things had been happening. With my father I spent a week in Brussels and Antwerp. Brussels was the first capital I really enjoyed. My first memories of London are very confused, a medley of fog, mud, an endless rumble, the violent ammonia smell of horses at Victoria, the stifling coal-smoke in the underground, hansoms, growlers, panto-mimes, the Tower, the Abbey, the Zoo, the portentously solemn rooms of the Grosvenor Hotel, and the Natural History Museum. Belgium was very different. I feel some compunction when I think of how much I must have bored people after I got back. For several days I literally could not stop talking about all I had seen, from the dogs harnessed to market barrows up to High Mass in the Cathedral at Antwerp.

What I remember most vividly now is not the sight-seeing or even the first real contact with Continental life, but something I was quite unconscious of at the time. I mean the peaceful busy life of the Belgians which was so abruptly and cruelly ended in August 1914. One day my father took me to lunch at a large restaurant on one of the main streets of Brussels. We went up to the second floor and got a table by the window so that we could look up and down the street. There were throngs of people passing up and down, an endless procession of fiacres among the trams, and every café and restaurant seemed crowded. It was the beginning of a holiday, and there was an indefinable sense of good humour and well-being about the whole scene. A woman on the street-corner was selling flowers, and I watched a waiter at the café opposite joking and laughing with his customers as he served them.

If somebody had told me then that in a very few years an invading army would march down that street, I should have thought him mad. I should have thought him even more mad if he had gone on to say that I should be one of a vast English army levied to eject that invader. Certainly our inability to foresee the future is one of the most merciful conditions of our existence. I shouldn't have enjoyed my lunch at all if I had known what was coming.

Yet if I were superstitious I might claim one flash of prophetic insight. Soon after I returned from Belgium I had a very vivid dream, wherein I saw the angels of the Lord riding upon white horses and slaying the wicked. The gruesome part of it was that as this divine vengeance proceeded, the white angels and white horses became red with blood. I was so much impressed by this that I made a little story of it, the first piece of prose I ever wrote. I can't explain this apocalyptic vision, except that I was scheduled for an operation; and my subliminal self, or whatever it is that functions in dreaming, exaggerated the extent of the coming massacre and effusion of blood.

In a moment of artist's vanity I read this precious composition to my mother and one of my great-aunts. That excellent

53

lady paid me the flattering compliment of shedding tears. Since I had already had my first poem printed in a London periodical that week I naturally began to feel as if the Nobel prize were just around the corner. Whereupon my mother got hold of a copy of this work and—just imagine!—sent it to Bernard Shaw. What she wrote to him I don't know, nor what her motive was, unless she thought that Mr. Shaw might turn his satire on me and drastically cure me of the itch for writing. If so, she was disappointed. I haven't got Mr. Shaw's letter, but it ran something like this:

"*Madam,*

Your son has obviously too much literary talent to earn his living in an honest way.

I enclose a guinea which he is to spend in some thoroughly selfish manner.

Yours faithfully,

George Bernard Shaw."

I wish I could remember what I did with that guinea. I believe I was so revolted by Shaw's cynicism that I insisted on giving it to my mother. As to Shaw's opinion, who am I to dispute it? If earning money by writing is dishonest, I can only say that I have done my best to follow in his footsteps.

In spite of all this glory and the efforts of Mr. Grey, I still needed educating. Mr. Grey was angry with me for having a poem published, and quoted Horace about keeping a poem seven years before publication. If only that rule could be rigidly applied to all books, the art of literature might be saved; and all the publishers would go bankrupt. At that time it seemed to me a fantastic proposal; why, if I followed it, I should be an old man of twenty-three before I had another poem published. However, I heeded Mr. Grey to the extent that for a time I made no further efforts towards publication and settled down to other work, to prepare for the university.

Hitherto I have said little or nothing about my schools, because I wanted to look on the bright side of life. I can't agree with the men who won't allow any criticism of the old school and who grow maudlin about the happiest days of their lives. Nor do I suffer from the infantilism which makes them yearn to be back in those days. My days at school were far from being happy, were indeed a perpetual struggle against a conditioning which was repulsive to me. Unluckily this resistance was extended to the purely educational side, so that I was regarded as rather a dull pupil. And yet, as a greater man said, I cannot think that I was disqualified for all literary pursuits.

I have no particular criticism for the system as such. Later researches enable me to say with some confidence that it was an imitation of Dr. Arnold's imitation of the methods worked out by Vittorino da Feltre for educating Renaissance nobles. There was a time when I thought it fantastic to apply these methods to middle-class boys in the 20th century. But having observed the results of the various brands of reformed, scientific, practical, enlightened, and psychological education, I have changed my mind. Without the humanities education is defective, and I find myself unexpectedly in agreement with the classical don who saw no reason why scientists should not be educated.

I am not a Renaissance noble, but I should not in the least object if I had really had the education of one. It could not possibly be as futile as the smattering of innumerable more or less fake "subjects" now fashionable. "Modern" education is as certainly a recipe for making sciolists as the feudal system was a recipe for civil war. My objection, therefore, is not that they taught so-called obsolete subjects but that they taught them with miserable inefficiency.

One reason for this is that, even if they knew their subjects, they had no enthusiasm for them. Languid teachers can expect nothing but languid scholars. But a more potent reason was the conditioning or training, which laid far too much stress upon mere games and upon a narrow-minded bourgeois outlook. Backed by a quasi-military discipline this inculcation of prejudices was most harmful. Under the guise of turning out gentlemen it produced a pack of stupids. In their anxiety for the mass production of too respectable citizens incapable of reacting against the prejudices instilled in them, they forgot (if they ever knew) Vittorino's cardinal principle that instruction must be adapted to the individual. Consequently, I had to expend a great deal of nervous energy in preventing them from turning my silk purse into a sow's ear.

Everything comes to those who wait, even unconscious apologies. A few years ago I returned to the old school, and walked on the sacred close with the headmaster, who had been my housemaster. He talked very nicely about my books and then, turning to me with the most disarming naïveté, said:

"And now tell me, my dear Aldington, *where* on earth did you get your scholarly knowledge?"

The price paid for this successful resistance was considerable, both in nervous tension and in ignorance, which had to be made good by desperate hard work later. But suppose I had not rebelled, suppose I had succumbed to the conditioning and, what was worse, the suggestion of the provincial middle-class milieu? I think I can make a rough guess at what I should now be:

I should be a fairly prosperous provincial lawyer, married to the daughter of some local personage who could bring business my way. Daily I should drive between my office and a modestly opulent country house in an expensive but not flashy car. In politics I should invariably support the Conservative candidate, and should discharge various municipal offices with unintelligent integrity. I should attend church regularly and act as churchwarden, subscribing to the right charities and denouncing respectable trade union leaders as Bolshie agitators. I should not read much beyond journalism and detective stories, but for social purposes I should maintain an unread library. Much of my leisure would go to golf and tennis, and I should turn out to cheer the Old Boys when they played cricket against The School. I should be a modestly prominent member of the British Legion, a Freemason, and one of the Watch and Ward committee for the suppression of vice. Occasionally I should take my wife to London, and when we returned invariably express the original idea that there's no place like home. I should drink water with my lunch, and a couple of whiskies after dinner. My sons would attend the worst best schools, the kind which teach biology without reference to either evolution or sex. I might even have risen to the heights of preferring to see my daughters dead than reading Aldous Huxley.

In exchange for security and good opinion I should have lost nearly everything that has made life valuable—freedom of living, thinking, and utterance; the exercise of a natural aptitude or talent, disinterested friendship, passionate love, travel, the arts, idleness.

If there was ever any danger of my falling a victim to respectability, it was averted by a sudden change in the family fortunes which took me to London. Not that London doesn't swarm with respectable people, but there are enough of the others for them not to have to live completely isolated. This change, so eagerly looked forward to, was at first a disappointment. There were three or four lifeless months at Harrow, which even then was becoming a mediocre suburb. I had few friends, and apart from the public galleries and the book shops in the Charing Cross Road (an Alma Mater to those who know how to use them) London gave me little. I dropped into moods of melancholy when I would walk up to Harrow churchyard and sit on Byron's tomb, finding the present distasteful and the future unattractive. So great is the vitality of youth, so immense its imaginary expectation of life, that it plays willingly with the idea of death, an abstract etherialised death:

"Now more than ever seems it rich to die."

When too soon the harsh reality came upon him, Keats found nothing rich in death, only a bitterness of frustration which is hardly to be borne.

A move to Teddington and enrolment at University College, London, put a period to this morbid gestation.

Teddington also was a suburb, though not nearly to the extent it is now, and far more attractive than Harrow. The appearance of the street we lived in was dull enough, but the houses had been built on a large orchard which had belonged to R. D. Blackmore, the author of that sugary *Lorna Doone*. Most of the fruit trees had been spared and were well grown, so that in spring all the gardens showed ragged pyramids of white or pink blossom, and in autumn ripening fruits. Whatever Blackmore's taste in heroines, he knew that a man cannot serve the future better than by planting trees. Those fruit trees and the blackbirds calling from them at dawn and sunset were a princely gift to posterity.

Near at hand were Mr. Pope's Twit'nam and Mr. Horace Walpole's Strawberry Hill and once aristocratic Richmond, all grown shabby and abandoned to the little people who dominate our age. There was the Thames, where one could be very happy pottering about in a canoe on summer afternoons and evenings. But the greatest asset was that we were only a couple of hundred yards from the entrance to Bushey Park, where you may walk to Hampton Court on turf under trees planted by Charles II. True, it is one of the common playgrounds of London and much scorned by intellectuals who probably never visited it except on a Bank Holiday, but I loved it. Even when it was thronged with people, something of its charm remained, but at various times during a couple of years I had it more to myself than the kings of old ever had.

The recipe for this is no secret. The park and the Palace gardens are open at 6 a.m. in summer, and there is seldom anyone about before ten. In the early morning, when the dew was still on the grass, there was a wonderful freshness under that majestic avenue of elms and chestnuts, four deep on either side. Out in the sunlight moved little groups of red and fallow deer. At the end of a mile or more of avenue comes the Palace gate, the so-called wilderness with its daffodils and primroses and crocuses and hyacinths, then the main garden with its great herbaceous border, which must surely be the longest in the world. Throughout the year it was a changing wonderland of flowers, which were raised in large greenhouses and then bedded out. It was said that in pre-1914 days the flowers alone cost 6000 pounds a year, and the money was well spent, not only because of the superbly beautiful result but because of the effect on the surrounding country. In the autumn the royal gardeners gave away the surplus of roots, cuttings, and bulbs, and for twenty miles round every garden, big and little, was enriched with the spoils of Hampton Court and the good taste of its gardeners.

In addition there were the great lawn, with more flower beds, ending in a terrace overlooking the river; the Long Water, reminiscent in a small way of Versailles; and the Privy Garden, where the melancholy King Charles I walked under guard when he was a prisoner. Now to have all this to oneself, by the simple process of getting up two hours earlier, was a very great privilege. Moreover, there were often times when I could be almost alone in the state apartments, and study in peace the Mantegna cartoons, the Raphael tapestries, and the pictures.

There are finer buildings and better galleries in Europe, but I never enjoyed any quite so well as Hampton Court. The attendants never begged for tips under pretext of giving information, which is the curse of Italy. The privilege—and it was a very great privilege—of being able to look at works of art in virtual solitude was far more valuable than I realised at the time. When we are jostled by a crowd, when people unintentionally keep crossing our line of vision, when we cannot help hearing inept remarks and expressions of fake enthusiasm, how is it possible to reach that state of contemplation which art aims at creating in us? If we do manage to reach it in spite of the difficulties, how devastating is the sudden intrusion of an ignorant ill-bred servant abusing his trust to try to get a little money! We should not tolerate such things in the concert hall. Why, then, in the art gallery and the beautiful building?

The fact is that the world no longer values the visual arts as it did in the past, no longer understands them. The palate of an alcoholic loses the ability to distinguish the infinitely different flavours and bouquets of wines, and craves only the brutal stimulus of stronger and stronger doses of spirits. In the same way modern sensibility is brutalised by a thousand crude and violent sensations, and becomes incapable of perceiving, let alone enjoying, the infinite variety of the arts. Moreover, the modern crowd is unconsciously but intensely destructive. It flocks to the mausoleums of art, not from any generous impulse, but to exercise a democratic right over booty wrested from dead aristocracies. It arrives with curiosity, passes with indifference, and departs with sneers, having gained nothing and merely prevented a minority from enjoying. Those who flung open to the mob all the art sanctuaries of Europe were perhaps well intentioned. They may have believed that they were "educating the people up to the level of art." Alas, the people have only dragged art down to their level.

How deeply I respect the ancient Japanese! In the solitude of their own exquisitely simple homes they really enjoy the full use of artistic sensibility, contemplating a simple arrangement of flowers or a single work of art. But in its heroic struggle against the white peril even Japan has lost or is losing that exquisite distinction of feeling.

At all events, Hampton Court gardens were a contrast to the arid precincts of University College. The façade of that learned institution is classical, but it was designed by an architect who either didn't know or forgot two essential facts about Greek architecture. In the first place Greek buildings were designed for a land of vivid sunshine; in the second place, they were brilliantly coloured. Under the influence of the soot and acids of London air, the columns and pediment of University College were dark grey streaked with unnatural white, so that the place looked like the rusty skeleton of a Greek temple. And there was a similar rustiness about what went on inside. In a laudable effort to set a higher standard of learning than the two old universities, London went a bit Teutonic. I should say that it was designed to turn out philologists rather than scholars, and ten thousand pedants for one poet. Somewhere about the place is a plaque recording that Robert Browning spent a year as a student there. I think I know why he only stayed one year.

I am not going to criticise London University. I am convinced that no ideal solution of the problems of education is possible, and the most a university can hope is to show a few lucky students how they may educate themselves. And in comparison with the drab task of trying to infuse an enthusiasm for learning in more or less indifferent young men, the proverbial casting of pearls was a hopeful enterprise. There seems to be a certain amount of superstition about universities and their degrees, on which topic the remarks of Gibbon are still entirely cogent. Moreover, popular clamour urges them to contradictory aims. They are expected to give their students a superior training, technical or otherwise, which will enable them later to make more money than non-university students; and at the same time the cry is that everybody ought to be allowed to go to a university. Where, then, will the material advantage be? They are expected to produce men who are at once independent thinkers and docile acceptors of the *status quo*. They are supposed to be able to test intelligence and knowledge by an ancient Chinese custom of written examinations. If they raise their standards and plough the incompetent, they are called highbrow snobs; and if they yield to popular demand and bestow degrees on everybody who can read and cipher, they are quenching the torch of culture. Exposing the uneducable for a number of years to the supposed influences of academic buildings and discourses is a waste of time and money; while insistence on rigid elimination is an offence to the sovereign people. And it is not easy to see what, if anything, all this has to do with genuine culture.

The result of the wholesale cheapening of learning will be exactly the same as the wholesale vulgarising of European art— destruction. The idea of having a whole nation of scholars is not only impossible but monstrous. The production of a nation of sciolists with no scholars at all would merely be another form of barbarism. Pure scholarship, like pure science and art, is entirely useless. That is why it is admirable, a demonstration that civilised man is neither an animal nor a savage nor a peasant, for whom nothing exists but what is immediately useful.

Among the sensible ideas of the Catholic Church is that which makes a distinction between the man and his priestly office. The efficacy of sacraments is not impaired by an unworthy officer. We can reverse this, and see merit in an individual while not wholly approving the system under which he functions. At any rate, that was how I felt about the professors

I knew at London. They inspired respect and sometimes even affection.

The two most eminent were A. E. Housman and Ker, with whom, unluckily for me, I had little contact. Housman was to be seen occasionally cruising gloomily about the corridors, probably depressed by the sins of German commentators on Manilius. It seems to me that he was the one member of the faculty (apart from the Provost) who was regarded with more awe than liking. We knew he was a real poet and probably the greatest Latin scholar in England, but he was too shyly aloof to be likeable. Yet he never refused to sign copies of *The Shropshire Lad* for his own students.

There was a legend about Ker which made him very popular. In those days London had a Poets Club, and for some mysterious reason they invited Ker to one of their dinners. I cannot imagine why he went, unless maliciously persuaded by Housman. At any rate the old gentleman got into his evening clothes and trotted off to the dinner, only to be bored for hours by having to listen to compositions by the sort of poet who belongs to poetry clubs. Ker had a mask-like face which you felt would not have changed if he were being tortured at the stake, and nobody noticed his indignant anguish. Finally somebody condescendingly suggested that perhaps Professor Ker would like to recite one of his poems. Whereupon Ker rose and with utterly solemn features and in a sepulchral tone said:

> "I'd rather be an emu
> Than a seamew;
> I'd rather be an eagle
> Than a sea-gull."

And then sat down, leaving a very perplexed audience. The more they thought about it the less they liked it.

Two or three years later I met Ker again, when he was acting as chairman to a lecture on Provençal poetry, delivered by Ezra Pound in Lady Glenconner's drawing-room. As the lecturer tied himself into a series of inextricable knots, consisting largely of "I mean to say," "what I mean is, er—er," I found myself watching Ker, who by the way was one of the best mediæval and Provençal scholars in Europe. It was the first time I had ever seen a real expression on his features. His wrinkled and slightly acid face seemed petrified with incredulous astonishment. I wish I could remember the little speech he made afterwards; it seemed to me a masterpiece of irony.

The lecturer in English at London then was Gerald Gould, at that time a white hope of English poetry. He was an amiable fellow and a good lecturer, though as far as I was concerned he had to expound authors already familiar. We all read and admired his poems and believed he had a brilliant career before him. He didn't quite achieve it. For years he had the dreadful job of reviewing half a dozen or more novels every week, work which was laborious, tedious, and intellectually below a man of his gifts. Moreover, he tied himself up with socialism, which has destroyed poets but never made one. He was a conscientious reviewer but apt to be diverted by trifles from the main theme of a book and rather stodgy in his taste. Towards the end of his life his column was read by young people à rebours; if he disliked a book they were almost sure to like it, and vice versa.

So far as I know, the name of Platt, the professor of Greek, never appeared in the newspapers, though it may be found in the rather more permanent pages of the *Classical Review*. Every genuine don seems to affect an eccentricity, and Platt's was Aristophanes. He used to put up the most disingenuous arguments to prove that Aristophanes was superior in every way to Shakespeare. Since Aristophanes had hated Euripides, so must Platt. I read *Hippolytus* and *Medea* with him, and he had the strangest method of inspiring his pupils with a love for classical literature. Every now and then he would interrupt with a remark of this sort:

"What nonsense! No human being but Euripides could perpetrate trash like this."

The other classical don, Solomon, had a winning nature and took great pains with us. His eccentricity was acrobatics. He generally lectured, not from the dais, but from the right-hand corner of the room, twisting himself in and out and up and down a rope which hung down from the lofty window. It was a strange spectacle to see him hanging by one arm and leg from the rope like a learned chimpanzee in blue serge, declaiming lines from Catullus or Vergil with unflagging gusto. His taste was as catholic as Platt's appeared to be narrow, and he had an enthusiasm for poetry which brought the classics vividly alive. A good many famous passages in English poetry are in fact translations or imitations of the classics. Whenever we came on the original of one of these, Solomon would challenge me to quote the English poet. If I couldn't, he always could.

I have forgotten the name of the mathematics man, from whom I took extra coaching in private. We soon became friendly, and one evening he lamented his inability to enjoy poetry and asked me to recommend something which might interest him. Without reflecting I mentioned Browning because he had belonged to the university, and suggested "The Bishop Orders His Tomb" because Ruskin says somewhere that the poem is an epitome of the whole Renaissance. At our next meeting I noticed an unaccountable stuffiness and coldness. What had happened was this: he had read along calmly though probably without much real comprehension until he came to the lines:

"And hear the blessed mutter of the mass,
    And see God made and eaten all day long."

As a Christian he was scandalised by what he thought a horrid blasphemy, cast Browning to perdition as an atheist, and entertained the gloomiest suspicions about me for having recommended him. It was useless to point out that Browning was a devout, a too devout, Christian; that the offending lines were not Browning's opinion but a piece of dramatic imagination, showing marvellous insight into the mind of the Renaissance. No, they were blasphemous, and Browning shouldn't have written them. When people now tell me that higher mathematics and poetry are closely akin, I am apt to be a little sceptical.

University College was co-educational, a mistake in practice however desirable in theory. Like English literature, sex should be a non-academic subject. A fair number of the men must have been killed in the war, but that fate befell none of my own few particular friends. One of them, who was obviously gifted as a writer and amused us with his wit, was drowned in a bathing accident before he was twenty. It is easy to exaggerate the talents of those who die young especially when they were the friends of one's own youth, yet it seems to me even now that if Arthur Chapman had lived he would have succeeded as a writer. I wrote a poem on his death which was published in the university magazine, and there was a project that I should edit for publication the MSS. he left. Eventually his parents decided against it, I think rightly. The true promise for the future was not in these youthful and derivative writings, but in the personality which was gone for ever. I was greatly impressed by a visit I made to his parents. I had never before been in a house so unmistakably haunted by the impalpable spirit of grief.

Another friend, after a short period of uncertainty, entered the diplomatic service and has had a very successful career. I have often thought that if I were not a writer I should like to be a diplomat; indeed there are times when I have regretted that I didn't make the required effort and combine the two. I was attracted by the cosmopolitan aspect, the opportunities for getting a thorough knowledge of foreign countries, the tradition of culture and good manners, and the certainty of having accurate knowledge of current affairs instead of the hotch-potch of fact and fiction, rumour and surmise, dished out by the press and veracious journalists who write books.

When many years later my friend was acting Chargé d'Affaires to the Vatican, I spent part of a summer with him in Rome and Vallombrosa. I had visited the Frascati villas several times as a tourist, but to go in the Embassy car was a new experience. I perceived that I had never before been allowed to absorb and enjoy the beauty of the places. I also perceived that the only kind of liberty worth having is privilege, i.e., a liberty which other people don't have. I forget whether it was on this or one of my later visits that I received a lesson in diplomacy which showed me that I lacked at least one important qualification—the ability to keep a secret in the most unguarded moments.

I don't know what gave me the idea, but I had a strong intuitive feeling that the long dispute between Church and State in Italy was on the point of being settled. We were sitting together talking of this and that as old friends do, and I had entirely forgotten the diplomat in the friend. Apropos of nothing in particular, I said I had a feeling the Roman question would soon be settled, and asked what he thought. He laughed carelessly and said:

"I don't see why you should think that."

Notice he didn't affirm or deny, even gave me an opportunity to say why I did think so. But there was something in his laugh which made me feel an awful fool for even making the suggestion; and something in his tone which reminded me that one must never discuss foreign affairs with a diplomat,

67

above all when he is an intimate friend. I apologised, and changed the subject.

About a fortnight later the big headlines in the *Giornale d'Italia* informed me of the accomplished fact and left me reflecting. It is quite incredible that my friend failed to know of the negotiations which must have been going on at the very time I made my remark. Therefore he had put me off a true scent very neatly indeed. In his place should I have been as quick and skilful? I felt perfectly certain I should not. Certainly, I reflected, I have missed a great deal that would have interested me through not belonging to the *corps diplomatique*. On the other hand by not getting me, H.M.'s diplomatic service hasn't missed much.

There was one other friend of those days whose character and fate are not without interest. He was the nearest thing to the historical Crichton I have ever met. He was handsome and something of an athlete. He wrote, he painted, he was a musician, something of a linguist, an amateur actor, a good ballroom dancer. At the university he was taking a special course in biology, and when I dropped in to see him in his laboratory I admired the skill of his dissections and the accuracy of his drawings. It seemed to me that here was a young man of my own time potentially equivalent to the many-sided man of the Renaissance I admired so much. I thought it altogether admirable that while he was making a delicate biological dissection he could talk of the opera we had seen at Covent Garden the night before, or of the poets we were reading, or of Whistler and the French Impressionists.

The war came, and seemed only to bring out another side of his versatile nature. He was promoted a field officer while still in his twenties, and was a great social success at Cairo. Soon after the war, he became interested in the cinema. When such expeditions were still something of a feat, he crossed Africa from the Cape to Cairo, made a film and published a book about it. Then I lost sight of him. Years later I heard that for a long time he had been living in retirement, "a complete hermit." Was it some weakness in him which rendered all his gifts useless? Is it a weakness in an era of specialists that the world could find no permanent place for him? Or, as I prefer to think, has he not seen the futility of all success, which he could have had in so many ways, and may he not be seeking in solitude and meditation some ultimate wisdom, some means of harmonising an exceptionally complex nature? Perhaps that renunciation is the supreme success.

There is a novel in that, if one could work it out.

Chapter VI

LEAVING University College for the last time I walked, as I had so often walked before, down Gower Street towards Bloomsbury, Soho, and Charing Cross. In this I detect an accidental symbolism which is rather pleasing—the departure from buttressed respectability towards the freer if frowstier fields of bohemianism. Not that I ever wholly shuffled off the bourgeois. Certain prejudices or standards of behaviour and material conditions clung to me. I could not, for instance, give up my daily bath and clean pocket handkerchief; nor could I ever endure the downright squalor in which some of my artist friends lived with seeming satisfaction. I am convinced they really liked squalor, because when they did get money they merely increased their hugger-mugger without any attempt at tidying up their lives or their surroundings. I should say I was naturally the eremitical kind of bohemian, far more akin to Mr. Eames in Douglas's *South Wind* than to the loafers who sat about gossiping and drinking Parker's poison at the Nepenthe club.

As I have tried to show, there were among the London professors men who were gifted, learned, and unselfishly amiable. (Artists are seldom amiable in that way; they are too self-centred, too preoccupied with their desperate strife against a philistine society.) For all their virtues, University College was a philistine stronghold. At least it gave me that impression, which comes to the same thing so far as I am concerned. There was something desiccated about it, something that froze the genial current of the soul. In the morning as I crunched over the gravel of the large arid courtyard I would feel a flagging of energy and spirits, a sense of discouragement. It looked as if the time of everyone concerned was being wasted.

There was every reason why I should go. By means of a complicated series of speculations my father contrived to lose his money, and was practising his profession in London, not very successfully. With characteristic energy and good sense my mother eventually solved that problem by buying and running a famous old Sussex inn. Obviously I could not continue to be an expense to my parents. What was to be done?

This is an ancient and fish-like problem, which in its innumerable forms will continue to occupy countless young men and women until such time as all humanity is enslaved by giant corporations and everybody does, not what he wants to do, but what he is forced to do. In spite of all the talk about liberty and opportunity, I have a suspicion that this is exactly what the great majority really desires—a mediocre security, a prescribed routine and no responsibility, above all no responsibility for its own individual life. Such was not my view, either then or now.

The bourgeois always rats in money disasters. To me it was a valuable lesson, though admittedly rather a shock at first, to find how people who had abounded in flattering expressions about my talents when my father was in a position to make me a handsome allowance, suddenly performed a volte-face, discovered that I was the most ordinary of young men, and formed a high-pressure group to force me into some inferior and underpaid job. There was one "friend," older than I, who represented a special type of bourgeois self-deception which seems worth exposing. He did not take the line that my father's financial losses had suddenly deprived me of my wits and any gifts I had hitherto been thought to possess. On the contrary, he sympathised enormously, but then, "my dear fellow, consider"—the inconveniences of lacking money. (I was considering them.) He himself intended to write, but was going about it sensibly. He would work at his profession for a number of years, say until he was thirty-five or even forty, and then retire with a modest competence and devote himself for the rest of his life to the Muses. He urged me, he entreated me to do the same, and offered an introduction to some large firm in the City of London.

Well, that conversation took place nearly thirty years ago. My "friend" prospered in his profession, and could long since have retired with his competence. He must now be about fifty-five and is still climbing up the climbing wave, hoping presumably for some further "honour" (he already has one title) and the security of a few more thousands. But he certainly hasn't done any writing, for I looked up his name in the catalogue of the British Museum a few years ago, and found the most eloquent of blanks. And that failure is of less consequence than the fact that he lacked either courage or ability to live the life he so vehemently affirmed he longed for and intended to live.

Naturally, I could not foresee the future. All I knew then was that his advice made me feel depressed and aroused a vague instinctive suspicion that this plan might be all very well for him but didn't look so good to me. I took the letter of introduction he forced on me, but I did not tell him of an alternative line of action I was considering which, perhaps owing to a streak of pig-headedness in me, his arguments in the opposite direction made suddenly attractive.

It is with a feeling of gratitude and affection that I speak of Mr. Beare and his kindness to me. At that time he was sports editor of one of the big London dailies, and I had met him more or less casually through friends with whom I went rowing on the Thames. I won't flatter either him or me by suggesting that he had any particular sympathy with my studies or literary plans or with the way of life I had in mind, but he had some respect for literature and he was a good-hearted man very willing to help a beginner. And in spite of the differences in age and temperament we genuinely liked each other.

We had many talks together, and I now see that by innumerable anecdotes he tried to give me the advantage of his experience of life and his homely sensible wisdom. As a respectable journalist, who for many years had earned a good income in his profession, Mr. Beare naturally did not take the gloomy view of all forms of writing for a living which was held by my other advisers. He warned me that nobody could make a living out of poetry, though he thought he could help me to pick up a few guineas. He was proposing to take a flat in Bloomsbury and offered to let me share it on terms very advantageous to me, on condition that for two or three afternoons a week I acted as his assistant in covering sporting events he couldn't find time to attend, and for which I was to be paid the usual space rates. And he made this proposal just at the moment when others were trying to bully me into an office.

I fear Mr. Beare and I were at cross purposes without knowing it. I have little doubt that he believed I should settle down to his type of journalism when I found how easy it was and that eventually I should drop poetry and literature and foreign travel and all the rest of my nonsense in exchange for a staff appointment on his paper. To me it appealed merely as a stopgap until I could get established as a literary journalist.

I was still living at home and still had not given notice of leaving University College when I secretly made a first experiment as Mr. Beare's assistant. The secrecy was because I knew everybody about me would be scandalised and furious at me for doing anything so low and vulgar as sporting journalism. Primed with a press pass and Mr. Beare's instructions I went off to see Blackheath play the Harlequins, and was not a little disconcerted to find that the Blackheath captain was no other than the man who had been captain of the First XV at my own school. One of the real newspaper men—I'm almost sure it was

The Times correspondent—saw I was a novice and helped me. I had taken one of Maurice Hewlett's novels to read, and in the intervals we discussed his work and Thomas Hardy's, which somehow was a comfort.

It seems to have been a Victorian tradition, still lively in those days, that sordid surroundings and dirt were a necessary guarantee of all serious business. The filthiest and most squalid holes I have ever seen outside a really bad slum were the chambers of highly successful barristers. The next worst were pre-1914 newspaper offices. Bare dingy walls that had once been white-washed, unscrubbed carpetless floors covered with an insane litter of newspapers, spoiled sheets of paper, ticker tape, and what-not trampled by muddy feet, and a hurricane of draughts—such was my impression of the Fleet Street office where I found Mr. Beare that evening, chewing a cigarette and writing his article at a long inky deal table. I asked how much I should write and he, lost in the reveries of composition, answered absently:

"Stick—stick and a half."

I stared at him, not having the least idea what a stick was, whether five lines or five hundred. I sat down and devoted what seemed to me a more than adequate amount of space for a particularly futile form of human restlessness; and this turned out to be all right, though a bit on the short side. It seemed to me contemptible that grown men should waste their time playing a children's game and even more contemptible that other grown men should want to waste time reading about the event; but I kept this to myself, and, having delivered my copy, went home and re-read some Shelley.

Before committing myself irrevocably to these irregular ways I thought I should at least see the business man to whom I had the letter of introduction. The memory censor, who tries to prevent us from remembering unpleasant things, refuses to let me remember either his name or his business or even the address. I had to wait, I remember, for some time in a large outer office, and occupied myself by watching some twenty or thirty young men mysteriously working over papers and ledgers at desks. They wore lounge suits with creases in their trousers and starched collars, in contrast to my informal undergraduate dress of flannel trousers, tweed jacket, soft collar, and no hat. Their voices were genteel, and all had close-cropped hair shiny with brilliantine, all except one who wore long ringlets and a most unhappy expression. I wondered very much how he got there and how he liked all those hearty-looking rugger players—I would have wagered anything they made his life a misery and that he was the sole support of a widowed mother. . . .

This story was just getting interesting as I ran over various ways in which the ringleted youth might escape to a more congenial life when I was summoned for my interview. I suppose it does often happen that two human beings take an instant and spontaneous dislike to each other, but I know I have rarely felt so much reciprocal hostility so speedily. My daimon, who always becomes internally clamorous when the accidents of life bring me to a situation he knows is not for me, was urgent that I should do something strenuous at once—insult the man or run away or both. However, I controlled myself, answered all questions politely, and even promised to come back again in a few days with more letters from the Provost of London University, parsons, lawyers, beadles, and what-not, which if satisfactory might privilege me to start work at a salary of forty pounds a year. If I behaved in a wholly satisfactory and exemplary way I should eventually be given five hundred a year, and at about sixty-five retire with a steady but inadequate pension. And then once more I found myself in the unfamiliar streets of the City.

I took an exceedingly gloomy view of this proposal for it seemed to me that in no circumstances could I endure that man's presence for a single day. It didn't look a hopeful way of subsidising a career in poetry. No doubt I was grasping and worldly-minded, but I couldn't help noticing that I was required to give the whole of my time in exchange for a token salary and vague conditional promises which (see how unfair these shifty bohemians are to men of integrity!) might easily be broken.

I had with me a portfolio containing among other things twenty or thirty of my poems and translations of poems, and also two or three letters of introduction to editors given me by Mr. Beare. On an impulse I took a bus to Fleet Street, and, choosing one of the letters at random, presented it and asked boldly for an interview. Here too I waited in the strange squalor of the newspaper office, which yet had something friendly and almost attractive after the Podsnappian mahogany and starch from which I had just fled; and here too I was eventually received.

Unfortunately I don't remember this editor at all clearly, because he has got mixed up with several others whom I saw in those days. I have a composite memory of a middle-aged Scot in gold-rimmed glasses, with an air of severity and philistine narrowness which failed to conceal the fact that he was intelligent and good-humoured. Instead of putting on airs and asking me how many dukes and beadles I knew, he questioned me sensibly about my education, and had me repeat an ode of Horace and some lines from Homer. Strange goings on in a newspaper office! I should almost doubt my own recollection, were it not that the Scots have always had a high regard for education. But now that respect for the classics marks an epoch. The successor of that editor today is no doubt just as genial a fellow, but in the very unlikely event of his having time to see an unknown free-lance he would certainly give the advice to forget such unprofitable and musty stuff as Horace and Homer as quickly as possible.

As a matter of fact my Scotsman had an original idea, and warned me that poetry didn't pay. Having paid this lip service to the ventripotent god of business, he proceeded to falsify it by immediately buying two of my poems. Moreover, he said that I might send him others from time to time, and that when they were "suitable" (whatever that might mean) he would use them. I then passed on to the office of Mr. Beare's paper, and proceeded to draw what I had earned there during the previous week.

On my way home that evening I did a little calculating. By giving up a couple of afternoons to reporting and by selling two poems which I should have written anyway, I had made as much as I could have earned by giving all my time for a month to the City dungeon, supposing that I knew enough respectable people to achieve that slavery. True, there was no guarantee that I could continue to do this regularly, but then was there any guarantee that I could be an industrious and exemplary clerk? I rather thought not, and I may add that I am now perfectly certain I should not.

Long before this I had given some attention to the problem of what I did and did not want in life, but on this journey I forced myself to make a summary. I had no objection, on moral, political, or any other grounds, to the enjoyment of filthy lucre. I regretted my father's carelessness in losing so much money; but as I have myself since been robbed of considerable sums by honest English lawyers, I can scarcely blame him. He, poor man, was part of the eternal swindle of society and could not, like his son, laugh at it and point a pen. The French always have the precise phrase; in this case it is *"la scélératesse des hommes."* Would he see it? No!

Even at that age I saw through the swindle, which in essence consists of enslaving oneself to the machine by acquiring multitudes of unnecessary objects and consumable goods, merely for the purpose of enriching a host of commercial parasites. I had read my *Walden*, and realised that my frugality was a supremely valuable asset. As Socrates walked through the agora, I could walk down Bond Street and perceive how many things there were I didn't want. What I wanted was freedom, and for me "freedom" meant something entirely different from the cant of "freedom"; it meant the disposal of my days and hours and thoughts as I wanted, and not as a predatory industrial system wanted. I saw clearly that this would involve a certain amount of sacrifice. Like a wild creature caught in a trap (and how I wish that the wild things could trap the trappers!) I had to sacrifice a limb to save my life.

Rousseau has a story (which I don't believe) of how he had a Damascus-road vision on the way from Vincennes to Paris, when in fact he merely saw the possibilities of an idea given him by Diderot. My vision on the suburban railway was genuine. I was fed up with petty snobbishness, and only too anxious to avoid social climbing and any dishonouring honour which a government can inflict. In religion and even in politics I was more or less a Gallio, caring nothing. What I wanted to do was to enjoy life, to enjoy *my* life in *my* way; and that in no wise depended on the three fatal vices, the exercise of power, the possession of property, the esteem of other featherless bipeds. I was not only willing but determined to make exertions, but not for the financial benefit of the social machine.

What interested me was a way of life, the way of life of the good European. I wanted to know and to enjoy the best that had been thought and felt and known through the ages—architecture, painting, sculpture, poetry, literature, food and wine, France and Italy, women, old towns, beautiful country. Greek was not too good, nor the refined civilisation of Catholicism too delicate, for me. By the luck of a shuffle of genes I was one for whom the visible world existed. I could twist to my own end the obviously apocryphal remark attributed to the humanist Giovanni de' Medici: "Since God has given us the Papacy, let us enjoy it." Since my parents had given me life, I saw no reason why I should not enjoy it. So long as I could keep myself intact and preserve most of my time, it was a matter of indifference that I should record the talents of young men throwing and kicking a leather ball about or even that I should be polite to Scotchmen in gold-rimmed glasses. I was exactly in the position of a woman who from time to time does a bit of whoring so that she may devote all the rest of her life to a fascinating but penniless lover.

So I didn't go back to the man in the City of London, and have rejoiced in that decision for almost thirty years. True, I must grow old and take the kicks from the donkeys' heels; and die and have them stale on my grave; but let come what come may, I shall have had my day, and a day such as the eunuch donkeys dare not dream of as their masters crack the whip.

I did not put any of these views to the Provost of London University when I said good-bye to him, but merely announced that I had a job in Fleet Street. Evidently he belonged to the same school of thought as Mr. Grey, for he asked frigidly if I considered it a good thing to be throwing myself about in print at my age. This kind of rhetorical question has endless possibilities of debate, but I evaded it as politely as I could, and was dismissed to my fate with the academic equivalent of a blessing. With a feeling of exaltation I turned my back on the statues of the marble strigil-user and discus-thrower who stood so patiently naked in rain and cold at the foot of the great flight of steps leading up to the classical frontispiece of the college, and for the last time walked down Gower Street.

As I said, to my excited mind there seemed something symbolical in putting that street behind me for ever. At that time there was only one break in the long monotonous façades which seemed almost to meet in the distance like two railway lines. Indeed architecturally they were not much more exciting than a railway track. Eighteenth-century ideals of symmetry and regularity and correctness had been craftily falsified in the interests of a bleak unashamed utility. The purpose had been to give an illusion as cheaply as possible; 19th-century burgesses were to have the illusion that they were living in the style of 18th-century gentry. The result was about as close to the original as a fireman is to a Roman emperor. It was a desolating example of the democratic attempt to standardise aristocratic luxury cheaply, an enterprise nearly as absurd as trying to supply every French farmer with a miniature Trianon to live in. There was a stagnant sameness about the street which became quite nightmarish, so that you seemed to remain for minutes in exactly the same place however fast you walked, until suddenly and amazingly you stumbled into Bedford Square. The monotony of

> "Window just with window mating,
> Door on door exactly waiting,"

suggested a similar monotony in the lives of the departed who had dwelt there fifty years before. One could imagine the same roasts steaming in every kitchen, the same over-worked servants stumbling up every identical stairway with heavy scuttles of coal, and in every parlour the same philoprogenitive matron reading *Dombey and Son*. It seemed as if you could truthfully write over every house:

> "We have not sighed deep, laughed free,
> Starved, feasted, despaired—been happy."

Whether such a regimentation of life ever occurred in precisely that way outside my imagination is of no importance. The essential fact is that respectable life was and unluckily still is regimented, and that I fled from it in horror. Bernard Shaw says that when he was young he decided it was better to see straight on a pound a week than to squint on a million. I have no claim to such an ideal of intellectual integrity, but I did feel it was better to live free on a pound a week than to serve for a million.

An escapist, of course. Taking risks which now look insanely reckless (but who then foresaw two European wars?) I gleefully escaped from every activity which engages the attention of statisticians. Never, I reflected as I hastened down Gower Street, should I trouble the tranquil graphs of Mr. and Mrs. Sidney Webb. There is a (probably apocryphal) story of those two, that they spent their honeymoon working on statistics at the British Museum. Sensible people. They did what really interested them, regardless of custom and fashion. And that was precisely what I proposed to do.

A year or two later I was present at a discussion of this topic in the house of a philosopher, who was something of an oracle to literary youth. Some civic-minded person said that a poet (most of those present were hopeful of being poets) had no right to independence, that economically poetry was utterly useless, that everyone ought to give an economic equivalent for value received, and that therefore every poet should be made to work and merely allowed to write poetry as a spare-time hobby. I confess I thought this was not illogical, if you took a purely utilitarian view of life, and I waited for the philosophic oracle's reply with some anxiety.

He began by saying that a wealthy country could easily afford the luxury of a few idle poets, especially in view of the fact that it spent vastly more on far less reputable amusements, such as prostitutes and prize-fighters. A complex civilisation could not function on the mere barter system implied by our economist friend. How, on his assumptions, could he dare to claim any economic value for the ravings of economists? They were hopelessly at variance with each other, and he was prepared to argue that nations were prosperous precisely because they ignored the alleged principles of professional economists.

It was true that strictly speaking no economic value could be attached to poetry, but that was equally true of all intellectual pursuits. (It flashed across my mind that philosophy is as economically valueless as poetry.) Economically useless parsons, he proceeded, might be defended because they gave spiritual comfort to primitive minds. While poets plainly were incapable of consecutive abstract thought, they had performed such services as refining the relations of the sexes, inventing many forms of beauty, and by forcing the world to study that wonderful human invention, that indispensable tool of civilisation, language. . . .

Naturally this led to a long philosophical-political-economic argument, from which I soon absconded.

It seems to me significant that during this time I never once attended a political meeting. I managed to find plenty of time to haunt the art galleries; I took some trouble to get into theatres and music halls; and I cheerfully stood in line for a couple of hours to hear an opera in Covent Garden. Now I come to think of it I neglected almost unlimited political opportunities of every brand, from the Young Conservatives to the anarchists of Goodge Street. Yet, comically enough, I should have been offended if anybody had questioned my devotion to republicanism and socialism.

I am now a bit of a realist in politics. It seems to me that, whatever the label, it always boils down to the same thing: the strong take what they want, the weak accept what they can get. The great mass of mankind is always exploited either by force or craft. Since the exploited so greatly outnumber the rest, a young man naturally concludes that the real power is in their hands and that all that is necessary is to point out what he thinks are their true interests. Unluckily this is not true. As Montaigne said long ago, the people are helpless without able leaders, so that politics everywhere boils down to a contest in leading or deceiving the people. Sometimes an energetic set of opposition leaders is able to profit by the weakness or embarrassment of the old leaders, and chucks them out. The oppressors are now oppressed; a lot of changes happen on paper; and after a few years the mass finds itself exactly where it was before, except that the new rulers probably are greedier and more ruthless. This is called having a revolution, during which futile proceeding many of the finer and gentler manifestations of civic peace are brutally stamped out. I don't say there haven't been ameliorations in the world, and I hope there may be many more, but I distrust utopias. Above all, I mistrust the violent short-cut to utopia. I think it improbable, for instance, that the average European was happier between 1790 and 1815 than he was between 1765 and 1790.

I can see cogent reasons why reasonable men may be republicans and socialists; I can also see cogent reasons on the other side. But I must admit that at the time of which I am speaking there were no very cogent reasons for my political beliefs. Like a good many other people, I based them on ignorance and emotion. My republicanism was a schoolboy affair picked up at second hand from Landor and Swinburne and American declaimers. The Gettysburg Address is a glorious piece of rhetoric which everyone should know by heart; but in point of fact it leaves all the practical problems of human organisation exactly where it found them. My socialism had no solid basis whatsoever. It was a figment derived from William Morris, Shaw, Wells, and forgotten journalists.

True, there was an emotional basis—I couldn't bear to see or hear of human beings deprived of the common essentials of life. I thought that was wrong at seventeen, and I still think so at forty-seven; but what the complete permanent solution is I know no more now that I did then. Much as I admire George Moore and Norman Douglas I have never been able to imitate their pose of turning away from misery with a contemptuous shrug. I say "pose" because I know from experience that Douglas is a compassionate man, and I dare say Moore was too.

Somewhere about this time a revolution occurred in Portugal, Dom Manoel was deposed from the throne, and a republic was proclaimed. At that time I knew rather less than nothing about Portugal. I did not know, for instance, that quite half the population was made up of illiterate peasants living mentally in the middle ages. Unconsciously I peopled the country with worthy and public-spirited abstractions, who had only to be freed from the tyranny(!) of Dom Manoel to enjoy an immediate utopia. I did not reflect that Dom Manoel's father and elder brother had recently been murdered by political assassins; that he was little older than I was and had not been given a chance to show whether he would rule well or ill; that he was probably quite as patriotic, well intentioned, and able as those who threw him out; and that in a Catholic and largely peasant country a king would probably have more chance of putting through necessary reforms than a junta of anti-clerical revolutionaries.

These and many other practical considerations touching the state and well-being of Portugal never entered my head, for the obvious reason that I was in total ignorance of them. All I went on was an abstract and unfounded belief that monarchies are corrupt and republics perfect *per se*. So I celebrated the tremendous victory of good over evil in a poem. I sent this to a leftist journal called *Justice*, which in the name of abstract justice advocated the very practical injustice of depriving a great many people of their property and probably of their lives. *Justice* printed my poem conspicuously. This filled me with joy, about seventy-five per cent of which was gratified vanity and about twenty-five per cent conviction that this finally clinched the whole matter for happy Portugal. Alas, utopia did not arrive in Portugal either then or later. Riots, disturbances, and more revolutions succeeded each other for twenty years, until finally Portugal became a dictatorship which revived in a harsher form the supposedly abhorrent features of the abolished monarchy. Long before this, however, I had begun to suspect the ability of revolutionary idealists to make good their glittering promises or even to maintain the *status quo* of comparative well-being they overthrew, or wished to overthrow, as unjust and oppressive.

Apart from this scepticism, I had another reason for avoiding any active part in politics. In Tillier's novel, *Mon Oncle Benjamin,* is a phrase which has stuck in my mind—*"l'homme constitutionnel est triste,"* which might be rendered: political man is a dull dog. Of course he is. The few people who actually rule compensate the inevitable worries and responsibilities by the pleasure of exercising power, which seems to have a great attraction for them. But the great mass of the community is supposed to worry and to feel responsible without any more power than casting an occasional vote which will very likely not have the slightest influence anyway.

In politics what is called public opinion is a farce, a matter of prejudice and personal interests. For a voter to have a truly informed and valid opinion on matters of internal policy he would first have to be intelligent and then spend all his time mugging up blue books and other sources of exact information. To have a correct opinion on foreign and world affairs he would have to possess a great deal of secret knowledge which governments either can't or won't make public. All the voter can do is to read the newspaper which supports the "principles" favourable to his pocket. Politicians long ago gave up attempts to appeal to reason and knowledge. The dictators simply tell people what to believe and what to do. The politicians of the democracies produce a certain amount of cant and appeal to prejudices and passions. I have never known an election which was not fought on false and usually trivial issues. Why, then, should I worry over problems I can't in any way control or delude myself into accepting non-existent responsibility?

As I reach the end of Gower Street on this memorable occasion, imagine me intercepted by a *Pilgrim's Progress* character, one Mr. Social-Revolutionary, with the following dialogue:

Mr. Social-Revolutionary: Tarry a moment, Young Man, whither dost thou hasten so fast?

Young Man: Sir, I am bidden to a great and excellent banquet to be given by my singular good lady, my lady Life, at the sign of The Globe.

Mr. S-R.: Out upon thee for a lewd fellow! Knowest thou not that this same Life is ill-reputed of grave and sober men, inasmuch as she keepeth a tavern or bawdy-house wherein she doth lure many a young man to perdition?

Y.M.: It is true, Sir, that such are your words, but that I do believe the same is not true. And therefore, Sir, I beseech your good mastership to let me no further in my journey, which I perceive must be long.

Mr. S-R.: Friend, I have a concern for thee and for all mankind, and will in no wise suffer ye to be lost. Hast thou never heard of Mr. Discontent and Mr. Cloud Dreamer, who will bring you speedily to the earthly paradise hight Perfect State?

Y.M.: Sir, of this somewhat I have heard, but . . .

Mr. S-R.: Tush! But me no buts. Answer me, thou losel, wottest thou not there is evil in the world?

Y.M.: Alack, yes, Sir, but . . .

Mr. S-R.: And knowest thou not that the faces of all poor honest men (for to be poor is honest and to be honest is to be poor), their faces, I say, are ground down ever, and upon their sweat do batten sundry hideous and corpulent fiends that are

86

ever clad in top-hats and morning clothes, with gold watch chains and diamond rings, and do never cease from smoking Havana cigars and drinking the drink of iniquity, even French champagne?

Y.M.: It is true that I have seen cuts of the same in certain diurnals, but never yet did I set eyes upon one of these same bloated fiends.

Mr. S-R.: Weenest thou that such as these would consort with such as thee? Methinks thy doublet is none of the best and thy shoon are clouted.

Y.M.: Why truly, Sir, these be my workaday habiliments, yet others have I, rich and of good conceit, wherein I may present myself before ladies and worshipful men.

Mr. S-R.: Now well do I perceive that thou art a most pitiful prevaricator. Art thou not poor?

Y.M.: Alack, yes, Sir, but . . .

Mr. S-R.: How much hast thou in good unclipped coin?

Y.M.: But sixteen pence, Sir, yet do I not lack for gold from my lord Paper-Blast and e'en from my lady Poesy.

Mr. S-R.: Thou dotest and sinnest grievously. That same Paper-Blast grindeth thy face and doth batten on thy sweat.
. . .

Y.M.: Under favour, Sir, I sweat not, neither is my visage marred, as thou mayest perceive.

Mr. S-R.: And that ill-favoured wench, Poesy, doth naught but cozen idle fellows with empty words. She shall be banished from Perfect State, I warrant you. But hearken to me.

. . . [*He discourses for twenty-five minutes on the wrongs of men, and for twenty minutes on Perfect State.*]

Y.M.: Sir, somewhat of all this have I heard before, and yet I know not, and I have no stomach for wrangling. I perceive thou art a learned man, and I would fain be resolved of a certain question.

Mr. S-R.: Ask on. I have witty answers to all questions culled from my Capital Bible.

Y.M.: Tell me then, thou who hast conned the chronicles of wasted time, in what ages and among what peoples has Perfect State been extant?

Mr. S-R.: Why, truly, in none, forasmuch as men were oppressed by tyrants and evil lords. But wherefore musest thou?

Y.M.: Sir, I muse that ye should believe ye can achieve in a trice that which for so many ages hath baffled all mankind.

Mr. S-R.: We only have found the way. In us alone is truth.

Y.M.: Sir, there be certain folk hight Christians, from whom I most vehemently suspect ye have pilfered. For many an age they have awaited Perfect State through a certain second coming, yet it comes not.

Mr. S-R.: Thou errest and reasonest most vilely. ∴ . .

Y.M.: Not so, Sir. This same dream of Perfect State is right ancient. I am a poor scholar, and under one Master Holofernes I have read in right Greek lettering Plato his *Republic*. Where he failed why should a braggart such as thou win? You would have me put off living until you have brought us all to Perfect State. Had all men done this, thou and I had never been, nor would any man have laboured to fashion the multitude of things wherein I delight. Moreover, Sir, at the banquet of Lady Life, whom thou scornest, I am avised that there awaiteth me a fair damsel with whom, though as yet I know her not, I would fain be cater-cousin. You bid me wait, but belike I must wait till my hoary beard reacheth my knee or I be in my grave. And what reck I of Perfect State then? A fico for it. You must know that we poets have our wise men, and thou hast doubtless heard of worthy Master Herrick?

Mr. S-R.: A foul malignant, a base Arminian . . .

Y.M.: Yet, Sir, is it not wisdom that he uttereth?

> "Then be not coy, but use your time,
>   And while ye may, go marry;
> For having lost but once your prime
>   You may for ever tarry."

Mr. S-R.: I do not forbid thee to marry. I bid thee set thy hand to the plough and labour with me and my fellows that thy children may not be of the oppressed but rejoice with me and Mr. Discontent and Mr. Cloud Dreamer in Perfect State.

Y.M.: Why, as touching that, thou knowest my mind. Yet there is a saying among the French . . .

Mr. S-R.: These Frenchmen be exceeding hot fiery whoresons . . .

Y.M.: It may be, yet is it true that *le mieux est l'ennemi du bien.*

Mr. S-R.: Yet shall thy chap-book and losel ballad quips avail thee nothing on the day of Judgment, when there shall be weeping and gnashing of teeth by the rich and idle. In their blood and in thine shall iniquity be quenched.

Y.M.: Why, verily, Sir, I had as lief perish as dwell in Perfect State built by thee and thy fellows.

Mr. S-R.: Now I perceive thou art utterly damned, and until the day of vengeance thou wilt waste thy days in penning of bawdy songs and gaping at trinkets in rich men's houses, and thy nights in junketing with wenches and idle fellows!

Y.M.: Pauvre âme, c'est cela.

Chapter VII

Hinc incipit vita nova . . .

For some minutes I have been wondering why at this moment I should want to quote Dante's *Vita Nuova,* a book I have not looked into for years. Gradually I have recollected. In those days, as now, there existed a snob culture, emanating from university sets and London cliques, which refined all literature to three or four fashionable authors. An exaggerated and simulated admiration for these chosen preciosities alone constituted intellectual salvation; while not to admire them or, still worse, not to have heard of them, put the unlucky person in the ranks of the inferior. The high-hatting and looking down the nose which the English unfortunately cultivate in their social life are also imported into the free commerce of the republic of letters. (Exactly parallel imbecilities exist in Montparnasse and Greenwich Village.) From the centres, whatever they may be, these snob values spread slowly in concentric circles until finally they hit the suburban-Soho crowd.

The time-lag in those days must have been terrific, for, believe it or not, the three indispensable books were Fitzgerald's Omar, Rossetti's *Vita Nuova,* and Andrew Lang's *Aucassin and Nicolette;* all translations, you perceive. Illustrated editions of these works were freely handed about at Christmas, concrete evidences of extreme good taste, much as an edition of Gerard Manley Hopkins and a bottle of gin would be now. Naturally I studied these works. I am inclined to think that Fitzgerald's Omar is better than the fashion of the moment allows, a kind of Elegy in an Oriental Wine-Shop. (I surmise that it is no longer fashionable to quote it over a one and three-penny bottle of Algerian claret, labelled St. Julien, in a Soho restaurant.) Being ambitious I determined to study these works in the original, though after a glance at the original of Omar I wisely decided that I was both unwilling and incompetent to study Persian without a teacher. But I plugged away at Dante and *Aucassin,* and felt rather grand about it, though obviously it was a senseless way to begin the study of Italian and Old French.

But that is why a quotation from the *Vita Nuova* came so unexpectedly to mind at this point.

Somebody—I forget who—at this time took me to what I firmly believe was my first literary party. It was in the flat of an ardently climbing lady novelist, and to get in at all you had to know the passwords—Omar, *Vita Nuova, Aucassin,* there pronounced Aw-cassin. Evidently primed by my friend, the hostess introduced me as "a poet who reads *Aw-cassin* in the original," and then vanished into another room. It was whispered to me that the inner room contained a Great Poet, and I gradually realised that in this salon there was an outer room for the unknown and an inner shrine for the illustrious.

So highbrow was this salon that there was talk of French poetry, and the ladies shivered chastely as they denounced a dreadful man with the mysterious name of Bawdy L'Air. An elderly gentleman in a dinner jacket opined gravely that he was "very Gallic," and the ladies said: "How true!" At that moment Edward Clodd was announced. I should explain that Clodd was a survivor of the Darwinian.epoch, and bore the stigmata through his pronounced likeness to the missing link. He was hustled off to join the Great Poet, and after a certain time was re-conducted to the outer door by the hostess with profuse expressions of extreme not to say fulsome politeness, while we sat in frozen awe. Returning to the centre of the room, the hostess clasped her hands, and in tones of religious pride uttered an oracle:

"Ker-wight a celebrity."

A couple of years later I met that Great Poet on more equal terms at Violet Hunt's, and he had to listen to Ezra Pound, Gaudier, and myself playing verbal ninepins with the Post-Victorians, the Royal Academy, and a variety of other pompiers' institutions. Ford Hueffer saw him down to the door, and came back chuckling. We asked what the joke was, and he said:

"When we got to the front door he asked very anxiously: 'Are all the young men like that?' and I said: 'Oh, they're comparatively mild,' and he said: 'Oh, my God!' and ran away."

The first months of this *vita nuova* were lonely. That is one of the inconveniences of a rigidly Spartan regime, such as I had so blithely undertaken. But I was very far indeed from being unhappy. There is happiness in personal freedom, especially when it is enjoyed for the first time; and a further satisfaction in taking full responsibility for one's own life. Except for a couple of afternoons a week and an occasional evening, I disposed of my time exactly as I wished. I hasten to add—in view of the human aptness for swift and charitable judgments—that I did not prize this liberty because it gave opportunities for what are known as vicious courses.

On the contrary, I was too absorbed in other interests to think about such things, even if I had had the money for them. In order to have more money for books, I cut my diet down almost dangerously, and gave up smoking and drinking entirely. A lifetime of such asceticism would be dull, though it might be good for one's health; but a year or two of it, especially in the late teens, is excellent discipline. The insolence and selfishness of very young men and women, children of wealthy parents who have never denied them anything, make a very unpleasant spectacle. Nobody has a right to wealth who has not experienced poverty, or to privilege if he has not known its absence.

As for purchasing females for the sportive lusts of the flesh, there was never a time when it didn't seem to me both repulsive and ridiculous. He must be a poor sort of chap with whom no woman falls in love; and who that has known this felicity would pay a poor woman to degrade herself and him? I was amused at the time—and still am—by a precaution taken by my father to disgust me with vice at the tender age of sixteen. He, dear innocent man, had no higher standard of vice than a Leicester Square café. But fate was kind to us. On one of the red plush divans sat a parson in his choker, tight as a tick and embracing a couple of tarts. He certainly looked an ass, but my father was scandalised because I laughed. In point of fact, it wasn't a laughing matter. The man must have been miserably repressed; he certainly must have lost his watch and cash, and probably his benefice.

On the whole I enjoyed this period of quasi-solitude, and got through a prodigious amount of work. I had to, because it was my chief recreation. The only thing that bothered me was what used to be called the Sabbath peace of London. If that's the Lord's day, he can keep it. The lifeless streets, inhabited only by a few people creeping about disconsolately in Sunday clothes, needed only a howling dog and an occasional corpse to reach a peak quotation in dismalness. Except for an occasional concert of a supposedly improving kind every form of civilised occupation was suppressed. The only way to meet this was to stay in all day and work. But even this was an incomplete protection. Itinerant out-of-door sects too frequently chose my street for bellowing with a brass band to the Lord of Hosts. And there were the bells,

"Where never bells have knolled to church"—how enjoyable such places are! It is one of the attractive features of the Sahara. Very likely campanology is a fascinating study, but it repels me; and if there is one thing worse than church bells, it is a carillon playing hymns on one finger, so to speak. This

dislike for bells is one of the prejudices I share with Moham-
med; the other being his respect for cats. Another anti-bell
person is Ezra Pound. When he lived near St. Mary Abbots,
Kensington, he engaged in a fierce guerrilla warfare of letters
with the Vicar on the subject. I sympathised with Ezra—half
an hour of that ear-splitting, brain-paralysing din was enough
to drive anyone mad. Luckily the laws in most countries now
restrain bell-pullers, those noisy self-advertisers who if left to
themselves would be jingle-jangling away all day and half the
night.

My solitude was short-lived, and before I was weary of it I
began to meet people. Within a few days, and almost by accident, I came across Ezra Pound, H.D., and Harold Monro,
poets who were to have some influence on the development of
art, people who had personalities of their own.

Ezra was the first poet I met on equal terms. There was no
particular inspiration in seeing Housman wandering moodily
about corridors or in listening to Gerald Gould's views on *The
Faerie Queene* and *The Hind and the Panther*. There are contradictions and perhaps a real disharmony in Ezra which make
him one of the problem children of modern poetry. It seems
to me hard to deny his flair or that he has at least a streak of
genius. In proof of the first I would cite the number of writers,
from Joyce to Hemingway, whom he picked out and boosted
when they were practically unknown. I think he lacks funda-
mental originality and self-confidence, which explains why he
has put up so many stunts. He has tasted an enormous number
of books, yet I doubt if he has ever read one with concentration
from cover to cover. There are lovely things in his short poems
and astonishing flashes in the *Cantos;* yet it must be admitted
that most of his poems are derived or even paraphrased from
earlier poets and that the structure and aim of the *Cantos* are,
to put it gently, not immediately apparent. His prose is so

violent, so mannered, so incoherent and lacking in judgment that it often seems senseless. Ford Hueffer used to say that Ezra is so ignorant of the English language that it is impossible to understand him. I should say myself that Ezra would rather perplex his readers than please them.

Yeats used to worry himself a lot about Ezra, who seemed to support one of Yeats's numerous fads, the theory of the anti-thetical self. In the winter of 1928, Mr. and Mrs. Yeats dined with me at my hotel in Rapallo. We were given a room to ourselves; I fear because Yeats was an Irish senator, but I hope because he was a great poet. It was a cold night, and Yeats arrived with his hands thrust into a pair of grey woollen socks, because he had lost his gloves. Recovering from this shock, we went to dinner. But with the spaghetti a long thin lock of Yeats's hair got into the corner of his mouth, and the rest of us watched with silent awe his efforts to swallow his hair with a strand of spaghetti. Giving this up in dudgeon, he suddenly turned to me and said in portentous tones:

"How do you account for Ezra?"

I still don't know what the answer to that is; so I said nothing. Fortunately with Yeats that never mattered. He proceeded in his pontifical style:

"Here is a man who produces the most distinguished work and yet in his behaviour is the least distinguished of men. It is the antithetical self . . ." *Und so weiter.*

I am not competent to say whether Ezra or anyone else has an antithetical self. In the first place I don't see the antithesis. In his work Ezra can be abrupt and barbarous; when he wants he can be a pleasant companion and the most generous of men. He is sensitive, highly strung, and irascible. All this throwing down of fire-irons and sputtering of four-letter words is merely Ezra's form of defence against a none too considerate world. I should say Ezra has had to put up with far worse annoyances from other people than they ever have from him.

At all events in 1912 Ezra was great fun, a small but persistent volcano in the dim levels of London literary society. London was interested and amused by him. The evening papers interviewed him at length and published his portrait; and even *Punch* had to notice the existence of a certain Mr. Ezekiel Ton who had achieved a new synthesis of Wardour Street and the wild and woolly West. Unluckily, Ezra had read Whistler's *Gentle Art of Making Enemies,* and practised it without the "gentle." And in his chivalrous generosity he made the absurd mistake of taking on himself the feuds and dislikes of his cronies, Yeats and Hueffer; for which there was no need whatever. Consequently, in spite of his endearing qualities, Ezra does not inhabit The White House at Chelsea, keeping one half of London perpetually irritated and the other half perpetually delighted with barbed gibes. He is a Rapallo troglodyte, suffering from the mental indigestion following on a feast of fascism plus the too-too solid hokum of Social Credit. *Que diable allait-il faire dans cette galère?*

Chiefly through Ezra but partly through Harold Monro I soon got to know quantities of people in very different social sets. One of the advantages of an artist's life in England is that he can be on friendly terms with practically every social group except the working class, who are dreadfully exclusive. Nothing less than a European war was needed for me with my middle-class manners, accent, and standards, to be accepted on terms of equality by working men. The aristocracy, on the other hand, were extremely easy—up to a point. There always came a moment when you felt that their charm, high spirits, and wit were a kind of gracious electioneering or slumming among intellectuals. It isn't really the haughtiness or class prejudice imagined by tweedy socialists. Or it wasn't then. They were so certain of their own position they never bothered about it. But owing to their rigid training all other people seemed dim and fabulous, and the attitude towards these surprising phenomena was dictated by the fact that Cousin Dick, Uncle Arthur, and Brother Aubry would need votes at the next election, and by a naïve and obsolescent tradition that the aristocracy are obliged to be the patrons of the arts. Unluckily their tastes were a little out of date, and dictated by prestige, historical association, and patina rather than genuine æsthetic flair.

With one or two exceptions I found the formal dinners and even more formal drawing-rooms of the wealthy bourgeoisie tedious and intolerable. Similarly with the successful trade writers, who were all secretly members of the Social Alpine Club. With the rather arty gatherings of Hampstead and Golders Green one was returning perilously near to the salon of the "ker-wight a celebrity" lady. There was a pretentiousness about such people which I couldn't stand. Why they should have been so self-conscious is a mystery, for their selves weren't much to be conscious about.

Vastly more entertaining were the evenings in Yeats's bachelor diggings in Woburn Place. The talk was often good, though after a time one grew a little weary of spooks, fairies, elementals, sorcerers, Lady Gregory, and the feud with George Moore. Yeats specialised in anecdotes and gnomic remarks, most of which have already been printed either by him or others. A curious trait in Yeats, which I have not seen mentioned, was a misplaced intellectual loyalty. Every influence, however distant, which had come into his poetical life had to be cherished and somehow reconciled with all the later influences and Yeats's own continuous development. He seemed unable to take the more rational position of admitting frankly that such people had once been valuable to him, but that while he was grateful to them he had gone on to something new. This persisted even in Yeats's later years when he made

D

that remarkable recovery and wrote some of the most beautiful lyrics of our time.

Thus, he was cluttered up with defunct tinkers who had said something funny in Sligo in the eighties, with hoary Irish liars who had positively seen a fairy, with Rossetti and Morris and Wilde, and a hundred other persons and artists from whom he had long since emancipated himself. He would talk frequently and admiringly of "my friend MacGregor," much to the perplexity of the newcomer until he discovered gradually that MacGregor had been a Scotch sorcerer of the nineties in Paris when Huysmans had made Satanism a fad. I never heard any evidence of Mr. MacGregor's powers as a sorcerer, except that he caused two "elementals" to appear on Yeats's bed, a contretemps which the poet solved happily by pushing the elementals out of the window. Or perhaps it was "my friend MacGregor" who pushed the elementals. It doesn't matter.

One of the most difficult evenings I spent with Yeats was when a party of us took Marinetti, the Italian Futurist, to see him. Sturge Moore, Ezra, and I acted as interpreters, for Marinetti spoke no English and Yeats would not talk a language of which he was not a master. Yeats read some of his own poems, which Marinetti would have thought disgustingly *passéistes* if he had understood them; and then Yeats through Sturge Moore asked Marinetti very politely to recite something of his. Whereupon Marinetti sprang up and in a stentorian Milanese voice began bawling:

> "*Automobile,
> Ivre d'espace,
> Qui piétine d'angoisse,*" etc.,

until Yeats had to ask him to stop because neighbours were knocking in protest on the floor, ceiling, and party walls.

Another trying time was when the inner group of London

literati decided to put over Tagore. Of course, he hit Yeats bang in the Blavatsky. Ezra too had a streak of superstition—hence perhaps his kinship with Alberta rain-makers. We had pi-jaw stuff about Tagore for weeks, and Yeats would read the same things over and over from *Gitanjali,* as if they had been the Book of Common Prayer and we a congregation of fanatical Episcopalians. I wasn't allowed to see Tagore, as being too profane; but I could always tell when Ezra had been seeing him, because he was so infernally smug. The snob appeal was worked with consummate skill, and the first edition of Tagore's book was limited to five hundred expensive copies. May Sinclair gave me one, which was stolen long ago—anyway I didn't want it. But by the time the popular edition was out, all the cliques were chattering Tagore like mad though most of them had never seen a word he had written. Naturally it was a best-seller, and Tagore even got a knighthood. But he blotted his official copybook by taking up an anti-British attitude in India, and the Tagore boom collapsed as quickly as it had been manufactured.

One of my best evenings with Yeats happened because I mistook the date of one of his evenings and found him alone. He wouldn't hear of my leaving, and we spent a couple of hours together by his fireside. He could not have been more pleasant and unaffected, and told me a lot about his early life in Ireland and London. During the evening he offered to read me a lyric he had finished that morning. It was:

> "Romantic Ireland's dead and gone,
>   It's with O'Leary in the grave. . . ."

Something worth remembering.

I greatly enjoyed these contacts with people in the pre-war years. It was an epoch comparatively free of fanaticisms, so that I had the experience of meeting human individuals and not merely embodied opinions. True, I had not much more than a series of glimpses of the varied yet orderly society which was England before 1914, but they sufficed. The flaws in the structure were not nearly so apparent at the time as they are in retrospect. But there was a stuffiness, almost a stupidity about the more formal groups which made me infinitely prefer the informal meetings where everyone was free to expatiate on anything and everything that interested him. That camaraderie of minds—how can one express it? I could write pages of character sketches, descriptions, dialogue, and yet fail to give an adequate expression of what I enjoyed so much. One might as well try to describe the perfume of a flower which has vanished from the earth.

Above all I was fortunate in my friendship with Ezra and H.D. It may seem strange that, with most of my English prejudices still strong, I should turn away from the English poets who became "the Georgians," and whole-heartedly throw in my lot with the two Americans. I can give one example. At a "Dutch" Soho dinner collected by Harold Monro, everyone was deploring Ezra and running him down. Finally I could stand it no longer. I stood up and said: "Ezra Pound has more vitality in his little finger than the whole lot of you put together," and walked out. That queered my pitch with a large and powerful clique, but I have never regretted it. On the contrary, time has showed and will show even more decisively how right I was.

There was more to it than that. The Georgians were regional in their outlook and in love with littleness. They took a little trip for a little week-end to a little cottage where they wrote a little poem on a little theme. Ezra was a citizen of the world, both mentally and in fact. He went off to Paris or Venice with vastly less fuss than a Georgian affronting the perils of the Cotswolds. Instead of wasting time on debating whether Walter was greater than Rupert, or whether Ralph was more of a *singer* than Jack, he invited my attention to the literature of Europe. True, he was bigoted, dogmatic, and capricious, but he did not say:

> "A little seed best fits a little soil,
> A little trade best fits a little toil:
> As my small jar best fits my little oil."

On the contrary, he talked of Arnauld Daniel and Guido Cavalcanti, of Homer and Dante, of Ronsard and El Cid—in short, of the European tradition. Instead of pap, he fed me meat. He gave me Villon, he gave me Verlaine, he gave me the Symbolistes, he gave me Flaubert, and carelessly threw in the Neo-Latins. We have come to differ over a lot of things but—I find I'm a bit like Yeats in this respect—I can't go back on the Ezra of 1912–14.

I would say of H.D. that she was more distinguished (to use one of Yeats's favourite adjectives) than Ezra, both as a person and as a mind. I have never known anybody, not even Lawrence, with so vivid an æsthetic apprehension. Lawrence was more keenly aware of the living world, but he was almost blind to the world of art. To look at beautiful things with H.D. is a remarkable experience. She has a genius for appreciation, a severe but wholly positive taste. She lives on the heights, and never wastes time on what is inferior or in finding fault with masterpieces. She responds so swiftly, understands so perfectly, re-lives the artist's mood so intensely, that the work of art seems transformed. You too respond, understand, and re-live it in a degree which would be impossible without her inspiration.

Addington Symonds said that nobody could hope to understand Italian poetry unless he were exceptionally gifted æsthetically. The same is true of H.D.'s poetry. It is the expression of a passionate contemplation of the beautiful, as the young Plato must have felt before Socrates lured him into the fictitious world of abstractions. . . . But why do I speak of such things? What possible interest can they have for the contemporary world?

Chapter VIII

IN the spring of 1912 I went to Paris.

Needless to say, this harmless step was strongly opposed by those who had my best interests at heart. It was pointed out that I had my job with Mr. Beare, that I was selling poems regularly to the evening papers, that I had had an article in a daily and another in a weekly, that I was doing reviews (unpaid, by the way) for Monro's *Poetry Review,* and that I was meeting all sorts of people. I had to earn a living, hadn't I? I wanted to write, didn't I? Well, then, here I was with the doors beginning to open, and yet at a season when "everyone is in town" I proposed to go off to the city of nameless iniquities for an indefinite period.

It did seem rather silly, but a stubborn mule of a daimon in me insisted on going. The mule-daimon might not have been so confident if at that time I had not been given a small monthly allowance by my parents.

Going down to the coast on the boat train I got into conversation with a Frenchman. He was pleasant, but gave me the impression of one under an emotional strain. As I walked from the ship to the train at Calais he came up to me, and in tones of dramatic emphasis I cannot hope to reproduce, said:

"You are now in France. You will have food that can be eat. They will *give* you WINE!"

I received this communication with British phlegm, for in those days I had little interest in food and none in wine. Sheer ignorance, plus a violently youthful scorn for material comforts. But now I understand that Frenchman, I sympathise with his emotion. I know what he meant. There is a similar plaint somewhere in Verlaine's correspondence, though I can't at the moment put my hand on the passage. If I remember rightly, he was particularly offended in England by what he poetically called "violet-hued suet puddings."

My nice Mr. Grey fully approved of this expedition, sent me his blessing and the large edition of Liddell and Scott's Greek dictionary, which I had long coveted. But he disapproved strongly of some free verse I sent him. "You were once a singing bird, Dickey," he wrote sadly, "and now you're just a beastly modern poet." To compare small things with great—so must Whitman have felt when Emerson denounced *Children of Adam,* and with a like sadness and determination disregarded his old and revered friend.

Mr. Grey also advised me to stay in the Rue de la Grande Chaumière, to avoid all cafés, and not to miss Versailles and Fontainebleau. My father told me to visit the Musée de Cluny, to study the stained glass in la Sainte Chapelle, and to stay at a "nice quiet little hotel" in the Rue de Rivoli, the name of which I forget—it may have been, I suspect it was, the Meurice. As was proper I began by obeying my father and booked a room at his hotel, only to find that its cost was exactly equivalent to my whole daily income.

Slightly incensed by this further though unnecessary proof of my father's practical ideas, I went forth at once with a map to seek the Rue de la Grande Chaumière, and almost at once found myself in the Jardin des Tuileries. The late sunshine of a cloudless May afternoon was warm and golden, and there was the faint but unforgettable smell of Paris in the air—a delicate mixture of savon de Marseille, hot rolls, lilac, and sewers. People were strolling up and down. There were grave gentlemen with red rosettes in their buttonholes, high stiff collars, and Henri IV beards, but not, alas, the sharp moustaches, pointed beards, and slightly conical top-hats I had been led to expect by ill-informed cartoonists. There were pretty ladies with very long skirts, which they held daintily, very wide-brimmed hats, and parasols. As they passed, the gentlemen looked hard at the ladies, and the ladies pretended neither to see nor to be seen, but saw everything, especially that they were looked at. There were mothers and nursemaids with children, who played without screaming, fighting, or quarrelling. There were two hand-worked merry-go-rounds with tricolour flags, one for little children which went gently, and one for older children which went fast. In the distance stood a classical triumphal arch and statues and the long façades of the Louvre.

"Linnæus fell on his knees and wept when he saw for the first time the long slope of some English upland made yellow by the tawny aromatic blossoms of the common furze."

I did nothing so timely and dramatic, but I certainly fell in love with Paris at first sight. Perhaps it is fanciful to say that central Paris *looks* the most intelligent of cities, where people not only work and strive and suffer, but live, love, and think. Yet vaguely, confusedly, I felt something of the sort. More keenly in retrospect I feel the vivacious peace of that moment. The phrase is not really an oxymoron. There was the vivacity of a race intelligently in love with life, and at the same time they were tranquil and assured, at peace with themselves and the world. It has not been the same since 1914. Even during the best years of the long armistice, there was something a little hectic, uneasy, menacing. Shall we ever see again the peace and the vivacity?

That day I didn't get as far as the Rue de la Grande Chaumière; there were too many distractions on the way. But I moved in there next morning. Much amusement and some horror were caused by my insisting on a cold bath every morning, and as there was some difficulty in pronouncing my name I was known as *"le-monsieur-qui-prend-le-tub,"* a rather startling sidelight on the other guests.

Numerous books are published on the remote places of the earth, in spite of their being monotonous and repetitious. Arctic books, for example, consist chiefly of ice-bergs, frost, ice-floes, glaciers, snow, blizzards, the midnight sun, the long Arctic night, polar bears, walruses, seals, Esquimaux, igloos, sledges, dogs, the Aurora Borealis, and what we listened to on the radio. Tropical books are largely made up of steaming heat, thunder storms, prodigious rain, gloomy forests, stinging insects, leeches, snakes, bad or good natives, mud, fatigue, rivers too flooded to cross or too dry to navigate, where we camped, I tread on an alligator. All this we have heard before, and unless the book is written by an artist in words (which it never is) there seems no good reason for its existence. The plea that such books have scientific interest is exaggerated; the science is cut down to a minimum and the real stuff goes to specialist publications. Once, surprised in an unguarded moment by the author of one of these books, I allowed myself to be persuaded into asking the opinion of Norman Douglas about a travel book. He sent me this devastating but true judgment: "Not a single original observation in it."

On the other hand, any attempt to give personal impressions of the great art centres, with their extreme variety and possibilities of discovery, is at once dismissed as guide-book stuff. From which I deduce, as from many other indications, that contemporary readers are not particularly interested in art. It is perhaps worth noting that the most popular exhibit in the Musée de Cluny is the *ceinture de chasteté*. Contrary to popular belief, this barbarous and ungallant device was extremely rare, and there is no proof that it was ever used. But the people who dawdle indifferently past the exquisite tapestries and sculpture brighten up as soon as they find this indecent relic, and nothing on earth will persuade them that it was not in common use.

I wrote a few poems and made some translations in Paris,

but most of the time was given up to seeing the city and living the rhythm of its life. Ezra and H.D. were there, so I didn't lack companionship. Ezra took me to see the American composer Walter Morse Rummel, who has since made a reputation in France as an interpreter of Debussy. Walter was taking us on to see a French woman who lived in a house which had been Maeterlinck's, and in which he was alleged to have written *La Vie des Abeilles*. I was much interested in this, for in those days Maeterlinck was a big name in England. As Rummel was in his working clothes he retired to change, and by way of passing the time Ezra started playing Debussy with one finger on the open grand piano. Suddenly Rummel, dressed only in his underclothes, rushed furiously in, shouting: "Ezra! Ezra! If you touch that piano once more I'll throw you out the window!" I expected an explosion, but Ezra merely blinked and desisted. Later on, at Rummel's request, H.D. and I wrote some children's verse for him, and he made charming settings of them which Augener published.

But the greatest piece of luck on this trip happened when by accident I ran into Henry Slonimski just outside the Luxembourg garden. He was a Polish American who had recently taken his degree as doctor of philosophy at Marburg, with a thesis on Parmenides and Heraclitus. I had met him earlier in the year in London, and had been impressed by his skill and eloquence in refuting the arguments of the English Bergsonian, T. E. Hulme.

Of course I am incompetent to discuss Slonimski as a philosopher, but as a personality he stands for me alongside Yeats and Lawrence. He is one of those distinguished men who by accident are known only to a comparatively small circle. He is the victim of our infatuation with the printing press and the written word. Slonimski talks books better than most people write them, but though you listen spell-bound and enchanted by his grave eloquent voice and marvellous gift of finding the right phrase, the brilliant image, the books vanish with the sound of his voice. In another age he would have been appreciated. He should have walked and talked with the Peripatetics in Athens, before professorships were invented and when human intelligence was undimmed by cloudy theologies.

I am glad to think now that at nineteen I had the sense to appreciate him and to respond to the stimulus of his thought and talk. Indeed, for me it would have been impossible to resist. He made philosophy as attractive as a Persian tale. He had wide literary culture and a sensitive æsthetic appreciation. He presented philosophical ideas so poetically that what for me was the dark forest of abstractions became temporarily real and living; and he talked of poetry so profoundly that it took on fresh significance.

Ezra never appreciated Slonimski, because Ezra never listened to him. But H.D., with her swift unerring response to whatever is beautiful and lofty, at once comprehended his greatness and his charm. What evenings we spent listening to him in Paris! *Noctes Atticæ*. On a bench under the trees in the Petit Luxembourg, away from the noise and glare of the cafés, we would sit for hours while he talked to us of Hellas and Hellenism, of Pythagoras and Plato—"a kingly man"—of Empedocles and Heraclitus, of Homer and Thucydides, of Æschylus and Theocritus. We knew just enough to understand, to be moved by the beauty and grandeur of what he set before us.

Curiously enough, it was from Slonimski that I first heard of the possibility, even probability, of a European war. The French, he said, were convinced it would happen soon. I listened incredulously, and dismissed it as mere gossip. I knew, of course, that the newspapers occasionally started such scares, but nobody I knew ever believed them. There was a general idea that the age of any but colonial wars was finished for ever. Like all such popular delusions this was embodied in a catch phrase; in this case, "war between civilised nations is unthinkable." I heard it, I believed it, and I repeated it. But, unlike a good many of my contemporaries, I had lost the romantic-heroic idea of war inculcated by histories, adventure stories, and persons over military age.

It happened this way. At London University I was invited to read a paper on some poet to the Literary Society. At that moment I was deep in Whitman, and was greatly excited about him. While preparing my paper I read *Specimen Days,* and the pages recording Walt's experiences in the Civil War made an unforgettable impression on me. I re-read *Drum Taps* with a totally different viewpoint. Up till then, the killings, the maimings, the sufferings and miseries of war had been as unreal and conventional to me as the murders in a detective story. Whitman made me see the reality; and I believe he has the honour of being the only poet of the 19th century to tell the truth about war. This partial realisation of the true nature of war made it all the easier for me to believe the "war is unthinkable" stuff.

So, when I returned from France, and was offered a part-time job on the Garton Peace Foundation, I accepted. These worthy people were not pacifists in the more recent sense of non-resisters. At any rate, the committee I belonged to was engaged in making investigations of various problems of war and peace. One man, for instance, examined the consequences of the Franco-Prussian war from an economic point of view; and I was assigned the task of criticising Admiral Mahan's views of naval strategy, of which I knew rather less than nothing. But it was all pleasant and friendly, though it didn't occur to us that we were in the position of a group of very little mice planning to put bells on an extremely large and intractable cat. But amateur peace-makers in comfortable security very seldom do make that reflection.

The text-book of the group was Norman Angell's *Great*

Illusion, which at that time was about the most intelligent contribution to this hitherto unsolved problem. As I lacked the knowledge necessary for any serious criticism of the book, I was naturally convinced by it. But so far as I was concerned Mr. Angell soon lost prestige. He was being asked questions at a conference and somebody (probably a submerged socialist) suggested that war would be less likely if human life were better and happier. Mr. Angell replied rather to this effect:

"Well, after all, what is human life, but getting up in the morning and having breakfast, going to work, and coming back at night to slippers and the newspaper?"

That wasn't my ideal of human life, and I couldn't help thinking that if it was no more than that we were taking a lot of unnecessary trouble to try to preserve it. That chance remark, which was most probably merely intended to squelch an irrelevant question, made such a deep impression on me that eventually I left the group. Meanwhile another group, far more interesting to me, had been got together by Ezra and called the Imagists; and that enabled me at last to go to Italy.

Winter mornings can be unpleasant almost anywhere in the North, but London can turn out a truly spectral brand. On one such morning I sat at the large work table in Mr. Beare's apartment. There was a heavy brownish fog outside, a Holmes and Watson fog, and a steady drizzle muddied the pavements. By an almost sardonic irony I was working in this murk and gloom on a verse translation of Charles d'Orléans's *"Les courriers d'été sont venus"*—The heralds of summer are here—which some forward-looking editor thought he would like on hand for "the first real spring day." The postman rat-tatted at the door, and I found a letter and a picture postcard in the box.

The postcard came from a friend in Genoa, and showed a hillside of blossoming almond trees on the Italian Riviera. Underneath was scribbled: "These will be full out in a few weeks." The letter was from Chicago, with a draft in English currency for the equivalent of forty dollars, in payment of my first free verse poems, and a letter saying the editor would be glad to see more. This was entirely due to Ezra, who used all his influence with this periodical to make it publish what was then called the new poetry.

The thought: "How pleasant to be in Italy!" was followed by the more daring one: "Why not go?" The more I looked at the gloom outside and at the photograph of the almond trees on my table, the more I liked the idea. I had my allowance, a few pounds in hand, two or three small cheques due to me, and now this unexpected forty dollars. I felt rich. Moreover, Orage of the *New Age* had published some of my translations of Neo-Latin poetry without payment, but had promised to publish and pay for a series of articles if I found an attractive subject Perhaps . . . ?

To my delight Orage consented to take a series of articles on Italy. This was generous, because neither the subject nor my treatment of it could have interested his sedentary Guild Socialists. I also discovered that one could travel as far as Rome for as little as three pounds. I bought a ticket.

Italiam petimus! This has been the cry for centuries of thousands of enthusiastic northern pilgrims, but it can seldom have been echoed with more excitement. However much we may gain in knowledge and width of appreciation with time, we can never quite regain the first fine careless rapture of discovering Italy. Perhaps the course of true love runs all the truer for not being smooth; and very possibly my enjoyment of these wanderings was made keener because I had been forced to wait so long, overcome difficulties and take risks. In spite of very high anticipations I was not disappointed. I started out hoping for two months in Italy at the outside, but in fact I stayed nearly seven, during which I saw Rome, Naples, Pompeii, Sorrento,

Amalfi, Capri, Florence, Venice, Padua, Vicenza, Verona, and Lake Garda.

This may seem far too much for a brief visit of seven months, but actually nearly all my time was spent in Rome, Naples, Capri, Florence, and Venice. The others were visits of a day or two only. In Padua, for instance, I saw only the Giottos and Mantegnas, and in Vicenza I missed the Renaissance theatre and the admirable Tiepolos.

My longest stay was in Rome. In his inimitable way Gibbon has described how he "trod the Forum with a lofty step" and visited every Roman ruin with a Scotch antiquarian. My first day and night in Rome were less dignified and ideal. In London my friend John Cournos had given me a little book of addresses of hotels and lodgings in Italy frequented by American students and artists. In a fine frenzy of economy I chose the cheapest, which turned out to be in a swarming tenement on the Via Principe Amedeo. The room was clean enough, but those who have ever looked closely at an Italian tenement will not need to be told that it is not an ideal spot for literary work. I looked out disconsolately on a vast panorama of washing over a courtyard littered with debris. Slatternly women screamed information or insult at each other, and more children than I had ever beheld in my life played, fought, and shrieked with a demoniac energy. Was it for this I had so hopefully abandoned my quiet if murky room in Bloomsbury?

I was so fatigued by the long journey that I decided to stay the night and look elsewhere next day. The place I was taken to for dinner was a cavernous *trattoria,* dirty but extremely cheerful. There was a large fire at the end, with various smoky pots and a kid on a spit. The place was crowded with Italian working people, who could easily have been mistaken for brigands by a romantic eye; and the barrel roof echoed with tumultuous talk and the restless activity of children. The patience, the loving patience, with which Italian parents continue to bid a child: *"Sta fermo"* (keep quiet) is only exceeded by the cheerful energy with which the child continues to disobey. I felt some reluctance to eat in a place so dirty and noisy, yet the meal was unexpectedly good and cheap. A large bowl of minestrone, roast kid and beans, an enormous hunk of bread, a half-litre of red wine, and an orange (all for less than a franc) restored my shaken optimism. I needed it to survive another shock to British prejudice. The woman who waited on me carried a small child, and by way of being amiable I asked in my faulty Italian if it were a boy or a girl. With the utmost simplicity she lifted its clothes and exposed the little naked body. *"E un maschio,"* she said proudly.

Fortunately I had brought some letters of introduction from London, including two from Violet Hunt—to R. B. Cunninghame Graham and to an English resident in Rome, Mrs. Violet Gibson. As soon as I decently could I presented myself to her, explained the situation, and by afternoon was installed in the Via Sistina. I had a large though plain room, with a prospect of blue sky and a quiet garden of orange trees and cypresses. Just at hand were the Spanish steps and the walk along to the Pincian, past Santa Trinità, the Villa Medici, the old ilex trees, and the great Roman fountain bowl. At the far end of the terrace one looks across the Piazza del Popolo and to the roofs of Rome to St. Peter's. Three blind musicians were often to be found beside the walk, playing little primitive airs on stringed instruments. They were as out of date as a Romantic engraving of a girl with corkscrew curls, yet strangely melancholy and pathetic. At other times a crippled child on a crutch sang snatches from operas in an amazingly pure strong voice, which he was doubtless ruining by over-straining. There was still music in the Italian populace of those days. One evening in the Piazza Venezia a boy began playing a violin. He had a delicate wistful face and played with some skill and sensitiveness. In half a minute a listening crowd was round him.

"*Bello, bello,*" they said as he finished, and his cap was almost filled with soldi which had not been easily earned by the givers.

About four in the afternoon the daily promenade of carriages rolled up and down Verdier's ascent from the Corso to the Pincio. In this way the Roman aristocracy, especially the women, took an airing and what used to be called "carriage exercise." There were few motor cars in Rome then, partly because of the bad state of the roads but also because the Romans could not bear to give up their handsome equipages. Cunninghame Graham, who knew everything about horses, assured me that the Romans owned some of the finest carriage horses in the world. And as I watched the high-stepping champing pairs I could well believe it. Their beauty and breed were all the more conspicuous because of the contrast with the poor hacks drawing the public cabs which were here and there mixed in with the nobility and gentry. As I watched this cavalcade of cheerful, gesticulating, laughing people I had no idea that I was seeing the very end of a venerable custom.

In Rome, as in London, I touched simultaneously very different strata of society. I was accompanied on excursions by Mrs. Gibson, who took me to see some of the places then practically unknown to tourists. Or I lunched with her and an American friend, one of those accomplished cosmopolitan women who speak three or four languages perfectly, and appear to have gone everywhere and seen everything. Through Graham I was introduced to some of the Roman aristocracy, who lived in great outward splendour of marble stairways and columns, frescoed ceilings, crystal chandeliers, and white-gloved footmen. Graham himself was staying in a large hotel with his mother, Mrs. Bontine, one of those amazing old ladies who at eighty remain energetic and interested in everything. One could still see where Graham got his fine hidalgo looks and supple energy.

From these opulent places I would plunge directly into the life of the people. Most nights when I was alone I dined at a little *trattoria* (long ago vanished) in a street behind the Via Sistina. It was clean, cheap, and comparatively quiet, as it wasn't very successful. The waiter there was called Attila, a tremendous name bestowed by an over-sanguine parent. Poor Attilio! He was one of the world's meekest, most put-upon creatures. However gently one treated him, he always seemed to be flinching from some anticipated gibe or insult. And indeed the Italian customers could scarcely have been more domineering to him if they had been senators of old Rome and he a barbarian slave. They sometimes played on him the same shabby trick Prince Hal and Poins played on the drawer.

"Attilio!" somebody would shout.

"Subito, signorino, subito!" And Attila would run forward obsequiously. Immediately two or three other prodigious Roman voices would call imperiously:

"Attilio!"

"Attilio, vieni qui!"

"Qui, qui, Attilio!"

And the unhappy Attilio would run up and down like a frightened hen trying to get through wire netting, pitifully squealing his obligatory:

"Subito, signorino, subito!"

Attila was always the goat, always in trouble. One evening at the table next to mine sat a young man reading a Greek newspaper. It must have been just after Christmas, because I remember the headline was *"To tou Christou genethliacon,"* i.e., Christmas Day. We got into conversation in French, but I was soon bored with him. He was a student sent over to learn Italian by a doubtless conscientious father, but he was one of those horrible little political students who used to swarm in Continental universities to the increase of the world's confusion and folly. He had no real interest in art, literature, history, or any form of culture; he grumbled bitterly at being in Rome; all he wanted was to go to Paris, meet the socialists there, and pick up women. *Il me dégoûtait, ce petit voyou.*

Next evening Attilio hovered round my table, and at last plucked up courage to ask if I knew the name and address of the Greek *Signore*. I explained that I had never seen him before. Whereupon Attilio sadly drew from his pocket a two-franc piece and handed it to me. It was obviously false, and poor Attilio had to stand the loss out of his wretched wages. . . .

If I had stayed a week or a fortnight in Rome I might have thought I had seen it; but I stayed eight weeks and knew that I had barely begun. Fortunately when I left I was going south; it would have been miserable to leave Italy for the north so soon. There was no need to throw a coin into the great Trevi fountain; I knew I should come back.

The air was fresh, almost keen, on the high ground which was Tusculum, where Cicero had a house; and the sky was very blue. There was that silence so rare in Italy, but so deep when it does happen. In the soft turf grew wild crocuses, and there was a tiny Greek theatre. Beyond that a shepherd's hut built of rubble, with fragments of marble limbs and at one corner a whole statue of a naked faun with the face and sex mutilated and a piece of stick thrust obscenely in its place. And—happy fool—I never dreamed that the destructive brute in men would break loose again.

In Pompeii the bees hummed softly over the dwarf wild flowers among the ruins, while we rested and looked drowsily at the white smoke ebbing from Vesuvius. At Sorrento there were the freesias under the orange trees of the Coccumella garden. At Amalfi the two-sailed fishing boats rested like dark moths on the calm sea, and there was a crescent moon. At Cava in the pension they gave you large bowls of scented honey at breakfast; and the German poet, Stefan Georgs, talked to me of his French friends, Mallarmé and Verlaine and the Symbolistes, and said I must read no more Latin but only Greek, always Greek.

At Pæstum the mourning asphodel grew profusely and there were tiny wild roses, descendants I liked to think of the once famous rose gardens. From whatever point you look at the temples, each column is in harmonious proportion with all, each temple with the others. On the squalid track to the station a haggard beggar whined incessantly: *"Cieco, signori, cieco"* —blind, gentlemen, blind—and so we were, but didn't know it.

In Anacapri time stood still between Monte Solaro and the blue waves far below. Beside the rocky paths grew white violets, purple anemones, star-of-Bethlehem, cyclamen, and scented jonquils. When I got back to Naples the locust trees were in flower along the Mergellina, and after dark the people strolled there—softly it seemed for a southern crowd. There were warmth and friendliness, nothing tense, no hatred.

At Fiesole a Franciscan monk showed me the not very interesting church, but the cloisters, as nearly always, were attractive. Later, looking down on the dome and towers of Florence, I saw the cool violet evening slowly gather over the Val d'Arno. In Venice there was brilliant sunshine on the Grand Canal, and in the narrow streets a slowly moving chattering crowd while the black swifts screamed and darted overhead. Heavy serious Germans bearing rucksacks crunched in their huge hob-nailed boots over the pavement of the Piazza and the ancient floor mosaics of St. Mark's. . . . That should have been a warning, but like the beggar of Pæstum—*cieco, cieco.*

These are a few, a very few of the picture thoughts I brood over between these paragraphs. To live at all in these agonising days of Europe's torture I have to live in memories, and try to persuade myself that they may come again, if not for me, then for others. In those days one could say "Yes" to life with no hesitation, and there was a near infinity of hope ahead. It was wonderful, it was even—as Rochefoucauld would have denied—*délicieux* to be young and alive and in Italy in the spring then; and shortness of cash was a mere inconvenience which in no way hindered or tarnished the splendour and the enjoyment. Besides, I soon learned to live with the Italian people as they lived, which was far indeed from expensive, and yet so much more pleasant than our northern ways. Yes, I thought, this is a good place, and when I am really established as a writer I shall live here, and only sometimes go to France and England.

I put in the blind man, the unkind joke played on poor Attilio, the hob-nailed Germans, as a hint that all was not well, all was not perfect. Far from it most obviously, in view of what has happened since. But what freedom we enjoyed, what tranquillity! I had no passport and was never asked for one; I was never questioned by an immigration officer, never required to report to the police. Except in Russia and the remote parts of Spain, we then travelled as freely in Europe as in our own country. The sense of stability, of security, was complete. A trifling episode may bring this out. The first time I cashed money in Italy I received more for my pounds that the statutory 25.25 exchange of the Latin union. I thought the bank had made a mistake, and pointed it out. But no, the cashier explained that owing to the Italian war in Libia the Italian exchange had fallen slightly. I was astonished. Since in England and France we always used gold and silver, of presumably fixed value, it had never occurred to me that a currency might vary.

Undoubtedly the evil game of power politics was being played. There had been the Boer war, the Russo-Japanese war, the Balkan war, the Italian-Turkish war, the Agadir incident; but none of these things had touched the essential camaraderie of Europe, the unquestioned belief of the educated classes that we were all part of a common civilisation. The stay-at-homes and the cranky super-nationalist minorities were disregarded. My impression was that on the Continent the arts were taken far more seriously, were much more widely and sincerely practised and enjoyed than in England, where sport usurped their place in all classes. Certainly there was in England no respect for the artist such as existed in France and Italy. On the contrary, the artist in England was an object of suspicion, dislike, and contempt—unless he happened to make money. Of course there was also a highly civilised and cultivated minority surrounded by a host of pretenders, but the minority was small and the pretenders irritating.

I may be doing an injustice in saying this, but I don't claim to be giving more than personal impressions. English political institutions are excellent, and that is certainly one factor towards the good life. But I found what seemed to me on the whole a better way of living among people whose political institutions were not so good. Moreover, I have always found difficulty in getting on terms of friendship with most of my own countrymen.

An instance of this incompatibility occurred during my first two months in Rome. Somebody wrote me from England that Alice Meynell was there and would be glad to see me. I had read some of her poems and thought them good, so one afternoon by appointment I called on her for tea. I was taken into a large gloomy Italian room, where I gradually discovered, as my eyes grew accustomed to the pale light, the masses and outline of an elderly lady wearing a hat. (It was rumoured by the ribald that Mrs. Meynell had never been seen without a hat in living memory.)

Almost immediately she began lamenting the "destruction" of Florence—somebody had put up a factory, it appeared—and of Rome, where the government neglected "the bew-tiful mediæval churches" and spent money on digging up ancient Rome. Now I thought this rather silly, for after all the modern

Italians have to live in the industrial epoch. Moreover, I was interested in ancient Rome, and grateful to the Italian government and Commendatore Boni for excavating the Forum so intelligently. Why shouldn't the Italian government spend its money on investigating the antiquities of its own country in its own way? And if the mediæval churches were falling down (whereof I had seen no evidence) it was surely up to the Church to do something.

Mrs. Meynell had espoused Catholicism with female ardour, and these common sense remarks were not well received. The moral temperature of the room fell several degrees. By way of retrieving the situation I hastily turned the conversation on to poetry. All went well until I said something mild in praise of Swinburne. The lady bridled—I think that is the right word—and said she couldn't admire a man who started a poem "Before the beginning of years" and then went on to talk of "sand From under the feet of the years." I pointed out that this was a trifling blemish in a long and magnificently rhetorical poem like "Atalanta." Whereupon she asked me if I admired Coventry Patmore, and I said cheerfully: "Not a bit."

The temperature was rapidly approaching zero, and she then asked sarcastically what poets I did admire. I said, Swinburne for one, but at the moment I was very much interested in modern French poets and their interesting experiments in form.

"Oh, but *surely* nothing could possibly be better than our *bew*-tiful *English* forms?"

So I left.

Chapter IX

IMAGISM is now a matter of literary history, but it occurs to me that none of the English members of the group or tribe has yet told his tale of transactions which had some effect on the course of recent poetry, particularly in America. What did the Imagists achieve between 1912 and 1917? Well, they did some useful pioneering work. They dealt a blow at the post-Victorian magazine poets, whose unappeased shades still clamour for Imagist blood. They livened things up a lot. They made free verse popular—it had already been used by Blake, Whitman, and Henley and by many of the French Symbolistes. And they tried to attain an exacting if narrow standard of style in poetry. As a purely personal opinion, I may add that I think the poems of Ezra Pound, H.D., Lawrence, and Ford Madox Ford will continue to be read. And to a considerable extent T. S. Eliot and his followers have carried on their operations from positions won by the Imagists.

It will doubtless be an instant relief to the reader to be told that I don't claim to be the Fuehrer of the Imagists. I was five years younger than the next youngest member of the group, and when the first Imagist poems appeared I was all of twenty. The fame or otherwise of Ducedom must go to Ezra, who invented the "movement" (how often would Ezra obliterate a literary figure by the simple assertion: *"Il n'est pas dong le mouvemong"*) and to Amy Lowell, who put it across.

That I can swear to, but I wouldn't make an affidavit that I remember all that happened concerning the "mouvemong" or exactly what was said. I have only more or less capricious memories. My old friend, John Gould Fletcher, has written at length about these proceedings, and unlike myself he has an excellent memory, so that he has reported long conversations he had with me of which I don't remember a single word. Yet in details even he sometimes falters. Thus, he records a very interesting conversation he had with me in London during the month of February 1917; in defiance of the fact that I was at the front in France from December 1916 until June 1917. Perhaps he met my *Doppelgänger*.

Like other American expatriates, Ezra and H.D. developed an almost insane relish for afternoon tea, a meal with which I can most willingly dispense. Moreover, they insisted on going to the most fashionable and expensive tea-shops (which I thought a sad waste of money) not only in London, but in Paris. Being merely an oppressed minority I had to yield. Thus it came about that most of our meetings took place in the rather prissy milieu of some infernal bun-shop full of English spinsters. However, an extremely good time was had by all, and we laughed until we ached—what at, I haven't the faintest recollection. No doubt, we all got off some splendid cracks, but for the life of me I can't remember one of them. I suspect that the cream of the wit lay in the fact that we were young, entirely carefree, and having a glorious time just being alive.

Naturally, then, the Imagist *mouvemong* was born in a tea-shop—in the Royal Borough of Kensington. For some time Ezra had been butting in on our studies and poetic productions, with alternate encouragements and the reverse, according to his mood. H.D. produced some poems which I thought excellent, and she either handed or mailed them to Ezra. Presently each of us received a ukase to attend the Kensington bun-shop. Ezra was so much worked up by these poems of H.D.'s that he removed his pince-nez and informed us that we were Imagists.

Was this the first time I had heard that Pickwickian word?

I don't remember. According to the record, Ezra swiped the word from the English philosopher, T. E. Hulme; and anyone who can find a copy may read in Ezra's *Ripostes* the five or six poems Hulme wrote to illustrate his theories. They are pretty good, especially the one about the moon like a red-faced farmer looking over a gate. Ezra's note on Hulme's poems contains the ominous threat: "As to the future, that is in the hands of the Imagists." But at that time who and where were the Imagists? My own belief is that the name took Ezra's fancy, and that he kept it *in petto* for the right occasion. If there were no Imagists, obviously they would have to be invented. Whenever Ezra has launched a new movement—and he has made such a hobby of it that I always expect to find one day that Pound and Mussolini are really one and the same person—he has never had any difficulty about finding members. He just called on his friends.

I have no exact memory of what was said at this bun-shop meeting, but I do remember that H.D. looked very much pleased by the praise Ezra generously gave her poems. I didn't like his insistence that the poems should be signed: "H.D. Imagist," because it sounded a little ridiculous. And I think H.D. disliked it too. But Ezra was a bit of a czar in a small but irritating way, and he had the bulge on us, because it was only through him that we could get our poems into Harriet Monroe's *Poetry,* and nobody else at that time would look at them. (My impression is that even so Ezra had to bully Miss Monroe to get her to accept this "new" poetry.) So we had to give in.

If I am not mistaken these poems of H.D.'s were the first to appear with the Imagist label. Three of mine (which launched me on my Italian trip) had appeared a month or two before without the label, though Ezra afterwards included them in the first Imagist anthology. I think this fact (which can be established from the early files of *Poetry*) lends considerable support to those who say the Imagist movement was H.D., and H.D. the Imagist movement.

I believe it was at this same tea—though it may have been later—that Ezra proposed we should all three publish a book of our poems together. H.D. and I were in favour of this, because it seemed the sort of thing the three musketeers would have done. But Ezra soon changed his mind. He gravely pointed out to us that he was internationally famous while we were miserable unknowns, and that consequently the whole attention of the world's press would go to his poems and ours would not even be noticed.

Evidently Ezra was having a good time compelling them to come in. With Fletcher he discovered a poet we were glad to welcome, and he accepted our friend, John Cournos. We liked F. S. Flint, although the nearest he had got to Imagism was reading masses of young French poets and imitating Verlaine. Ford Madox Ford (né Hueffer) was a well-established author and we liked his poems, though there was nothing very imagistic about them until he started to imitate H.D. Joyce and Carlos Williams were also most acceptable. But we objected to Allen Upward, Skipwith Cannell, and Amy Lowell.

This may sound ungrateful to Amy in view of what she afterwards did, but at that time she had published only one book, which H.D. and I agreed was the fluid, fruity, facile stuff we most wanted to avoid. We wanted clear outlines, directness, concision, unhackneyed rhythms. True, the poem of Amy's Ezra showed us seemed to demonstrate a sudden conversion to free verse and (probably owing to Ezra's blue pencil) a more austere style, but would they last? These scruples disappeared as we began to know Amy. It would have been difficult to resist that vivacious intelligence, and her conversion was obviously sincere. She lacked H.D.'s classical knowledge and taste, but she knew French better than any of us except

Flint. He introduced her to a whole new generation of French writers, the foundation of her book on that subject.

Through the good offices of John Cournos and Alfred Kreymborg, Ezra's collection of Imagists appeared in New York in February 1914 under the fantastic title *Des Imagistes*. What Ezra thought that meant remains a mystery, unless the word *"Anthologie"* was assumed to precede it. Amy's anthologies were called *Some Imagist Poets*, so she may have supposed that Ezra thought *"Des Imagistes"* meant *"Quelques Imagistes."* But why a French title for a collection of poems by a bunch of young American and English authors? Search me. Ezra liked foreign titles. His own include *A Lume Spento, Personæ, Ripostes, Quia Pauper Amavi;* and where other people wrote a preface, Ezra pretentiously indited prolegomena. It was rumoured later that he was responsible for making T.S. Eliot use the title *Ara Vos Prec,* a snippet of mediæval Provençal which I imagine is unintelligible to most people. It seems a rather childish form of high-hatting, especially since Ezra was apt to get into ludicrous difficulties with his languages. Thus, in his Propertius, he rendered "nocte canes" by the schoolboy howler "night dogs," when of course it means "thou singest by night"; and in the text of his Cavalcanti, instead of "Donna mi prega" ("A lady asks me") he printed "Donna mi pregna," which made the Tuscan poet claim to be a biological monstrosity, since it means "A lady impregnates me."

Under that ridiculous ensign, *Des Imagistes,* our little boatful of poets was launched, only to come at once under fire from apparently the whole American fleet of critics. I say "apparently," because we didn't bother about press cuttings, and only saw some of the many abusive ones which kind friends sent us. Columnists parodied the poems, or reproduced them (without payment) accompanied by derisive remarks. I seem to remember that the poem which gave most offence was a lovely little epigraph by H.D. which revolted the journalists by its perfection of taste and sobriety. The edition sold out. Evidently we were at least a *succès de scandale*.

Very likely some of the sales were to the kind of people who will always pay two bits to see a bunch of freaks. The serious part of the success was very largely due to H.D. Of course, the majority of poetry readers have little real judgment and practically no flair for good new work. But genuine obtuseness to art, such as is requisite in a successful journalist, was needed to overlook the fact that H.D. showed an original sensitive mind and an almost faultless craftsmanship.

This craftsmanship was the result of infinite pains. Version after version of a poem was discarded by H.D. in the search for perfection, and the pruning was ruthless. I had thought I was fairly exacting, but I was staggered by this relentless artistic conscience. The fervour with which ten generations of Puritan ancestors had sought moral righteousness was here devoted to æsthetic righteousness. I think it significant that H.D. was a close student of St. Paul, but obviously her version of the famous tirade ran: "Though I speak with the tongue of men and of angels and have not *style* . . ."

In the summer of 1914 Amy was again in London, occupying her usual suite in the Berkeley Hotel, with its view across Piccadilly to the Green Park. With her usual energy and vivacity she had been battling valiantly for us all, but was fed up with Ezra. So were others. I have a notion that Fletcher was particularly restive—his high-strung nature made him particularly sensitive. Moreover, Ezra had now attached himself to the *Blast* group, and was busy patenting a new movement, Vorticism, whatever that may have been. The first number of *Blast* was indeed a brilliant production, but most of the brilliance was due to the editor and chief contributor, P. Wyndham Lewis, and to a short story which I think one of the best ever produced by that gifted writer Rebecca West. But *Blast* didn't seem quite the right medium for the rest of us.

Amy arrived with certain proposals, to which she had evidently given a good deal of thought. She proposed a Boston Tea Party for Ezra, the immediate abolition of his despotism and the substitution of a pure democracy. There was to be no more of the Duce business, with arbitrary inclusions and exclusions and a capricious censorship. We were to publish quietly and modestly as a little group of friends with similar tendencies, rather than water-tight dogmatic principles. Each poet was to choose for himself what he considered best in his year's output; and the anthology would appear annually. To preserve democratic equality names would appear in alphabetical order. Amy undertook to do all the practical work, to get the books published in Boston and London, and to account to us for the royalties. And well and loyally she discharged that task, which involved a good deal of work and correspondence.

On these terms Ezra was invited to contribute, but refused. There is said to have been a row between Amy and Ezra, but I certainly knew nothing about it. I seem to remember that H.D. and I pleaded with Ezra to stay in, but he refused to play ball. But if we lost Ezra, we gained a much greater writer, D. H. Lawrence. The whole credit for this is due to Amy, who made the suggestion and carried it out successfully. Lawrence was already publishing in the anthologies of the Georgians, who affected great scorn for the Imagists, so the situation looked delicate. Luckily, Lawrence was such an individualist that he didn't care a hoot about groups and their alleged principles. As anyone can see from his *Collected Poems*, even Lawrence was for a time influenced by H.D.; so that his work fitted in perfectly.

I have one or two vivid memories of that evening when I first met Lawrence. It was the end of a sunny tranquil July day and, if we had been able to see into the future, the end of tranquillity in Europe for many a long and bitter year. There were several people in Amy's large private room, where the Austrian waiters (already called to the colours) were setting out an elaborate dinner table with ominously quiet deftness. For some reason I sat apart at an open window, looking down on the endless traffic of Piccadilly and the warm golden light on the Park. At the corner of the Ritz opposite was a news stand, with a flaring poster: "Germany and Russia at War, Official." As I sat there men and boys came rushing along with hoarse shouts: "Special Edition," "Extra." Someone tossed a bundle to the news man and he unfolded another poster. It read: "British Army Mobilised."

Until that moment I had felt certain that England would not be involved (war is unthinkable, etc.) in these senseless European squabbles. That mobilisation poster was the first stab of doubt. I looked back at the room where friendly people were talking unhurriedly of civilised things. At that moment the door opened, and a tall slim young man, with bright red hair and the most brilliant blue eyes, came in with a lithe, springing step. As a rule I don't remember people's eyes, but I shall not forget Lawrence's—they showed such a vivid flame-like spirit.

Before Amy could start the introductions he said quickly:

"I say, I've just been talking to Eddie Marsh, and he's most depressing. He says we shall be in the war."

Eddie, the Mæcenas of the Georgians, was then private secretary to the Prime Minister, and obviously in a position to have real knowledge. There was a pause of something like consternation, and then somebody said: "Oh, nonsense." Plucking up courage, we all said it was nonsense. Did we all believe it? I know I had a sickening feeling of doubt. But a few minutes later dinner began, and we forgot all about the threat of war.

As guest of honour Lawrence sat next to Amy, and they

made a curious contrast, if only because one was so lean and the other so plump. Probably Fletcher and H.D. appreciated more than I did the spectacle of the coal miner's son sitting at the right hand of a Lowell. H.D. had told me the rhyme about the Lowells, the Cabots, and God, but I hadn't then grasped its full significance.

Amy came out well that evening. There was not a trace of condescension in her and she did a difficult thing.well—she expressed her warm admiration for Lawrence's work without flattery or insincerity and without embarrassing him. It is the fashion now to write off Amy as a society woman, who would never have been heard of as a writer if she hadn't been a Lowell. That is unfair. In Amy there was something of an artist and a real æsthetic appreciation. She could not have felt such enthusiasm for Lawrence and H.D. without it.

When the war came, Amy was a little alarmed at the idea she might not be able to get home. Reassured on that point, she became the patriot anxious to help her fellow-countrymen, who were crowding into England from the war areas in considerable panic; and she pestered the American Ambassador for something to do. That ruthless humorist made her meet every train arriving from the Continent with a large notice hung from her neck: "American Citizens Apply Here." Amy was extremely sensitive about her abnormal size, and it must have been agony to her to display herself in this way. But she had pluck, and went through with it to the end.

The sales of the new Imagist anthologies greatly exceeded our hopes. If I ever knew, I have forgotten the figures. But I do remember one unexpectedly large cheque representing my sixth share of the royalties, and on the basis of that it seems to me that we must have sold about twenty thousand copies of the first two. I may be wrong in my calculations, but anyway

E

the anthologies were widely read; and Amy kept the publicity going with superb generalship.

She did one thing I can't approve. She published her *Critical Fable* anonymously, and then broadly insisted that it was in fact the work of Leonard Bacon. That was putting a gentleman on the spot with a vengeance, for Mr. Bacon highly disapproved of the Imagists. He had either to prove the lady a liar, or to remain silent while appearing to deny his most cherished literary opinions. It would have served Amy right if he had walked up and down outside her home in Brookline with a striker's banner:

"Amy Lowell Unfair to Leonard Bacon."

By way of insinuating that the Imagists were merely an unimportant clique (for the sales of *Des Imagistes* were only a fraction of the Imagist anthologies after Ezra left) Ezra raked together a number of miscellaneous poets in a *Catholic Anthology*. Apart from causing astonishment and consternation to a few pious people, this compilation achieved nothing in particular. When America entered the war in 1917, Amy decided that we had better quit and each go his own way. The Imagist "movement" then was at an end, and it was left to others to carry on.

In 1929 my modernistic friend, Walter Lowenfels, suggested to me in Paris that I ought to get out another Imagist anthology. Of course I knew Walter thought the Imagists were as dead as Shelley, and that the suggestion was ironical. By way of snubbing him I promptly took a taxi to the cable office, and as I had just published a successful novel I had no difficulty in selling the non-existent anthology to London and New York within two days. When I got the cables of acceptance I confess I was a little perturbed at what I had done. Suppose I couldn't collect any poems? However, I got to work, Ford and H.D. laboured nobly, and the *Imagist Anthology, 1930,* contained poems from everyone who had ever contributed (including James Joyce and Carlos Williams) except poor Amy who was dead, Skipwith Cannell whom we couldn't trace, and Ezra who was sulky. Ford wrote one of his genially discursive introductions, and we sold several thousand copies between the two countries.

That I fancy was the original and unforgivable sin of Imagist poetry—people bought it.

In order to round off the little episode of Imagism I have gone ahead in time, but, if only from a feeling of nostalgia, I should like to return for a little while longer to those days when we were all laboriously marching or gaily capering on our way to the precipice of August 1914.

My own life was fairly occupied. I wrote poems, and did a lot of reading in the British Museum. I had articles in some of the literary weeklies and was literary editor of the *Egoist,* a job inherited by T. S. Eliot when I joined the army. I should not say I was a good editor, but as I had practically no funds to pay contributors it was something of an achievement to keep the paper going at all. But I had a lot of fun, and managed to publish a good deal of poetry—good, bad, and indifferent—by young French, American, and English poets. Through Ezra's influence we were able to run as serials a novel by Remy de Gourmont and then James Joyce's *Portrait of the Artist as a Young Man.* At the same time I was planning a series of very cheaply priced translations of minor Greek and Latin authors, with the intention of leading up later to the more important works. The nearest we got to that, owing to the war, was H.D.'s choruses from Euripides. I published these pamphlets myself at my own expense, and made more out of them than the total cost. Later on, T. S. Eliot in his lofty way remarked in an article that "none of these translators has showed himself capable of translating the *Agamemnon* of Æschylus." Since the text of the *Agamemnon* is a chaos and we were only amateurs, it would have been foolish to try. I wrote to him at once, offering to publish his version of the *Agamemnon* in the series; but the manuscript was never sent in.

So far as my limited funds permitted I tried to publish the work of young and unknown artists. About the best of the young ones was Nina Hamnett. Among the unknowns was a lean elderly man called Horton, a friend of Yeats, who made crayon drawings of his mystic visions. (I believe he was introduced by John Cournos.) In his style was a bit of Blake, a bit of Odilon Redon, a bit of Gavarni, and a bit of himself. I didn't greatly care for the mysticism, but Horton was poor and neglected, and I thought there was some talent there. Anyway, I published some of these fantastic drawings; but forgot to put his name under them. Horton was dreadfully offended. Which only goes to show how fitted I was to be an editor.

During my stay in Rome somebody suggested to me that the nuisance of guides, attendants, and the like could be avoided if I had one of the free passes which the Italian government granted to foreign students and writers. I called at the British Embassy for the formal recommendation, and was refused rather insolently by the Third Secretary, presumably because I was not wearing an old school tie as he was. A few days later I mentioned the matter as a joke to Cunninghame Graham, who surprised me by being very angry about it. Having eviscerated the manners, morals, and methods of the British Diplomatic Corps, he gave me a letter of introduction to the Ambassador, Sir Rennell Rodd. By return of post His Excellency made a personal appointment, and once more I entered the majestic portals of the palace in the Via Venti Settembre.

But what a change! To my way of thinking I was exactly the same person as I had been a week or ten days before, but now I no longer waited in the ante-chamber, nor was I repulsed by an underling. At the magic words "personal interview with

His Excellency," flunkies flocked to me, the portentous major-domo himself deigned to receive my cloak, and I was conducted at once past waiting and envious fellow-countrymen to the ambassadorial study.

I have to confess that I was immediately captivated by Sir Rennell's conversation and manners. He apologised winsomely and whimsically for the "mistake" about the pass, and, as I was leaving in a day or two for Naples, he promised it should be sent on within the week. (It never was.) Then he talked with knowledge and enthusiasm of Rome and the classics, and ruefully showed me a large pile of documents on the Balkan war—another straw in the wind—which had rudely laid waste the cultured leisure traditionally enjoyed by a British Ambassador to the Quirinal. Altogether a very pleasant talk, which I enjoyed.

But one remark made in those august halls—whether by Sir Rennell or his understrapper I don't remember—has stuck in my memory. I happened to mention Orage, editor of the *New Age,* for whom I was writing. The comment was:

"Why does he publish such nonsense about foreign affairs?"

Among the avant-gardistes and leftists of that time there was a superstition about the "brilliance" of Orage as editor and writer, which I could never wholly share, in spite of his kindness to me personally. Certainly he was an amiable man and good company, but his literary articles were based on insufficient reading and were liable to be infected by his taste for theosophy. True, he published a number of young writers, but as an editor he could not be compared with Ford Madox Hueffer. He was an authority on theoretical socialism, and I believe had invented a special brand of his own, but who cares? There have been ten new brands of socialism since then, and we shall have more anon.

The justice of the diplomat's remark was demonstrated by the fact that on the Friday before England went to war in 1914

Orage published a "strong" editorial proving that there would be no war, it was a capitalist ramp to play the stock market, etc. That article wrecked Orage's reputation, much as the far superior and more solid writer, Hilaire Belloc, damaged his by his omniscient but, alas, too often chimerical analyses of war strategy in *Land and Water*. In point of fact neither Orage nor Belloc knew much, if anything, more about their subjects than other people; they were good hard-hitting journalists who happened to guess wrong. In both cases—particularly Belloc's, for he is a fine writer—it was bad luck. If they had guessed right, they would have been revered as prophets.

> "Alas, what perils do environ
> The journalist who makes a try-on."

So far as the *New Age* was concerned, I was always a fish in the wrong tank. I cared little about their Guild Socialism, nothing for their theosophy and notes on the present kalpa, and disliked the vulgar and often spiteful articles which passed as literary criticism. Nevertheless, I liked Orage personally and was grateful to him for printing me. Many years later I had a chance to show this when he returned to England and tried to revive the *New Age*. He applied to his old contributors for financial help, and I at once sent him a cheque. A little later Orage told me that out of all the writers he had helped to launch only one other had responded, and that was Michael Arlen, who wrote a very generous cheque indeed. So much for the tangible gratitude of "intellectuals."

The anthology *Des Imagistes* was published in London at the Poetry Bookshop by Harold Monro, after a good deal of hesitation and misgiving. One copy was angrily returned from the Savoy Hotel by an American, and an old gentleman came into the shop and made a row. Moreover, except for the ultraconservative *Morning Post,* which gave us a column of praise, all the newspapers, particularly the "liberal" ones, were against us. No doubt Monro had to take a lot of chaff from his Georgian friends, but he did not wholly drop us, and eventually published my first book of poems along with one by F. S. Flint. That juvenile work was issued at the modest price of eightpence, but such is the folly of first-edition collectors that I have seen a copy advertised for sale at twenty-five dollars. An even more insane example of this mania came my way more recently. A friend of mine wasted forty good dollars on a copy of some other early poems of mine, which had the combined merits of being privately printed, hand-set, and strictly limited in number. As I further enriched this valuable work with my signature, I reflected with interest that neither I nor the amateur printer had ever received a penny for it.

Through Monro or by other means I had some fleeting acquaintance with the Georgian poets, such as de la Mare, Hodgson, Brooke, Abercrombie, Gibson, Squire, and Shanks. I had a last glimpse of Rupert Brooke when Flint and I bumped into him in Piccadilly, not long after the outbreak of war. He was dressed in a shabby macintosh, and looked a little sallow and less handsome than his pictures. He at once informed us that he had a commission, and was about to join the Naval Division at Antwerp. We wished him luck—a gallant but pathetic figure, the last English poet who really believed in the romance and chivalry of war.

I was so little intimate with these poets and saw them at such rare intervals that I have only vague and possibly inaccurate impressions of them. Hodgson was conspicuous, because he invariably wore a bowler hat, a briar pipe, and a large saliva-dripping bull terrier, and affected or felt a great interest in boxing. Gibson was a kindly cherubic person with a troubled social conscience, which vented itself in poems about bread and coal and similar domestic commodities. De la Mare was gentle as well as kindly, immersed so it seemed in a dim other-worldliness which left him with an imperfect grasp of realities. Squire also was kindly, but definitely one of the world's less gifted poets; he had a great popular success as a parodist, anthologist, and editor of the *London Mercury,* but has since retired into obscurity and a knighthood. In his youth Squire translated some of Baudelaire, but didn't like to have it remembered after he discovered that Britishism and moral disapprobation for "the Gallic" went better with the multitude.

All these people struck me as insular, not to say provincial, with little interest in what was being done on the Continent. Not long after the war Squire's *London Mercury* published a Letter from Paris, written by a Frenchman who devoted a good deal of space to Proust, who was then very much to the front. Throughout the article "Marcel Proust" had been changed to "Marcel Prévost," a popular novelist of a former generation. Also, their standard of criticism struck me as a little out of line. If one ventured a mild disapproval of the poetry of one of their innumerable friends, the answer invariably was:

"Oh, but he's *such* a nice fellow."

So what?

Vastly more entertaining to me were the people round Ford Madox Ford, and above all Ford himself. Ford had many enemies, who took advantage of his weaknesses and misfortunes to attack him personally and to disparage his work. He had friends with more affection than judgment. So on the one hand you had a Mr. Hyde Ford and on the other a Dr. Jekyll Ford, to the complete detriment of truth and a human, lovable, absurd, vain, mendacious, gifted creature well worth the attention of the world. Though I steered clear of him after I got my second wind as an adult, I wouldn't have missed him for anything. He was more like the great Sir John Falstaff than any human being I have ever known, with touches of that kindred spirit, the legendary Marius of Marseille. Indeed, Ford himself seemed to realise that his character more nearly resembled fiction than fact, and lavished on his legend all the imaginative resources a novelist would devote to a favourite character.

Ford's origins were highly respectable, not to say distinguished. His father was a cultured German who is said to have come to England to spread the musical gospel of Wagner, and who certainly wrote a nice book on the Troubadours. He married the daughter of Ford Madox Brown, the Pre-Raphaelite painter. Ford claimed to be related to the Rossettis, and this may very well be true—at any rate, I am not sufficiently well acquainted with the filiations of Pre-Raphaelite marriages to dispute it. Obviously Ford grew up in a large and well-known group of artists and writers, but his memories of their sayings and doings should be accepted with caution.

I have a vivid recollection of a dinner my father gave Ford and me early in 1914. The food and wine were good, and Ford, ever susceptible to the genial influences of the table and good fellowship, opened the flood-gates of his discourse and babbled o' green fields—I should say, of celebrities—in his most imaginative strain. A scholarly recluse like my father, with a passion for books and very little acquaintance with writers, was an ideal subject for Ford's experiments. He sensed the virgin sucker at once. So we had the stories about Ruskin, and my uncle Gabriel and my aunt Christina; the Conrad and James stories; the story of the abbé Liszt's concert and how Queen Alexandra took the beautiful infant Ford on her knees and kissed him; the "old Browning" stories, and the Swinburne stories; gradually working back through the 19th century. My father was swimming in bliss, although once or twice he looked a little puzzled. And then Ford began telling how he met Byron. I saw my father stiffen.

Yet there was probably a substratum of fact—impossible to

excavate—in all this, and even the Byron story may have been an authentic tradition which Ford over-dramatised in his devotion to artistic form.

When I first knew Ford he was in a mess, rather through imprudence and airy indifference to fact than any particular wrong-doing. For a long time he had been separated from his first wife, whose Catholic principles made a divorce impossible. It was one of those very early marriages which often go wrong through nobody's fault. Apropos this, I was once arguing with Ford about sexual education—I was all for openness and correct information at adolescence, he for Catholic ignorance and the longest possible repression. Finding himself a little driven in the discussion, Ford hit a smashing blow. "Why, my dear fellow, I myself . . ." and what possible reply could there be to so illustrious an example? "I myself knew nothing whatever about sex until I was twenty-two." And yet barely a month earlier he had told me he was married at nineteen and a father before he was of age—this in order to wipe out my objections to people having children when they were too young.

At any rate, just about the time when Ford lost the editorship of the *English Review,* he decided he wanted to marry Violet Hunt. She was the daughter of watercolour Hunt, and hence also connected with the Pre-Raphaelites in her youth. She had several of their pictures in her home; and it was rumoured that Ruskin had once saved her (or her sister, I forget which) from drowning in a Venetian canal. There's glory for you. But Violet was somebody. She was a successful novelist and had been very beautiful; at fifty she was still a very attractive woman and devoted to Ford. She was also a tremendous and not very discreet chatterbox. Ford used to imitate her talking on the telephone:

"Yes, this is Violet Hunt. Who is it speaking? Oh, Lady de Lammermoor—how *are* you? What! What? I said you had a baby before you were married? Oh, nonsense, I said that about Lady Bridlington."

Law and the administration of law in England being what they are, there could be no legal marriage. But Ford was equal to this. He went to Germany and claimed his legal status as a German subject (presumably his father had never bothered to be naturalised in those easy days), got a divorce under the laws of the German Empire, and was duly and legally married.

This made a radical alteration in the Ford legend. Hitherto he had been an English country gentleman of an "immensely old" Sussex family, descended from Ford the Elizabethan dramatist (not Ford in *The Merry Wives of Windsor*) and probably from Shakespeare, not to mention Hengist and Horsa. Much of this arose from the fact that he and Conrad had lived at Aldington on the edge of Romney Marsh, which incidentally is in Kent and not in Sussex; on the strength of which Ford frequently assured me that I mispronounced my own name. He was, he said, a "baron five times over," and entitled to be one of those who hold the canopy over the King at his coronation. It is quite true that the mayors of the old Cinque Ports still have that right and were once upon a time referred to as barons; but to the best of my knowledge Ford had never been mayor of one of them, still less of all five at once.

On his return from Germany, he blossomed out as a Freiherr, and told most entertaining stories of his life as an Einjahriger in the Bonn Hussaren, and of his intimate conversations with the Emperor Wilhelm. Whenever possible he talked to his guests in German, and referred to us as "you English" or "you Protestants." For, ignoring the fact that he was living in mortal sin, Ford pedalled hard on the Roman Catholic organ in those days.

Violet had an ancient retainer named Child, who had been in the family for about half a century and still treated her mistress with that familiarity servants naturally have with infants. One day Violet gleefully related to us the following scrap of dialogue:

"Is Mr. Hueffer really what you would call a gentleman, Miss?"

"Well, he's a baron in his own country."

"Oh"—sniff—"we all know what those *foreign* titles mean"—sniff.

Unluckily, Ford could not let well alone and be content with the fact that everybody winked at the ambiguous situation and accepted it at its face value. He was not only conceited, but an incorrigible exhibitionist. Therefore he must needs give a pretentious interview about his marriage to an illustrated weekly, which ran a portrait of Violet with the caption: "Mrs. Ford Madox Hueffer." The first wife immediately brought a libel action, and of course won it.

I was very sorry indeed for Violet. It must have been horrible for her, who had lived all her life in Kensington, to see the High Street filled with newspaper placards: "Libel Action against Famous Novelist," "Violet Hunt in the Box," and then: "Verdict against Woman Novelist."

Before very long this was followed by two other misfortunes—the war started and Ford fell in love with someone else. For very good reasons Ford had the strongest objections to rejoining the Bonn Hussaren for active service. Indeed after the 4th of August it was impossible. What he had to worry about was the possibility of being interned as an enemy alien. Fortunately Violet knew a cabinet minister, and Ford was hastily naturalised—no doubt as the last scion of an immensely old Sussex family.

At this time Violet persuaded me to act temporarily as Ford's secretary during the morning, although it rather interfered with my own work. This also involved acting as Violet's confidant, a position which made me very uneasy, since it didn't seem wholly loyal to Ford. Actually, like most sufferers in such a situation, all Violet wanted was to be able to talk endlessly about it to somebody sympathetic and to be told that it would all come out well in the end. For this purpose we used to walk together in Kensington Gardens. On one occasion we came to a long and secluded avenue of trees. Violet suddenly broke off her tragical declamations, smiled coquettishly, and said:

"This is where I used to meet Andrew Lang by permission of his wife."

Every morning Ford dictated and I took down in longhand. He was industrious. At that time he wrote a long weekly article for a semi-literary paper, worked on a book denouncing German aggression, and on a novel about a splendid fellow who was married, but fell in love with somebody else and eventually cut his throat. Violet was terrified when she heard the dénouement; but, as it proved, groundlessly. I soon handed the secretary job over to a university friend of mine; and some months later through the influential M.P. Ford was given a commission in the Welch Regiment, which is not the same thing as the Welsh Guards.

I know nothing of Ford's feats as a soldier, except that after the war he managed to produce no less than four novels on the subject. There was an unkind story current just after the war which is subject to the special caution attached to all war stories. It was said that about two weeks after he got into the line Ford was sitting on the fire-step, sunk in gloom, and oblivious of everything that was happening. The Corps Commander came along on a tour of inspection, saw Ford, and snapped at the Colonel:

"Who's that feller?"

"Second-Lieutenant Hueffer, sir."

"Well, send him down the line at once. He's depressin' the troops."

My old friend, Douglas Goldring, who also acted as secretary to Ford in *English Review* days, has a fine collection of Fordiana. A few years ago he told me with great glee that he had run across Ford in Paris, and had managed just in time to smother an exclamation when he heard Ford narrating to a guileless American his (Ford's) experiences as an Etonian and a Major in the Guards.

I can't see why some people were so irritated by these foibles. These ingenuous metamorphoses did nobody any harm, and added to the gaiety of nations. Very few people see themselves as others see them, and if Ford embroidered on reality he did it extremely well. "By're lady, he doth it as like one of those harlotry players as ever I saw." Like Mistress Quickly, I applaud. Let me put it this way: the exuberant invention which flowed out in so many books often overflowed into life, and Ford drew no hard and fast distinctions between writing a novel and living one. Why should he? The world is full of dull, unimaginative creatures who are only too palpably and sincerely their own dreary selves. We ought to be grateful to an artist who in our own lifetime so successfully revived the tradition of the *commedia dell'arte*.

I have known many men in my time, but few so fundamentally innocent of real harm as Ford. He was a generous man. His often slender purse was always at the disposition of friends and brother writers. He took great pains, devoted much time to helping young or poor or neglected writers. True, a' did hanker after women. Who but a fool will hold that against him? It says much for his charm and real goodness that, in spite of his trying little ways, he could arouse real devotion and love from so many members of the more intelligent half of the human species.

Long years ago Ford wrote a poem with the line:
"God is a good man."

And I parodied it:

"God is a good man, God is a fat man."

I still feel that Ford was essentially a kindly, well-intentioned man who was made to suffer more for his human failings and misfortunes than was just.

The grounds on which the public forms its opinion of writers are often mysterious and seemingly irrelevant. Thus, many English writers take great pains to reassure their public that they are not artists at all (perhaps an unnecessary precaution) but healthy happy grown-up schoolboys, who do a little modest writing on the side. To prove it they spend long summer days sweating or snoozing in the cricket field, and vie with each other in protestation of their undying affection for that unclean animal the dog. The truly successful also develop a complicated literary strategy which demands a heavy toll of time and tact. A strenuous exacting life. But it seems to be necessary in order on the one hand to placate or stifle professional rivals, and on the other hand to reassure the suspicious reading public, so quick to resent any suggestion that its values are not the same thing as the eternal verities.

How else can one explain the indifference to Cunninghame Graham and Ford as writers? One would imagine that Graham would have gone over as an amateur, a Scottish gentleman of royal descent, a lover of horses; but he was a disdainful amateur, he didn't play the social game, and he loved horses like a Spaniard, not like an English fox-hunter. When a man who looks rather like King Charles I and is said to be the legitimate King of Scotland openly announces himself as a socialist and obviously scorns the claims of plutocracy, he arouses the worst suspicions in those who are able to buy books. Yet I venture to think that Cunninghame Graham is underestimated as a writer, and that if intelligence survives our present troubles his books will survive with it. Graham has not been treated with contempt—only a crude and ignorant person would attempt it—but people have been content to accept him as a legend, and to neglect the qualities of his writing.

Ford's case is different. He was too professional in his manner, too much given to highfalutin about prose and style and form and the like. He overdid the gentleman propaganda; and neither played cricket nor bred dogs. On the contrary, he talked incessantly about breeding pigs and growing vegetables, and may even have done so occasionally. He could only have got away with that if he had been rich enough to run a "model" farm, and pay somebody else to do the work while he took the credit. And of course he was involved in the sort of mild scandals which thousands of more or less wealthy people get away with annually.

But what on earth has all that to do with his abilities as a writer? Nothing, one would say; and yet apparently everything. Ford had to work hard for a living, and evidently produced too much. Yet he and Norman Douglas made the *English Review* the best literary journal issued in England in this century. He was a very good literary journalist. After a quarter of a century or more his earlier poems (particularly those written in Germany and "On Heaven") are still very pleasant reading. His novels and other prose works, particularly his book on Provence, deserve a careful survey. I haven't looked at them recently, but I would wager there are excellent things in them. Anyway, the man could write, and he laboured valiantly. Nobody can accuse Ford of being sterile. Some day, I hope, an enthusiastic but discriminating Fordian will select and reprint the best of Ford's output.

Ford had the rare merit of believing in the republic of letters. He thought that writers and artists, whatever their personal differences and rivalries, should always support each other publicly. I don't know anyone else who did so much to help other writers, with the possible exception of Ezra. In this

Ford was following the Continental tradition; and not the English, which sets so high a value on individualism. T. S. Eliot put his finger on a real defect in English intellectual life when he said that writers tended to go off and function by themselves like so many Robinson Crusoes.

Moreover, Ford was free from that blinkered literary chauvinism which can see nothing outside the walls of one nation, has only provincial standards. In his way Ford was a good European. That may have been—probably was—because he was half-German, half-English, and also because he was brought up as a Catholic. He believed in a common European culture existing above and beyond national rivalries, a conception which the modern Germans have destroyed as their ancestors destroyed the Roman Empire from which it was distantly derived.

So far as I know, Ford cared little or nothing about Italy, which seems strange in a German and a Catholic; but most likely he got too much of it in childhood from his Pre-Raphaelite connections. In a similar revolt against gushing English culture-seekers, Norman Douglas uses the word *cinquecento* as a term of derision. Ford's dearest love was the intellectual France of the north and the sensuous France of the south. But he could also understand and enjoy what was good in England and Germany and America. I liked to hear him quote German poetry and play German songs. And he knew a lot about mediæval England, as I discovered when we visited Bodiam Castle together. But Ford's ideals, his way of looking at life and art, belong to a vanished world. In the catastrophe of chaos they have become meaningless.

Chapter X

THERE is a great temptation (I find) to go on writing about people one has known, especially in that pre-1914 period. Each old acquaintance recalls others, and the process could be continued almost indefinitely. But it must be curbed, and these personal memories worked in later if possible.

There is something more than interest in people which subconsciously urges me to prolong the last chapter. I perceive I don't want to leave those happy days of peace and face the first war over again even in retrospect. With another worse war devastating the earth as I write—and how futile it now seems to write at all—the whole thing becomes unbearable.

During the long armistice of '19 to '39 I was jeered at by journalists for "an obsession with the war." Perhaps that obsession did exist, and it was certainly only natural that people should want to forget the stresses and miseries through which they had so painfully lived. Yet, in view of subsequent events, it looks as if those who were "obsessed" with the last war were closer to realities than those who tried to pretend it hadn't happened. The early books of Aldous Huxley hardly refer to the war at all; yet later on he too became "obsessed" with the problems of war and peace, though in an abstract and not very practical way.

All sorts of things were wrong in that pre-1914 world; they must have been, to end up in so lamentable a bankruptcy. But it had two advantages which were lost in the struggle. There was a rough and ready European order, even a world order, in which the great majority unconsciously believed. And though foreigners might be despised and laughed at, they were not hated merely because they came from the other side of a frontier and spoke another language.

I was not in the habit of buying newspapers in 1912—except when something extraordinary happened, but when I saw the first placard of the *Titanic* disaster, I immediately bought a paper. Another man bought a copy at the same time, and to my amazement turned it over, read the stop-press racing news, and then stuffed the paper into his pocket without even glancing at the main news item. I was shocked. I couldn't feel so cynically uninterested in the misfortunes of fellow-creatures. People have seen a symbol of coming disaster in that sudden wreck of the arrogant *Titanic*. And there is something suggestive about it. Even more suggestive to my mind is that on the 10th of November 1918, an old warship called the *Britannia* was torpedoed off Trafalgar.

Newspapers suddenly became important in those sunny late July days. It was so hot that H.D. and I (then married only a few months) went every day to the Art Museum in South Kensington, and sat in a large cool room overlooking a courtyard with a fountain, where we read books on Italy and Italian art. We intended to go to Italy about November. But the headlines flared larger and larger across the front pages, the street placards became more frequent and more disquieting. Yet, as I have already said, it was not until the end of the month that we became really anxious. We were assured on all sides that the government (meaning of course the British government) would certainly do something about it. Apparently it went off for a long week-end.

I received a telegram from Ford, who was in a remote part of Scotland, asking me to wire him a news summary each afternoon, as their papers were a day late. So every day I sent off what seemed to me the important things. One day at the end of a long list of European calamities I added: "France at war with Germany." The clerk at the post-office looked up and said:

"That's not official yet."

"I know, but it will be within a few hours of that telegram's arrival."

It was. After the invasion of Belgium I sent no more telegrams, being certain that Ford was sufficiently intelligent to draw the right conclusion. The excitement and the gravity of the situation may be judged from the fact that strangers actually began talking to each other in buses and trains. With that comical assumption of holding sovereign power which is still a common delusion of people in democratic countries, a bus conductor told me solemnly that "the country wouldn't stand it" (i.e., the invasion of Belgium) and that "we" should have to turf them out. I don't know why in times of crisis journalists cable across the Atlantic and the world the opinions of bus conductors and hotel porters. My own impression is that they merely echo the newspapers credulously and do what the government tells them.

Following a suggestion of T. E. Hulme's, I went down to the headquarters of the H.A.C. to register as a volunteer. I was asked if I had ever had any serious illnesses, and admitted that I had undergone an operation in 1910. I was told contemptuously that there wasn't the slightest chance of my ever getting into the army. I lost my way going out and wandered into the armoury, where I was promptly put under arrest by a city clerk dressed as a corporal. He suspected me of being a German spy because I wore a small beard and a French jacket. The aspect of that armoury depressed me. I had seldom seen anything so ugly, and the place seemed to radiate a peculiarly drab philistinism. When I was released from duress, I felt rather glad that there was "no chance" of getting into the army. With only too clear a prescience I foresaw that living with the British army would be nearly as unpleasant as fighting the Germans.

When I have heard people making optimistic predictions about later wars, I remember that in 1914 most people said the war would be over in six months; some said, three. When they are pessimistic, I remember a certain Sunday evening in August. We were dining in Soho, and got out of the underground at Piccadilly. The streets were crowded, and immediately one had a vague feeling that something awful had happened. News boys were yelling: "Special edition, *The Times*. Total destruction of the British army." If it had been anything except *The Times* I should have been sceptical—Sunday afternoon is a great breeding ground for rumours. But it was *The Times*.

This was the famous or infamous despatch authorised by Winston Churchill with a view to stimulating recruiting, although he knew the information was exaggerated. Troops who have been in heavy fighting which ends in retirement are always sensationally pessimistic—they exaggerate in order to excuse themselves for what they think the disgrace of falling back. Some uncritical reporter had bumped into a few of these stragglers, and by the time they had told their story and he had told his version of it, truth was limping far over the horizon. I think Mr. Churchill was wrong to let that be published. It did no good and some harm. As for recruiting—the government was already incapable of dealing with the rush of volunteers. At noon on the 5th of August, the H.A.C. man told me they had received over a thousand applications that morning at that one regiment.

Those war rumours! The angels at Mons, for instance. Some people believe in them, although it has been proved that they originated in an article by Arthur Machen, in which he imagined something of the sort in a sentimental way. Very soon numerous members of the B.E.F. were to be found ready to swear that they had seen the angels in action. But any real old sweat would swear to a wagonload of angels or cherubim or any other supernatural phenomenon for a couple of pints of beer. As for journalists, they don't even require beer—*c'est leur métier.*

One evening in 1915 we dined with May Sinclair. On this occasion Ezra distinguished himself by alternately leaning forward to spear potatoes with his fork from a dish in the middle of the table, and then lolling back to munch his capture. By way of covering this *gaffe,* which evidently scandalised Miss Sinclair, I said the first thing that came into my head—that I didn't believe the stories about Canadian soldiers having been crucified by Germans. The elderly maid servant waiting at table suddenly broke in passionately that it was true, she had a nephew in the army who had told her so. When you consider the training of English servants, this breach of discipline shows how keen people were on believing these stories. Why? Because all but a few persons of exceptional and possibly abnormal natures prefer the sensational to the true, and are mentally incapable of critical judgment. Certainly, truth prevails in the long run, but only when it is too late to have any real influence on affairs.

The mental temperature of London fell imperceptibly but rapidly. Business as usual, so popular a slogan among merchants, did not apply to intellectual activities. Literary papers quietly disappeared, literary articles were not wanted, poems had to be patriotic. The old camaraderie disappeared, and along with it the old simplicity. Before the war *les jeunes* were perfectly happy to dine simply and to spend the evening in talk on nothing more expensive than tea and cigarettes. But as the young men began coming on leave in khaki, they wanted more violent and expensive amusements, good dinners, theatres, dancing, girls. I don't say it was the artists and writers who did this—they are always an insignificant minority—but somehow the majority began to set a more hectic standard which persisted until long after the war. Very few were content with art only any more; they had to have art and champagne.

Moreover, we began to have casualties among our friends. The first was the French-Polish sculptor, Henri Gaudier-Brzeska. During the Albert Hall exhibit of the Allied Artists in 1913, Ezra went round with his mother-in-law, Mrs. Shakespeare. They came to a statuette in what was then loosely called the Futurist style, and Ezra began capering about and making fun of it. Suddenly a gaunt sharp-faced young man, with flaming eyes and long dank hair, rushed at him and threatened him with immediate personal violence. Ezra prudently declined the combat, and at once became a warm admirer of the young man's work. Thus we came to know Gaudier.

He was probably the dirtiest human being I have ever known, and gave off horrid effluvia in hot weather. One summer day he came to see us in our small flat; so we prudently placed him on a couch at one end of the room and ourselves retired to the other. Who should come in but Ford, who had been to a fashionable luncheon, and wanted to display his shiny topper and formal morning clothes with a red carnation in the buttonhole. Unluckily he had to sit beside Gaudier; and soon left. The next morning Ford gave me a paternal lecture on my wickedness in permitting such a creature to be in the same room with H.D. It was, he said, not done. However, as the weather cooled, Gaudier was frequently at Ford's evenings; and eventually his phallic statue of Ezra was erected in Ford's front garden, much to Violet's distress.

Gaudier had fled to England to avoid compulsory military service in France—before the war, of course. He was extremely poor, and his "studio" was a railway arch somewhere near Putney. As he could not afford to buy stone for his statues, he and Epstein (so Gaudier informed me) used to go out late at night and steal pieces of stone from a mason's yard near the

Tate Gallery. As they were limited to what they could carry, practically all Gaudier's work was limited in size to statuettes. Such are the disabilities which afflict artists in the 20th century.

With the war came the slogan, so irresistible even to half a Frenchman, *La patrie est en danger*. Gaudier determined to go back to France, though he was liable to severe punishment as a deserter. However, the French Consul told him it would be all right, and a number of us went down to Victoria to see him off. He left in high spirits, assuring us repeatedly that he would bring back the Picassos from Düsseldorf. To our surprise, he returned to London in a couple of days, without the Picassos.

What had happened was this. On arrival he had been taken before a peppery French colonel, who denied that *la patrie* was in danger, threatened Gaudier with ten years on Devil's Island, and put him under arrest. By some means he escaped from his prison, boarded a Channel boat in the general confusion, and returned to London for a safe-conduct from his consul. Evidently a resourceful young man. We walked together across Hyde Park and Kensington Gardens on his last day in London, and he told me gravely that being in prison had entirely changed his views on art—he was going to abandon the modern style entirely, and follow "the Greeks." He even offered to do a classical statue of me as the youthful Hercules. If this had ever happened, I suspect I should have emerged in stone as a prize-fighter afflicted with microcephaly, elephantiasis, and superb appendages.

We heard from Gaudier from time to time, and he was evidently a good soldier, as he was soon promoted to sergeant. He was killed in a scrap at Neuville-Saint-Vaast in 1915. Two years later, when I was on that sector, I tried to find his grave, but without success. T. E. Hulme, who had been wounded at Ypres early in the war, transferred to the heavy artillery. He was killed somewhere in Dunkirk. We were told it was a direct hit from a very big shell, which literally blew him to atoms—a horrid fate for anyone, but particularly ironical for a philosopher who had doubted the reality of phenomena. Phenomenal or noumenal, the shell got him; and he walked and talked no more among us.

In his lifetime Gaudier made little out of his work. I believe Ezra was his most generous patron. On the occasion of Wilfrid Scawen Blunt's seventieth birthday, a small subscription was raised, and Gaudier made a little alabaster box in which a number of poets put autograph copies of their poems for presentation to Blunt. They were W. B. Yeats, Sturge Moore, Ezra Pound, Victor Plarr, F. S. Flint, and myself. Blunt entertained us to lunch, and gave us roast peacock, with a magnificent peacock's tail spread over the table as decoration. Blunt obviously hated Gaudier's "futuristic" work; and said politely in his speech that he wasn't sure at first whether we were a deputation of poets or horse-breeders. Hilaire Belloc came in for tea; which in his case consisted of a pint of claret in a large crystal goblet. Later on, Ezra and I spent a week-end with Blunt. He astonished us by appearing at dinner in the full dress of an Arab sheik with gold-mounted pistols in his sash and drinking damnation to the British government, which treasonable toast we were forced to accept. In the library on Sunday morning I found a number of books (including a Bible) all inscribed: "George Noel Gordon, Lord Byron." I believe Lady Anne Blunt was descended from the poet. In the same room was a couch on which, according to Blunt, Francis Thompson used to sleep off the effects of opium.

I have no views of Gaudier's work as a sculptor, though of late years I have come across it in one or two national collections. But, like many modern sculptors, he was a good draftsman. He showed me a large collection of his sketches, chiefly of nudes and animals; and they seemed to me to show real talent. He had a beautiful, almost calligraphic line in drawing deer

153

and antelopes. But when he worked in stone, all that grace disappeared and he was enslaved by pedantic abstractionist theories. "Abstractionism" is peculiarly inappropriate in a piece of detached sculpture not intended as part of an architectural design. What is the point of such work, except as a technical study in planes and masses? However, there is perhaps more to be said for abstractionist art than for abstractionist poetry. In the early days of Dada (predecessor of Surrealism) I received for review a book which contained the following "poem":

"A B C D E F
G H I J K L
M N O P Q R
S T U V W X
Y Z."

On which I commented:

"1 2 3 4 5
6 7 8 9 10."

I still think that was the most snappy review I ever wrote; but unfortunately *The Times* refused to print it.

I see I have said very little about Hulme. There has been a revival of interest in him of late years, and I have often been asked about him. Unfortunately I remember extremely little. My impression is that he was a burly fellow of about thirty, whose pockets were generally bulging with a French book and a set of proofs. He translated Bergson with F. S. Flint, or rather Flint did the translation and Hulme revised it and put his own name on it. Hulme had a coarse and cynical way of talking about women which repelled me; but he had the rare gift of being able to keep a large group discussing some problem of art or literature without their breaking up into side talks and without monopolizing the conversation himself. I only saw Hulme angry once, and that was when a man with a voice like a buzz-saw insisted on telling us theories about Homer which he had just discovered. Since most of us had been made to read up this subject at school or at the university, it was extremely boring. As nothing would stop the man, Hulme announced in a loud voice that we would all adjourn (meaning to the Café Royal), which we accordingly did, carefully losing the buzz-saw *en route*. Hulme had a flair for picking out gifted young men, and most of the people who frequented his evenings have made reputations in one way or another. One of them was David L. Murray, novelist and editor of *The Times Literary Supplement*. He amused us one evening by telling us that he had written to the *Manchester Guardian* offering to do reviews, and they had replied portentously that they thought he hadn't quite the "right ethos." The joke would have been even better if we could have known they were turning down a future editor of *The T. L. S.*

The brief carefree days were gone, never to return again so far as I was concerned. Under the stress of inner conflict I lost the serenity and harmony which form a large part of real success in life. I thought it was a plain duty to be in the army, and cowardly to be out of it. As the need for men grew more pressing, I first suspected and then became convinced that the old operation, which had seemed so decisive to the H.A.C. man in August '14, would no longer be considered important. On the other hand, I thought war an insanity, and I had the deepest suspicions about the motives of the combatants. The blather and bunk of the newspapers certainly suggested that the whole thing was a ramp, with very unidealistic motives behind it. I was infuriated by the cool assumption of the governing class that the nation must continue to pay by a prompt, servile, and profuse shedding of blood for their incompetence in peace-keeping and war-making. I wanted to keep my head during the catastrophe, and not be swept away by mass emotions or the puerile propaganda which showed such contempt for one's intelligence. I realised, too, that the situation must look entirely different on the other side of the battling armies; to a German his country must have seemed a beleaguered fortress. There were then no Hitler and Goebbels in command, to make the issue unmistakably clear.

I exaggerated, I think, the economic motive behind war. Certainly, it was there, but I now incline to think it was largely a rationalising of other and often unconscious desires for dominion—a psychological problem. One solid fact established by Norman Angell was that war did not pay, either immediately or in the long run. In 1914 Germany had become the leading export country, and the problem of the Berlin–Baghdad railway had been settled in its favour. Where was the economic gain in making war? The German thesis that the war was an Allied plot to destroy that prosperity seemed to me rather incredible. On the other hand, I thought there was a good deal in the population-pressure argument, though not in the way it was put forward. The earlier stages of the industrial system had brought into existence an enormous mass of Europeans, mostly of an inferior kind, who were less and less required as the system was perfected. The governments hadn't the faintest idea what to do with these people; and war seemed to offer a temporary solution.

Thus I argued with myself interminably, with a fatalistic instinct that sooner or later I should be involved in the massacre. It was not possible for me to be a conscientious objector, though I thought the attitude was entirely logical. Equally logical was the attitude of the ruthless militarist. But neither humanity nor the universe wholly obeys the rules of logic; and in any case it seemed to me ridiculous and presumptuous to set up one's little conscience against the conscience of a nation. The only effective method of "objection" was to pair off before-hand with someone in the enemy country, be sure you both kept your word, and have enough of you to be able to wreck both war machines. Otherwise pacifism is simply playing into the hands of the opposing militarists, and is a futile gesture.

I envied but could not imitate the airy arrogance of the intellectual presented with a white feather by a lady, who said melodramatically:

"Don't you know men are dying for civilisation?"

"Certainly, and *I* am the civilisation they are dying for."

A pretty jest; but only possible so long as the men in the line held it, and the navy kept the seas.

In the interim I thought that something might be done in a small way to maintain the tradition of the arts and of a Europe above nationalism. It was a forlorn hope, but not obviously so then. By way of giving a practical turn to this ideal I turned my attention to Remy de Gourmont, who had every claim to being considered a good European in matters of the intellect. I had been in touch with him for some time, and had translated some of his essays for the *Egoist*. His letters showed that he was in great difficulties. He was elderly, in poor health, and largely dependent on journalism for his living; but practically all literary journalism was suspended in Paris. A large part of his savings was in Ottoman bonds, which had become practically worthless. So for some time one of my occupations was to translate essays, articles, and poems by Gourmont for English and American periodicals, and to send him on the money. The letters I received from Gourmont during this last year of his life were printed at the end of the American edition of the two-volume selection I made from his books in an English translation.

Gourmont died in September 1915, and almost immediately I began to receive letters from Mme. de Courrières and from Mme. Jean de Gourmont. Each of these ladies claimed to be the heir, and besought me not to send any money due to Gourmont to the other. This was very embarrassing, but I solved the problem by writing them polite letters of condolence, and sending the money to Gourmont's account with the *Mercure de France*.

I never saw Remy de Gourmont. He was a complete recluse for a very sad reason. As a young man he had been very handsome, but contracted a form of lupus which disfigured him badly. He was exceedingly sensitive about it, and disliked meeting strangers. Only the influence of Miss Natalie Barney could bring him to a social gathering, and even then he usually hid unhappily in the conservatory. My contact with him was solely through his books and by letter; and yet it was a real friendship. I admired his range of interests, his erudition, his French culture, his unbiased judgment, his original point of view, his scepticism, his individualism. He was free from every fanaticism, any form of cant, any subservience either to authority or public opinion. He made a small income by his pen, but he never wrote for money. His integrity, his pure intellectual detachment were never betrayed. He was not widely known in his lifetime, even among his fellow-countrymen, who were not always friendly to him. Yet in 1922, seven years after his death, more copies of Gourmont's books were sold in France than of any other writer. His sanity and wisdom were obvious correctives to the disorders and fatuities of the war and post-war years. Recently he has again been neglected—he provides no encouragement for political fanatics. I should think it a hopeful sign if his books became popular once more.

Gourmont's work suffers from certain disabilities. He was slow in developing, and he wrote too much. Consequently, there is a good deal of his writing which either doesn't quite come off or is repetitive. But the best of it is so good that nobody who cares for European literature should miss it. For this reason I devoted a lot of time and trouble to making a comprehensive selection, and I modestly think that the two volumes published by Covici in America contain all and omit nothing of Gourmont's work that is essential.

From its foundation in 1890 until the war, the *Mercure de France* was one of the best, if not the best, of the independent literary periodicals in France. Nothing like it has existed in England and America, though the *English Review* under Ford, the *Dial* under Scofield Thayer, and T. S. Eliot's *Criterion* did succeed in reproducing some of the *Mercure's* features. But for years the *Mercure* introduced many of the best European writers, so that one bought practically any book with the familiar caduceus and wings on it. Moreover, its notes on French and international literature, art, and thought were unrivalled.

I will not claim that Gourmont was the sole inspirer of all this, but for many years it was an open secret that he was the real power behind the throne. The *Mercure* was a faithful mirror of Gourmont's catholic tastes and interests. How great his influence had been we only perceived when the *Mercure* reappeared without him. Immediately after the war its place was taken by the *Nouvelle Revue Française,* which had been in unsuccessful rivalry since 1907, under the inspiration of André Gide. There is said to have been a coolness between Gide and Gourmont, which may explain why the *N. R. F.* has always failed to do justice to Gourmont. Yet when I sent my Gourmont Anthology to Jean Paulhan, then editor of the *N. R. F.,* he wrote me that he now realised there was far more in Gourmont than he had believed and that he intended to study Gourmont's books more carefully. This may have been only politeness, but I was glad to have wrung from the opposition even that moderate tribute to *mon vieux ami et maître.*

There was an interlude before I was actually involved in the war. London had become depressing, and we decided to go to the country. John Cournos suggested that we should go to north Devon, where two of his friends were living, and that he would join us later. We all agreed that the mild climate of Devonshire would be pleasant after the winter days in London.

We left a foggy and rainy London, and arrived at a hilly landscape under six inches of freezing snow. This was a slight shock, and so was the fact that no vehicle was available. We had to leave our bags, and plod a couple of miles through the snow. It was rather fun, really, and those dull rounded Exmoor hills looked beautiful under the snow. But we soon got tired of living on a bleak snowy hill, and transferred ourselves to a valley, about a mile away, where the first primroses were already coming out.

I got to like that valley. In front of the cottage ran one of those rocky Devonshire trout streams, "warty" as Herrick calls them. Across a meadow there began a wooded hillside, and about a mile and half down the valley was the sea. There were only two other cottages and a large inn along the valley.

While the cold lasted, I cut down trees and sawed them up for firewood—astonishing how long it takes to get a couple of baskets of firewood and how very quickly they disappear in a fire. I spent nearly as much time in tree-chopping as in writing. Then, in the spring, we took long walks with our friends, Mr. and Mrs. Carl Fallas and J. M. Whitham, and recaptured the good fellowship and gaiety which had vanished from London. In the warmer days we made up beach picnic parties, and bathed. Quite an idyllic existence, if there hadn't been a war on.

Carl Fallas and Whitham were close friends, and yet each was the antithesis of the other, an epitome of two completely different types of Englishman. To liken them to Don Quixote and Sancho Panza would be unfair to both, yet there would be some truth in it. They might have been living models for some

17th-century writer of "characters"—The Realist and The Idealist.

Carl had the sense of adventure. He had been round the world, had lived in Ceylon, Japan, and San Francisco, making his way back to Liverpool on a wind-jammer by way of Cape Horn—an epic *Wanderjahr* for a young man. He was intensely interested in life as it is lived, in people as they are, and he had a very lively knack for telling yarns of his varied experience. He had a gift of alert curiosity about human beings and their ways which I envied him. Less apparent at first sight was a streak of poetic sensibility which came out in his novel about Japan, *The Wooden Pillow*.

Whitham was the prisoner of a cast-iron non-conformist conscience, against which he struggled in vain. Like John Morley and Mark Rutherford, he had cast off puritan doctrine but retained the puritan temperament. He disciplined himself unmercifully according to a rigid schedule—so many hours for writing, for reading, for strenuous exercise, with scarcely a minute for living. Without knowing it, he was ardently seeking salvation, both for himself and the world—it was as much a moral duty as cleaning his teeth and abstaining from flesh. His philosophy was pessimistic, and he illustrated it by a series of novels about rural tragedies which terrified the subscription libraries. A man of inflexible character and *idées fixes,* yet warm-hearted, unselfish, and an eloquent talker.

It was delightful to see the two of them together. Carl had a low opinion of human nature, not the faintest interest in abstract utopias, and didn't think the world was worth saving even if it could be saved. Yet as a rule he was as blithe as a lark on a May morning, and would chirrup over his pint of ale as merrily as Friar John of the Funnels. Whitham, who had the highest standards about everything, and prodigious ideals, was often as melancholy as a gib cat; though on occasions he could cheer up wonderfully, when human nature broke in.

F

For such a man there were only two possible attitudes towards the war. Either it would be a crusade and he would go into it with the grim courage and determination of a Cromwellian ironside; or it would be of the devil and he would have nothing to do with it. Whitham chose the latter view, and pleaded conscientious objections on non-religious grounds. His discourse on Tolstoy and the brotherhood of man was naturally brushed aside by a tribunal which had heard of neither; but Whitham refused to yield, and I fear he had a very bad time indeed.

Carl and I agreed that while we admired such resolution, we could not accept the grounds on which it was based. Carl was intensely curious to see the war, and pointed out that it would be a shame to miss the greatest event of our lives. I saw that argument too; but it also struck me as a high price to pay for gratifying one's curiosity. We agreed to join up together and to keep together, so that at least we should have someone to talk to.

Chapter XI

EVERYTHING or almost everything I have to say about the war of 1914-18 has been said in *Death of a Hero* and *Roads to Glory*. It is impossible for me now to re-capture the passion and indignation which inspired *Death of a Hero*. I worked them out of my system. And even if I could re-live those emotions, they would seem pointless with another and more disastrous war in progress. The European War, the World War, the First World War—whatever you like to call it—is no longer *the* War. It drops back into history, and takes its place with the other fading or unheeded calamities in the long tragedy of human suffering.

When I stripped for the medical examination I was handed a filthy grey flannel dressing gown, which had obviously been worn by thousands of the unwashed, and for all I knew by the lousy, the syphilitic, and heaven knows what infected bodies. A sergeant told me to put it on, but when I pointed out how dirty it was, he did not insist. How characteristic that is of British casualness and inefficiency. Millions are spent on a Ministry of Health, yet with the nation's manhood passing through the recruiting stations the authorities could not or would not go to the slight trouble and expense of avoiding so obvious a source of possible infection as those revolting gowns.

I had another instance of this carelessness—to give it no worse a name—when I was first inoculated against typhoid as a private soldier. We stood in a long queue, our left arms bared, and filed past a doctor. I noticed that he was jabbing the needle indifferently into arm after arm without sterilising it, although there was boiling water beside him for that purpose. When I got near I said aloud:

"He's not sterilising his needle."

The doctor glanced up sharply and caught my eyes, which met his steadily. I was fully determined to refuse inoculation unless he did sterilise the needle. He did so, ostentatiously, after each man until I had passed. When I had dressed and was leaving, I looked back from the door. He had ceased to sterilise.

I slept ill on my first night in barracks. The blankets were old and dirty, the "biscuit" mattresses lumpy and hard, the unventilated air foul, and the men groaned and snored in their sleep. I lay awake, thinking of Italy and France and the sea and the clean brook running past my Devonshire cottage. I think I can imagine what it must be to spend one's first night in prison, though prisons are clean and one has the privilege of solitary confinement. It was a relief next day to be shifted to the open Dorset country, into wooden huts with plenty of cracks and crevices to let in air, scrubbed plank beds with mattresses we stuffed ourselves with sweet-smelling straw, and shower baths which Carl and I had to ourselves at almost any time but Saturday night.

I knew that country well; I had walked over it on one of my excursions across England on foot. In the marshes I knew there would be nodding cotton-grass and blue gentians, and on the downs clear air and silence except for a distant curlew note or the caw of passing rooks or the clink of a sheep-bell. Standing to attention on the barren ugly parade ground, I sometimes reflected that not far off sat or slept Thomas Hardy, brooding on the iniquity of dynasts, but doubtless convinced that the war to end wars must be won at all costs. Like every new war, that one was different while it lasted.

In the early days of the war, training and discipline had been lax, if only because such essential military equipment as uniforms, rifles, and camps had been absent. All that had been changed into "intensive training." But was it really efficient? Was it intelligent? What was so vehemently and blasphemously instilled into us was not so much training for war as spit-and-polish soldiering; turning to the right and left by numbers, slow march, quick march, standing to attention ("the first duty of a soldier is obedience"—not, you observe, to defeat the enemy), sloping, ordering, presenting arms, platoon and company drill, polishing brass buttons, scrubbing or polishing equipment, took up most of our time. The most sensible things were physical jerks, marching, and musketry. But the actual firing was not a hundred rounds, and the route marches were languid affairs of a few miles. There was also a certain amount of distance-judging and "taking cover" (carried out gingerly because we didn't want to soil our uniforms or tarnish our buttons) and ferocious-sounding bayonet fighting. Dear me, those "lectures" on the spirit of the bayonet! They ought to have made the German army tremble.

This would have been all right if there had been time, but only three months elapsed between a man's enlistment and his being pushed out to face the trained troops of Germany. It is really astonishing that the new armies did as well as they did, and that they were not all wiped out. Their real training virtually only began when they got into the trenches.

Naturally, the men immediately directing this "training" were not responsible for it; that was devised by veterans of other wars in London. All the men doing the job cared about was to give proof of zeal by incessant barking and harrying of their victims, and to be able to put up plenty of eye-wash for visiting firemen of the brass-hat variety. So that while we shone in drill and button-polishing, we knew no more how to fight battles than a military expert on a newspaper.

The absurd rushing about and over-exercise were a severe strain even on Carl and me, who were in excellent condition when we started. We pitied the unfortunates from the tail of a plough or from behind a desk or counter, who were driven on when they flagged, and might excusably have collapsed from heart failure. Here is a schedule of one particularly strenuous day:

5 a.m.: reveille; wash, shave, dress, re-arrange plank bed, and fold blankets; as orderly man help to fetch tea for 30 men; polish buttons. 5:30–6:30: drill. 6:30: fetch breakfast from cookhouse, and afterwards wash up 30 tea bowls and 30 plates, scrub plank bed, and be on parade at 7:30. Until 12:30, physical jerks and drills. 12:30: Fetch dinner and wash up, replace plank bed, polish buttons. 1:30–4:30: drill and bayonet 'fighting. 4:30: fetch tea, wash up, sweep hut. 7:30–10:30: night operations, including a four-mile march and trench-digging. 10:30: soup for those who wanted it—most of us too tired to drink it. 11 p.m.: in bed. Shortly after we were all asleep, practice fire alarm, at the double. We were so tired, that we stumbled along arm-in-arm to keep each other from falling. About 15 minutes standing on the parade ground, and then dismiss. Up next morning at 5.

This might have been cunningly designed to accustom us to the real fatigues of war. But, as a matter of fact, one of the orderly room clerks told me that our being sent on night operations when a fake fire alarm had been staged was due to a "mistake in orders." In other words, it was not policy and certainly not inhumanity, but merely casualness, which unluckily can often come to be the same thing as inhumanity. It wearies me to think how often that same casualness or downright incompetence produced similar results, even in my small experience.

The colonel in command of that training battalion was a fool who had been sent back from France for incompetence. Instead of being reduced to the ranks, or put away harmlessly, he was given a responsible job because he was a Regular Army officer. The real work was done by the young Adjutant, the Regimental Sergeant-Major, and the Regimental Quarter-Master-Sergeant. Here was the sort of thing that colonel did:

Thinking that in the circumstances I should do well to brush up my German, I had brought a copy of Heine's *Buch der Lieder* with me; and since there was no place provided for a common soldier's private property, I had to put the book under the towel on top of my folded blankets. The colonel had a most mathematical eye for maladjusted blankets, and immediately spotted the slight bulge of the book, and had it brought forth. Somebody evidently told him it was German. Horrors! Spies in our midst!

It took an infinite time to convince this dreary ass of his error. He kept asking Carl why, if he was not a German, he was called "Carl"? There was the further suspicious circumstance that I had been to Italy and Carl to Japan, both of which, as everybody knows, are contiguous to Germany. What had we been doing there? I was looking forward hopefully to an indefinite period of confinement in the Bloody Tower or Pentonville, when the R. Q. M. S. suddenly asked me if I were *Richard* Aldington. Somewhat peevishly I said I was. Whereupon he immediately assured the colonel that all was well. It appeared later that the R. Q. M. S. was a schoolmaster, and recollected seeing my book at that Mecca of the higher culture, poor Monro's Poetry Bookshop. So my poems got me out of the mess Heine's got me into.

What seemed to me the limit of old army cheek occurred one Sunday afternoon. By way of keeping some slight touch with civilisation, Carl and I had formed the habit of walking over to Corfe Castle on Sunday afternoons for tea. As we were good customers, they put us in the best public room, which is a large one. I had bought some good Turkish cigarettes, and after tea we each lighted one. Suddenly a waiter appeared and in embarrassed tones informed us that the *wife* of the Brigadier General commanding the district *ordered* us to put them out immediately. Now, this lady and her friends were seated so far away that we hadn't noticed them. Of course, if they had been close at hand, we should have asked permission to smoke; but at that distance they could not possibly have been incommoded by the scent of excellent Turkish tobacco. The action, therefore, was purely insolent and due to the fact that we were dressed as "common" soldiers.

We debated a little what to do. Plainly, the woman had not the slightest authority to command any soldier, and if we had stood on our rights and there had been a row, no court-martial could have convicted us. But we should have been marked and persecuted men. I am sometimes sorry we didn't face it out, but in fact we paid our bill and left at once, as the quietest solution. Making the world safe for Democracy, in fact.

If surviving the war was a benefit, and I must say I still think so, then I was extremely fortunate in several little happenings. Carl and I did not go to the front with the majority of the battalion. We were given Lance-Corporal stripes, and held back for training as N. C. O.s. It was rumoured that the men who went out ahead of us were involved in the battle of the Somme and severely handled. All rumours in wartime, particularly those among soldiers, should be suspected, but there is reason to believe there is some truth in this one. Plenty of battalions were cut up on the Somme.

When we did get out we arrived at the base in a chaos of huge reinforcements. Twenty-two men were crowded into a tent supposed to hold eight; and we slept there every night for three weeks in an almost solid mass, like wedge-shaped candies fitted into a round box. As fast as troops were sent up the line others came pouring in from England, and we seemed to have been overlooked in the general confusion and lack of organization. Apart from a little floundering about in full marching order, going through the gas chamber, and throwing a couple of Mills bombs apiece, we had nothing particular to do. And as the camp's rations had apparently not been increased to meet the huge increase of men, we were often hungry, particularly as the temperature soon fell below freezing.

It was here that I benefited immensely by Carl's common sense. We ought, he said, to go into Calais each evening and get a proper meal. I pointed out that we should be lucky if we got one pass a week. Carl maintained that we could easily bribe our way in and out. I demurred, pointing out that it was our duty to keep the spirit of regulations and not to tempt poorer men with our money. Moreover, so high was my estimate of human nature, I did not believe that sergeants and sentries could be bribed. However, I soon fell a not unwilling victim to Carl's persuasive eloquence, and so did the sentries and sergeants. Carl managed it admirably, though how he did it I don't know, but he certainly did it very cheaply. A five-franc note was a consideration to men who only got five francs a week spending money; it gave them an extra night of rum and coffee and gambling at "house" (lotto) in one of the estaminets.

How pleasant it was to taste French cooking and wine, and to talk French once more! The cooking in the British army would have disgraced a tribe of Bushmen, for not only was the diet coarse and inferior but it was prepared with a lack of skill which approached the miraculous. Severely rationed as the French were, they still were able to provide a civilised meal, with the little elegances which raise eating from a base necessity to a minor art. And even more delightful was the sense of home-coming, of being once again with people, however humble, who had the same values. By way of testing this I told them one evening that in civil life Carl and I were "poets." *"Des poètes, quoi!"* They were immediately impressed in our favour. And then came the inevitable, the adorable French *cliché,* always produced as if it had just been excogitated by Rochefoucauld himself: *"Un artis', c'est quelqu'un, vous savez."* And the chorus: *"Ah, oui, oui, par exemple."* I thought of the jeers and sneers and impertinences such an announcement would have aroused in a similar or indeed almost any milieu in England, if one had been stupid enough to make it there. I see why Mary Tudor had "Calais" written in her heart.

When we did go up the line, we had the further luck of being sent to a battalion of pioneers. The word "pioneers" sounds rather dare-devil and *en avant,* especially to American apprehension, but in point of fact it was a flattering term bestowed on a body of men who were something between amateur infantry and unskilled engineers. Our lives were a perpetual working party, digging new trenches, repairing old ones, clearing or building roads, pushing out saps into No Man's Land, removing old wire and putting up new wire in the same delightful landscape. I was very thankful when I was relieved of these wearisome tasks by being made a runner.

It would be tedious to enumerate at length all my lucky chances and escapes, but consider these facts. It was by chance that I was given just one night off in a period of two months; and that night happened to be one when a shell dropped on a group of our officers and runners, killing or wounding all except Carl and his officer. It was by chance that I lowered my head just as a shell burst beside me in a mine crater, so that instead of hitting my face a splinter merely crashed my tin hat. It was by chance that I shifted my foot a fraction of a second before a bullet neatly took the toe from my boot instead of smashing my ankle. It was by chance that, standing in a trench, I turned my head to speak to the man behind me exactly at the moment a large chunk of shell whizzed so close to my cheek that I felt its harsh and horrid breath. It was by chance that in the last attack of the war my field glasses shifted round over my stomach—when I went to use them I found they had been smashed and bent. And finally (though by no means completely) it was by chance that I missed the worst phase of two of the worst battles of the war.

If that isn't what novelists used to call "a charmed life," what is? In my opinion I was a very poor soldier, and not worth the money the government had to pay for me, still less the time they insisted on my wasting. Not only did I fail to get killed myself (which might have been some consolation to them), but I am perfectly certain I didn't kill anyone, and know I saved the lives of two wounded Germans. I also saved a British sentry from being court-martialled (and possibly shot) for the serious "crime" of being asleep at his post in the front line—the poor devil was much more tired than I was, and I was dead beat. Finally I was almost court-martialled for putting my servant to bed when he was drunk, instead of putting him under arrest. I was steering that happy but incapable person most unsteadily along a duck-board track when I bumped into the Camp Commandant; whereupon the following conversation ensued:

"What are you doing here in the servants' quarters?"

"Taking my servant to bed, sir."

"Don't you know that's conduct unbefitting an officer and a gentleman?"

"Yes, sir."

"You are under arrest pending a court-martial."

"Very good, sir."

The charge was withdrawn for the most unjust and ludicrous of reasons—the Camp Adjutant happened to be an old

schoolmate. That was the only time in my life when I even
unwittingly cashed in on the old school tie.

There is a superstition that drowning men live over all their
lives again as vividly as they first endured them. If this be true,
I hope I don't die by drowning, for I shouldn't like to live the
war—that little, old-fashioned war I knew—over again. It no
longer haunts me against my will, as it did for years. Deliberately what I have set down here has been the trifling, not the
tragical. To have re-lived it all once in the making of another
book was more than strain enough.

But memory is a faculty not understood, a capricious re-
sponder to strange calls. Unexpectedly, in a flash, it may break
through that laboriously built wall of forgetfulness. Certain
smells, sounds, and sights are the battering rams which suddenly demolish the wall and let the memories escape.

The smell of old wood burning brings back to my lungs and
nostrils the hot frowsty air from a dugout on a winter's night.
I can see the rough chalk steps going down through darkness
to the candle-glimmer, the trench in which I stand, the dark
patient sentry beside me, and overhead the cold stars dimmed
suddenly by a Very light. The scent of new-mown hay is no
longer delicious to me. It is like phosgene, and brings up a picture of dawn over a ruined village and stretcher-bearers bringing down gasping foam-mouthed bodies on stretchers. And
that stuff women use to take the pink from their nails is very
like tear gas, so that pink nails make me think of masked men
groping along muddy trenches. In the vaults of the Escorial I
smelled again that awful stench of corrupting corpse. I was
with my old friend, Hal Glover, and simultaneously and without argument we both agreed to drop sight-seeing and retire
to the nearest café for brandy and coffee. We had both smelt
battlefields.

Sounds next. The drone of an airplane high up (not near)

brings a blue sky filled with the little white cauliflowers of bursting shells. A distant train whining away into silence on a frosty night brings back the sad whine of shells flying away death-laden to burst, unheard by us, among the unseen and mysterious Enemy. An impatient motor-cyclist warming up his engine is no friend of mine; he echoes the more deadly machine-gun. Yet thunder is harmless to memory; it is so much milder than a barrage.

Sight is much fainter. Pavé roads and fields of beet bring back the dead horses, with huge starting eye-balls of terror, heads reared back like the horse from the Parthenon, and large pools of dark blood. The New England woods, wrecked by the hurricane, brought back other wreckage of trees and many men's bodies.

The thought that all this must again be endured and perhaps worse, and that it may be repeated until this malicious and foolish species has gone, is a thought not to be borne.

I have just discovered another and most unwelcome stimulus to memory. It is when the war communiqués mention the names of too familiar towns and villages—Hazebrouck, Saint-Omer, Dunkirk, Lille, Béthune, Lens. Fatal names to a generation which helplessly sees more dreadful memories clustering around other names for the children they hoped to save. I wonder how many remember the wooden sign over a confused mass of bricks and debris, the sign which read: "This Was Pozières"? That New Zealander of Macaulay's, or more appropriately that Middle Western senator, may one day contemplate a similar sign: "This Was Europe."

They say I am bitter. The trouble is that I am not bitter enough. Tragedy upon tragedy, destruction upon destruction, another generation lost—and in my "bitterness" I dimly foresaw it:

"And trouble deaf heaven with our bootless cries."

It is only after a war that the experience of the individual survivor seems to have either interest or value. During a war civilians can think only in terms of "our side" and "their side." All they ask of their men is that they shall win. The individual suffering and cost are veiled behind military phrases, which cushion the abrupt shocks of reality. How much human misery and unrepeatable calamity lie hidden behind such words and phrases as "curtain fire," "local bombardment," "clashes of patrols," "strategic retreat," "heavy fighting," "advance held up," "aerial bombing," "casualties"! We cease to think of Jack, Jean, and Johann, and talk of Divisions and Corps. We even rejoice—it is horrible—at "enemy casualties." Delicate women look pleased when they hear that "the ground in front of our positions is heaped with enemy dead." And yet they are shocked by the simple-minded and practical cannibal who makes a meal of his enemy or his grandmother. We should not say, "as savage as a wild beast," but "as savage as civilised man." How can we look on ourselves and our species with anything but disgust?

> "O Seigneur, donnez-moi la force et le courage
> De contempler mon corps et mon cœur sans dégoût."

Chapter XII

ON the 4th of November 1918, there was an armistice between Italy and Austria; and owing to somebody's error this piece of news was falsely announced in America as the end of the war. Seeing that 6 a.m. Western European time is 1 a.m. Eastern American time, I calculate that on the very morning when New York went crazy over the peace, I was looking at the luminous dial of my watch in the grey dawn and giving my headquarter signallers the order to advance. As far as eye could see to north or south a huge curve of flashing gun-fire lit up the sky, and the old familiar roar and crash of drum-fire beat on the ears.

Modern warfare is a most complicated piece of organization. My job that morning of the 4th was not to kill Germans, but to see that as my battalion advanced I kept my battalion head-quarters in touch with brigade and both flanking battalions with a minimum of break and delay. For this purpose my field service message book and those of the other relevant officers contained two pages of mysterious letters and numbers, showing my different positions and those of the other stations at quarter-hour intervals, until the final objective was reached.

I hadn't to worry about what was going on. What I had to do was to lead my little group of men forward for about five hundred yards, cross a road which my map assured me was there (it was), set up a lamp signal station at once, establish contact in three directions, send and receive any messages; and at 6:15 a.m. precisely move on to another point. These man-œuvres were carried out with such clock-work precision that, except when moving, we were never out of touch with the other stations for more than two minutes. I got through the German barrage with the loss of my corporal and one man, passed dead and wounded and surrendering Germans, and lost my knapsack. Our trench mortar bloke covered himself with glory. Somewhere, somehow he had pinched an old horse, and brought his clumsy mortar walloping into action at just the right moment to knock out two machine-gun nests which were punishing one of our companies. By 7:30 a.m. we had advanced two miles, captured six guns and two hundred prisoners, and could see the enemy retreating with undignified haste in the distance. Field guns galloped up, and went into action.

We had another weary week of marching and actions with rear-guards before our armistice, and when it came it was undramatic and undemonstrative. Yet it was not .without deep feelings. There was an uprush of confused poignant emotions—relief, gratitude, a stir of hope, a belief that this was the end of war, an overtone of profound sadness as one thought of the silent ruined battlefields and the millions who never saw the day for which they had fought. And one's own insignificant little life, saved, but in ruins.

There had been no leave for several months, and my name was at the head of the roster. On the morning of the 12th I was handed a leave warrant in the orderly room, with the laconic and somewhat cynical advice to get to rail head as best I could. During the long period of trench warfare, rail head had been only a few miles behind the line, but now it was at least sixty and nobody up in front knew exactly where it was. The best bet seemed to be to hitch-hike to Cambrai by jumping an army truck, but unluckily I couldn't find one going that way. Heaven knows how many trucks I rode on that day or where we went, but for hours and hours I was driven over an interminable landscape of ruined villages, battered trenches, wrecked guns and tanks, and a huge amount of scattered equipment of all sorts abandoned by the fleeing Germans.

Somewhere in the early afternoon I passed through Le Quesnoy, which was full of Australian soldiers cleaning up the debris of war and some of the filth characteristic of places which had been German rest billets; and at dusk reached the headquarters of another Corps somewhere in the advanced Somme area. That night I slept, with other officers returning on leave, in a large and rather chilly marquee tent; and some time on the next day got to Cambrai, only to find that the leave train had left and I should have to wait overnight.

Not long before, I had been among the first troops to enter Cambrai, while it was still being shelled and was on fire. The streets then were littered with dead men and horses, fallen telegraph wires and the debris of ruined houses. Even in that confusion I noticed two things: the Germans had invariably fired the beautiful old Flemish houses, and the glowing woodwork still showed the beautiful Renaissance designs of the carving; and as we went along streets of unshelled houses, we could see they had been looted and that in the centre of each room was a pile of clothing, books, pictures, broken furniture, torn cushions, and similar objects on which the Germans had urinated and defecated. I am quite sure of these facts, because I saw them myself. In 1917 on the outskirts of Lens we discovered the same peculiar form of German insult in trenches and dugouts they had been forced to abandon by the Canadian advance at Vimy. On that afternoon of the 13th of November I went round the town and verified what I had seen. I could not go into any house—that was forbidden—but I could see easily through the smashed ground-floor windows. Moreover, I could not find a single one of the old Flemish houses unburned.

That night Cambrai was full of officers returning on leave, and we were billeted in a large hospital which was not required for the wounded. It was still a strange and delicious experience to sleep in a real bed again, but about 5 a.m. we were roughly awakened by orderlies, who rushed in and shouted the sensational news that the German armistice commission had revealed the existence of a time bomb in the building due to explode in an hour. There was no need to urge us to dress rapidly. After a very quick breakfast we entrained in a hurry; the train moved out about a couple of miles from the town and waited. And waited several hours. I then had ample time to reflect that Cambrai had been in our hands for at least three weeks and that no time bomb could be devised to last for such a period; so evidently that was a little joke of the authorities to make sure we didn't oversleep and miss the train.

How slowly that train moved! At sunset we had only got as far as Péronne, whose ruins looked gaunt and tragical against a grey sky cut with a blood-red rift of light from the setting sun. We did not reach Boulogne until dawn of the 15th, and there I saw a curious and moving sight—French soldiers who had been prisoners of war since 1914. They still wore tattered uniforms of red and blue, which looked positively historic, they were so different from those of the later armies. The faces of these men were pinched and yellow with privation, and there was an eerie, slightly insane expression on them.

In all it took me about eighty hours to go from the Franco-Belgian frontier to London; and this little fact may give some faint idea of the confusion and disorganization behind the lines.

It was unfortunate for me that my leave came so promptly. Two days after I returned to my unit, a War Office order was issued permitting all officers on leave to remain indefinitely in England pending demobilization. My division was not among those which marched into Germany; and after a lot of wandering about and interviews with railway transport officers I found the battalion in a straggling Belgian village, a few miles from Tournai.

Here I spent twelve endless and miserable weeks, in bitterly cold weather, with a foot or more of snow, and no fuel except a little coal-dust and an occasional tree which I bought from the estate of the local Count. This gentleman owned a hideous drawing-room, full of lace curtains and chairs covered in yellow satin and innumerable *art nouveau* objects, such as elephants and naked nymphs and Sarah Bernhardt, all in sugar-candy marble. He wore a very high collar, never asked me to sit down, and charged about three times as much as his wretched trees were worth. However, we were glad to have them at any price, for without the wood we couldn't even have had our food cooked.

It was at this time that I began to notice some of the after-effects of the war. I slept badly, was subject to meaningless but unpleasant moods of depression, and was in a frenzy of impatience to get out of the army. And it seemed to me that my mind had deteriorated, because of the difficulty I found in concentrating on mental work. I imagine that this was not uncommon with men who had been in the war a long time, and that a good many of us felt the strain. Our mess was startled one evening by an announcement from the second-in-command of a company that he intended to take holy orders. When we had discovered that he wasn't fooling and that it wasn't a brand-new device for being demobilised quickly, we gazed at each other in consternation. A cheeky young subaltern whispered in my ear that these were the horrors of peace, and that we should soon have more of them.

We did. By way of a contribution to the ease and comfort of the heroes of Armageddon under its command, the British War Office blithely issued instructions that all junior officers were to act forthwith as schoolmasters to "other ranks," in an education scheme concocted by somebody who evidently had a lot of second-hand school books to sell. Anyone acquainted with the ways and habits of men that go down to the sea in ships or up to the trenches with rifles will fully comprehend how deeply this kind thought was appreciated, and with what ardour we all returned to the three R's, the use of the globes, music and dancing.

Among the numerous trials of those wretched days was our Major. He was a peculiarly ripe specimen of the red-faced fox-hunting Tory, with all the delusions and prejudices appertaining to that brand of infantile mental paralysis. He began peace operations by getting drunk at the officers' Christmas dinner. Contrary to all mess etiquette he appointed himself toastmaster, and kept on getting up to make hiccupy speeches and patriotic toasts. Finally he crashed heavily over the tapes by proposing: "The health of the dead." A stony silence greeted this revolting though unintentional piece of sacrilege. Luckily, the Brigadier was present, and took charge of the situation by proposing the correct toast: "To the memory of the dead," which was of course drunk standing and in silence.

Quite unabashed by this episode, which probably disappeared from his memory along with his hangover, the gallant Major carried on strenuously. During the Colonel's absence on leave, he issued such vexatious orders for parades that the men were on the verge of mutiny, averted only by a swift agreement among all other officers to disregard the orders except at such times as the heavy-sterned Major came bumping over the horizon on his charger.

As a matter of fact there was no disloyalty among the men. They were fed up, they wanted to get home, and they wanted reasonable assurance they would get jobs. They had some reason for grousing. They had endured many hardships and had risked their lives for years for a shilling a day, or, if married, sixpence a day and twelve and six a week to the missus. Meanwhile, their mates, working on munitions or other "occupations of national importance," had been getting wages up to ten pounds a week, and in some cases twenty. Imagine how a soldier felt when he went on leave and found his wife pinched and shabby, while his unenlisted mate's wife swaggered in a new hat and fur coat and boasted about her new piano. If the soldier didn't resent that sort of thing he would have been less or more than human.

By way of soothing these irate feelings the fox-hunting Major went into action in a big way, and was a tireless deliverer of pep talks to weary Tommies and tired subs. What was there to grumble about? Nothing at all. Every man's life belonged to the country (when there was a Conservative government, you understand) and we ought all to be jolly thankful that we had our lives. Look at the men who hadn't. Now we'd won the war, it was up to us to win the peace. Germany must pay. There would have to be an army of occupation for at least forty years (we had a vision of ourselves still watching on the Rhine with beards down to our knees), so let there be no more of this nonsense about demobilisation. I've never had to rope steers or break broncos, but I can imagine the sensation from my experience in having to handle a bunch of very angry men after one of the Major's soothing little talks. I shan't forget that Major. He's the kind of chap who gets England a bad name.

I certainly got a bad name with him. He was shooting off his mouth in the mess one day on one of his favourite topics, namely, that we must cut off all Germany's foreign trade and at the same time collect about two hundred billion dollars for ourselves and allies. I couldn't stand it any longer, and pointed out that indemnities can only be paid out of balances abroad, and that Germany could only obtain them by having a continual large export surplus. He gobbled like a turkey cock at this, and said I was a Bolshevist. A decent young feller like me, who'd been to a decent school and all that, ought to be, well, you know what I mean, a decent young feller.

Fortunately, the Colonel came back from his leave in the nick of time, and we officers were able to go on parade again without a haunting suspicion that we might be shot by some infuriated Tommy.

The order of release from the army had been laid down by the wisdom of government in a hierarchy, with coal miners and ploughmen first and a hodge-podge of professions and intellectuals last. My own papers came through while the Major was in command, but even when he was superseded there was still delay. At last the reason was revealed in orders—six officers were required to volunteer for that army of occupation whose magnitude and duration haunted the Major's ambitious imagination. Sixteen volunteered within an hour. Why? Some wanted a year or so of military loafing at government expense, but most wanted a job, any job, to keep going. As I knew from their conversation, they had all written home hopefully about jobs, and their later silence showed the result.

But there was no longer any pretext on which I could be detained, and about the middle of February I departed, feeling very much as I imagine a released prisoner feels. I am told there are people who like military service, but I must say I find it hard to imagine their minds. It was bad enough when the urgency of war made it inevitable, but when the war was over it was absolutely intolerable.

Twelve weeks of "cease fire"—you couldn't call it peace—hadn't improved means of transport very much. I had another fantastic and uncomfortable journey, beginning with seven miles in the mess cart through deep snow. There was a slow, all-night train journey in an unlighted, unheated train, lacking window glass and doors. I had been cold in the trenches, but seldom as cold as during that interminable frosty night. We sat packed together stamping our feet and beating our hands to keep them from frost-bite. At dawn we stopped at Armentières, which was a strange sight. The splintered trees and telephone wires were festooned with thick hoar frost, and the ruins looked black in the dead-white snow. We stumbled over to a shed where we were given bowls of hot soup, and the cases of frost-bite were evacuated to hospital.

Late in the afternoon we detrained at Dunkirk, and were sent to what was optimistically called an Officers' Rest Camp, which consisted of canvas tents pitched in snow. As we prepared for another miserable night we could see, not fifty yards away, German prisoners laughing and talking in a hut round a warm stove. If I had been commandant of that camp I should have done a brutal thing. I should have sent the German private soldiers to sleep in the tents, and I should have put the British officers in the warm huts. But evidently he was too chivalrous, or perhaps he was playing bridge.

Next morning all troops for England were disarmed (a wise precaution) except for officers, who were allowed to keep their revolvers and ammunition. As we walked onto the quay at Dover we encountered a quasi-clerical gentleman in a choker and a goatee beard, who quavered in a goat-like voice:

"This way, men, this way for your buns and milk!"

A young captain, with a couple of wound stripes and several ribbons, seemed to be annoyed by this, and shouted at him:

"Buns and milk! You blank blank old fool! What we need is whisky and blank."

Such was the home-coming and such the welcome to some of the men of Flanders, Artois, Picardy, and the Somme.

When I reached London, I walked from Charing Cross to an Italian restaurant in Soho, and as I was very tired I rented a room there for the night.

Chapter XIII

Ah! Freedom is a noble thing!
Freedom makes man to have liking;
Freedom all solace to man gives,
He lives at ease that freely lives.

It would be pleasant to be able to say that I remembered those inspiring words of the ancient Scottish lyrist on my first morning of post-war liberty. But as a matter of fact I didn't, and must be content to quote them as an afterthought. But I felt something of the kind as I dressed that morning. True, I had to remain in khaki until the tailor made me some clothes, and therefore still came under the jurisdiction of the Assistant Provost Marshal. I had to see that my collar and tie were of the prescribed shade of khaki, and that my puttees were correctly rolled. And as I was now denied what Gibbon so unctuously called "the decent comfort of a body servant," I had to polish my own brass buttons. But these were indeed trifles. I felt like the stiff and aching Gulliver when all the binding threads of the Lilliputians save one were broken. I even considered committing some enormity of dress—an opera hat instead of a service cap, for instance—and giving the A.P.M. a bit of cheek. But prudence prevailed. It is unwise to cock a snook at tyranny until you are immune from its revenge.

I stepped into the streets that morning, almost a free man, with the purest feelings of benevolence to all mankind. The war to end wars had been won by the right side; President Wilson was bringing us peace in one hand and justice in the other; henceforth we Europeans, good or otherwise, would love each other like little children—just watch the darlings at play; I forgave all my enemies, even the Regimental Sergeant-Major and the Kaiser. My belt seemed feather-light—it carried

184

no revolver. I had removed the field dressing and iodine from the inner pocket of my tunic. All was for the best in this best of all possible worlds. . . .

Pangloss, Voltaire, books. I hungered for books again, for the surprises and triumphs of the bibliophile's chase. I remembered the folio Euripides, published at Cambridge in the 17th century, and bought for the ridiculous sum of twopence from a junk shop; the genuine Aldine Apollonius Rhodius picked up for sixpence from a Whitechapel stall; the French poets snatched from bondage, the Italian Humanists released from squalor—that noble folio of Cælius Rhodiginus published by Froben of Basel. . . .

I had to go to Cox's Bank for the purpose of drawing some pay, but the Charing Cross Road was on my route, and I lingered over the outdoor shelves. Books were ridiculously cheap, doubtless owing to the fact that the whole intellectual class had joined the army. I found a complete edition of the Waverley novels for two shillings. I didn't particularly want them, but I thought that perhaps Sir Walter would be grieved to think of so many years of work exposed to the derision of the unlettered for so base a price. I rescued him, and the bookseller recognised me as an old though not particularly valuable client. We shook hands, and I again glowed with benevolence to my fellow-men.

A little further down was a display of French books. One shelf of about forty particularly held my attention. I thought: This is a remarkable coincidence; it's the first time in my life I've ever seen a row of second-hand books, every one of which I've read. Mechanically I pulled down one of them and opened it. On the fly-leaf was written: Richard Aldington. I took down another, with the same result.

My first thought was that the house where I had stored my books had been burgled; and full of righteous indignation I plunged into the shop to try to trace the thief. Again the bookseller remembered me, and at once looked up his records. If I had suddenly and unexpectedly been hit between the eyes I could not have been more stunned than when I learned that the books had been sold by a "friend," a Bloomsbury intellectual, who had rooms in the house and therefore access to the store-room. Evidently he had come to the conclusion that I was unlikely to return from the front, and that since the books were no use to him as books he might as well change them into beer.

This was my introduction to the standard of behaviour ingeniously described as "amoralism," which during the post-war period was so enthusiastically professed and practised by a certain section of enlightened intellectuals.

It was absurd of me to be so much affected by so trivial an episode, but, as I have explained, I was in a disturbed state of mind and hence easily affected by small things. It seemed a shabby kind of welcome, and took the zest out of the day.

In a very short time I realised that the London I had come back to was a different place from the London I had left in 1915, let alone pre-war London. Everything seemed askew. The streets were dirty and shabby—there were no men to clean them and nothing had been repaired or painted for years. There were holes even in the main thoroughfares. The decent, orderly, good-natured Londoners had become as snappy and selfish as the far more sorely tried French. There was a shortage of everything except returning soldiers and debts. People fought for places in the inadequate transport system—a man who was accustomed to make way for women could not get on a bus. Food was scanty and very dear. Lodgings or apartments were almost impossible to find, because London was crowded with enormous numbers of "war workers," who still clung to their jobs like limpets. There was a devil-take-the-hindmost scramble for money and position in the new world, and an extravagance which seemed incredible to one who had known the old sober England. I stood aghast at this degeneration of my people, visible to me, as it was not to them, because of my long absence. I asked myself anxiously if I too had not degenerated, and it seemed to me I had. I could no longer quote with conviction Baudelaire's *boutade,* that a man can live three days without bread but not a day without poetry.

Even more significant and disconcerting was the existence of an indifference verging on hostility towards the men of the returning army. It is not difficult to understand. There was a definite split in the nation. On the one side was an ever-increasing number of young men who for two, three, and in some cases four years had been cut off from their homes and civilian life except for letters and infrequent furloughs of a few days. They were turbulent, impatient, full of strange oaths, contemptuous of anything that looked like humbug, and confident that a grateful country would be eager to hand them out jobs for which they were often quite incompetent. They were old before their time from hardship and harrowing experiences, yet immature and often helpless in these suddenly changed circumstances. For years they had abdicated responsibility and had lived a hair's breadth from death; and now they were abruptly handed an indefinite span of life and required to take full responsibility for it. You could recognise them at once by the new clothes they wore so awkwardly, their tanned faces, a queer strained look in their eyes. They were bound together by a strong though diminishing camaraderie. They were always getting together in groups and talking in a strange jargon of their own about one topic—the war, which they refused to discuss with anyone who had not been in it.

On the other side was the civilian population, frayed in its nerves, crushed with taxation, anxious about its own future, with all its benevolence and emotional sympathy long since exhausted. Men and women had supped full of vicarious horrors, and yet not until the flood of war books ten years later did they realise what the young men had endured. Every privation they had been called on to endure themselves had been excused by the authorities on the grounds of the army's necessities. What London had seen was a constant succession of young men on leave, crowding the restaurants and theatres. It had forgotten how many of those who laughed and drank and sang so merrily would never return. In fact, these young men who did return were a nuisance, and even a menace to everybody whose job was uncertain. Already crowds of munition workers and supernumerary government servants were being dismissed; and the pawnshops were crowded with the junk they had bought in their period of prosperity. One could see rows of imitation sealskin coats, for instance, hung out for sale by the pawnbrokers, who refused to take any more.

By way of showing the young officer the way he should go, a play was hastily staged, and I was taken to see it for educational purposes by the editor of several magazines, for whom I was doing some articles. I beheld a demobilised officer so conceited about having held His Majesty's commission that he refused to know his old friends and considered ordinary jobs beneath him. Finally, under the genial nagging of his girl and family, he chucked away his sword and war medals, and gratefully accepted a commercial traveller's job on two pounds a week and a percentage. The travesty was bitterly unjust. Already, ex-officers were tramping the streets looking for any job, and within a few months thousands of them were sleeping in Hyde Park, absolutely destitute. The problem was never successfully tackled, and England was left with a permanent army of unemployed—not all of them ex-soldiers, of course.

It was not enough that the returning soldiers were snubbed and left to get on as best they could. Our dead were insulted; our battlefields were made a show for money. My French colleague, Henry de Montherlant, making a pilgrimage of devotion to the sacred field of Verdun, found skulls of our dead comrades on which tourists had scratched their names and the initials of their country. When I read the burning words in which Montherlant denounced this sacrilege, I knew what it was to feel murder in one's heart.

I have mentioned these facts because in other countries, more bitterly tried by the war, similar situations existed in a more acute form, and led to a violent reaction, culminating in that type of military despotism known as fascism. I do not say this was the only factor, but it supplied the material from which fascists were made. In England there was never any such danger, but much unnecessary bitterness and misery resulted.

For my part, I had little to complain of, and therefore can speak more freely of the less fortunate among my war comrades. True, through my own folly or worse, I had got my personal life into a tragical mess, which added to my difficulties, and resulted in separation from H.D. And I found that my nervous malady and insomnia increased rather than diminished. I still found it hard to concentrate on literary work, whether writing or reading. By way of dealing with this problem, my father gave me a volume of Congreve's comedies. He was working in London as an official at the Ministry of Food, and had covered himself with glory by inventing a miraculously economical sausage; the only trouble with this contribution to victory was that the British people refused to eat it.

Flushed with this success and his importance as a government official, he assured me that I exaggerated my symptoms—he himself suffered from sleeplessness owing to his heavy responsibilities towards The Country—and he delivered a splendid eulogy of Congreve's wit and charm and soporific qualities. I accepted the book dutifully but with suspicion. Invariably the latest book my father had read—and he read continuously in several languages—was one of the world's masterpieces, until it was displaced by the next. Must I confess it? I found Congreve dull and footling, his artificial characters and situations intolerable. Indeed, in my then state of mind, the gift was about as sensible as trying to entertain a man about to be hanged with Huxley's *Crome Yellow*. Yet for some mysterious reason I found I could read Scott, and night after night sat up with his synthetic romances until dawn, when I managed to snatch a couple of hours' troubled sleep.

During those dismal days in Belgium I had prepared myself for the worst. I told myself that since I had published practically nothing for over three years I should be completely forgotten, and would have to start all over again. I was pleasantly disappointed. A few days after I arrived in London I wrote a little sketch describing demobilisation scenes, and sent it to one of the big daily papers. To my surprise it was taken and paid for at once. This lucky publication served to advertise the fact that I was alive and in England, and I had what was for me the new and astonishing experience of receiving letters from editors asking for my work.

Austin Harrison wrote me from the *English Review* and I promptly sent him three poems which he had rejected in 1915. Either he was magnanimous or had forgotten his former action, for he accepted them like a lamb and added a letter which was as complimentary as his former letter of rejection had been sniffy. Since then I have felt a certain loss of faith in the infallible judgment of editors.

A new editorial acquaintance was Holbrook Jackson, who in happier days had edited a popular literary weekly and published books of criticism. The exigencies of war had driven him to the profitable ignominy of editing trade journals. Although he made a handsome income, he was unhappy at losing touch with literature, and out of his own pocket was financing a small literary periodical, called *To-Day*. (This was a revival of an earlier magazine of the same name, for which curiously enough my father had written in the nineties.) Jackson was partly Jewish, with the warmth and ebullience of his people, and hence much easier for me to get on with than the average cold-hearted haberdasher on the Thames.

Jackson invited me to the annual dinner of *To-Day*, when the reputedly best poems published during the year were read aloud. Mine was a romantic love poem, and came first. To my horror the young man who read it had an appalling cockney accent, which made the poem sound like a parody of itself. I noticed people near me hiding their mirth behind their hands and menu cards, and I had difficulty in restraining my own laughter. The only phrase to express the incongruity is a favourite one of Huysmans—*éminemment cocasse*. My vanity has seldom been more amusingly kicked off its high horse.

I was also a contributor to the *Anglo-French Review*, edited by Henry Davray, a *Mercure de France* man. Owing to the pre-war dislike for "Gallic" literature in England, Davray had some difficulty in finding English writers who knew anything much about contemporary French work, and so was glad to make use of me. It seems worth remarking that financially I bridged that transition between military and normal life by work from which I had never expected to make anything. I had jotted down poems in a small pocket-book during the war, for no other reason than the consolation of writing something; and unexpectedly I found I could sell them for five or six times as much as I got before the war. (That little note-book, which I carried through gas attacks, two battles, and many months of trench warfare, was given to Amy Lowell, and may now be reposing with the other papers she bequeathed to Harvard.) What knowledge I had of new French literature had been acquired out of pure intellectual curiosity.

Within a few weeks I had arranged with the Egoist Press to re-issue my translations and to add the Anacreontea to them;

Elkin Mathews bought a small volume of love poems; Allen and Unwin agreed to issue a popular edition of my war poems; C. W. Beaumont was at work on a limited edition of these war poems with illustrations by Paul Nash, and a little later commissioned a translation of Goldoni's *Donne di Buon Umore*.

Beaumont was an interesting character. He supported himself by running a small second-hand book shop in the Charing Cross Road; but his passion was for the Russian ballet, with hand-printed editions of new poets as a close second. He is an example of how much can be achieved by enthusiasm and pertinacious industry, in spite of strict limitations of time and opportunity. In his cellar he set up a hand-printing press on which he worked at night, and in time produced a very pleasant series of contemporary poets. Everything was hand-set and hand-printed, but it was necessary to look out sharply for misprints. At the last moment I caught a really terrible one in my book. A poem about the trenches had the line:

> "Out in those wire-fringed ditches,"

and it was set up with a "b" instead of a "d."

All this was encouraging, especially as I was making more money than I had ever done. But the cost of living had more than doubled; much of the work I sold was stuff in hand from the spare-time production of three years; and I not only had difficulty in doing literary journalism but found that my creative vein had practically dried up. I realised that it was likely to remain so until I got over the effects of the war, and I felt that for some time to come I would have to do some kind of regular work, however distasteful. This problem was solved in an unexpected way, and through one of those apparently flimsy coincidences we all reject with scorn if a novelist dares to make use of them.

One of my friends, I think it was most likely T. S. Eliot, gave me a piece of literary news: Middleton Murry was giving up his post as critic of French literature on *The Times Literary Supplement* to edit a revived Athenæum, and an assistant editor was needed. The post had been offered to Eliot, and he had refused it as not sufficiently secure. In this he showed his wisdom, for Aldous Huxley, who was appointed, only lasted one year, and judging from his remarks about Burlap in *Point Counter Point* did not enjoy the experience.

I did nothing about the Athenæum job. My experience with the *Egoist* had not given me any reason to esteem myself as a literary editor. I had splashed around happily, had a lot of fun, and printed quantities of new poets; I had also made a lot of mistakes; and this didn't seem a good preparation for taking on part responsibility for what was evidently going to be an up-to-the-minute super-highbrow production. Moreover, though I had nothing against Murry, there had been no outbreak of sympathy on the one occasion we had met. I thought *The Times* job sounded much more promising, and therefore wrote to that august institution. A stately and unbroken silence resulted, and I gave up all hope when I was told that you couldn't even be a cub reporter on *The Times* unless you had graduated from Oxford with honours.

Here is where the chain of coincidence begins. During the summer of 1918 I had received a letter at the front, expressing interest in the Imagist poets and asking one or two questions. It was signed "Winifred Ellerman," which meant nothing to me. I answered the letter, put the lady in touch with H.D., and carried on with my job of being stormed at by shot and shell. After I returned to London I received an invitation to dine with this lady and her father, Sir John; and learned with some bewilderment that he was reputed to be the richest man in England. I thought this portended a sticky evening, as the rich are seldom very amusing.

Evidently Miss Ellerman had "spoken to" her father on my

G

behalf, for over the port he made me a speech. After touching at length on the hardships suffered by the civilian population in general and himself in particular—it appeared that among other horrors the government had only allowed him one ton of coal a week from his own mines—he briefly acknowledged some obligation to returning soldiers, and wound up by offering to lend me fifty pounds. As Sir John only left forty million pounds when he died, this was generous. A streak of bourgeois in me has always prevented my accepting any loan or gift of money. I told Sir John I didn't want money but regular literary work, and lamented my ill luck at failing to get any response from *The Times*. Sir John watched me very attentively as I talked, and then said tranquilly that he would give me a letter to the editor of *The Times,* whom he knew, and another to his friend, Clement Shorter, editor of the *Sphere.* I thanked him, not very effusively I fear, because I had already experienced the inefficacy of outsiders' letters of introduction in the gladiators' school of journalism.

However, I thought I might as well see these birds, so at my leisure I posted the two letters with covering letters of my own. The replies came back with incredible speed, fixing appointments for the next morning, fortunately at different hours. I saw Clement Shorter first, and I could hardly believe my ears when after a few minutes' conversation he commissioned six articles at a figure three times higher than I had ever been paid before.

Feeling rather as if I had stepped into a dime success novel or accidentally purloined Aladdin's lamp, I walked rather cheerfully down to Printing House Square. There, after a comparatively brief wait, I was received by that Olympian creature, the Editor of *The Times,* who is popularly supposed to tell the British government what it thinks. He had Sir John's letter in his hand, and asked me what sort of job I wanted. When I told him, he looked considerably relieved. He wrote a few sentences on a sheet of paper, put it in an envelope with Sir John's letter, rang the bell for a messenger, whom he told to take me to the editor of the *Literary Supplement,* and then shook hands with me, telling me that if I could do the job it was mine.

I followed the messenger along the corridors in a state of high bewilderment. I had read of such things happening in children's story books, but I didn't believe they could occur in real life. The clue, if I had only known it, was a very simple one. Owing to my ignorance of high finance I was quite unaware that Sir John held a controlling interest in the *Sphere* and a large block of shares in *The Times.* Hitherto I had believed that the way to success, however modest, was through merit and hard work. I should have refused to believe the truth of Dr. Johnson's poignantly expressed line, embodying his own life experience:

> "Slow rises worth by poverty depress'd."

I was now being shown what wealth alone could do, more or less irrespective of merit.

I was still vainly hunting for some explanation when I found myself in the presence of Bruce Richmond, editor of *The Times Literary Supplement.* I am sure my old and revered friend will forgive my telling the truth about this interview—that he looked annoyed when he read the communication from his chief, and treated me with that polite insolence which is one of the valued privileges of the English upper classes. When later I knew the truth which was then hidden from me I didn't in the least blame him. He naturally resented dictation from "financial interests," and very probably had already promised the job to some deserving Oxonian.

I left the office with a bundle of new French books and the conviction that it would be very difficult for me to work with Bruce Richmond. In fact as I reflected on his manner I was tempted to return the books and tell him to take a trip to Tartarus. But I not only needed that job, I wanted it; because it seemed just the right framework necessary to rebuild my life. I decided to be patient and to give it a month's trial. If at the end of a month Richmond seemed still as disagreeable, I would resign.

The arrangement was that I should call each week, to bring the reviews I had done and to discuss what should be reviewed next week. There was no change in Richmond's attitude, and I went to the fourth interview in a gloomy mood, convinced that it was incompatible with my self-respect to continue on such terms. To my astonishment and relief I found a totally different Richmond, as cordial as he had been frigid and offensive. He discussed our various problems of reviewing in a friendly way, and wound up by inviting me to lunch.

To this day I have no idea what caused this sudden change. It couldn't have been due to any outside pressure, because Richmond was not a man to be influenced and anyway I had not spoken of the situation to anyone. I flatter myself that he discovered I was not such a crashing cad as he had apprehended and that I did know something about French literature. Whatever the reason for it, the change was permanent. A few months later my rate of pay was raised fifty per cent, without the slightest hint from me on the subject; and I continued to write regularly for *The Times* for ten years, long after Sir John had sold his interest in the paper.

All this was accomplished within two months of demobilisation, but I was far from being satisfied with my life in post-war London. Every night as I read or lay sleepless I heard the raucous shouts and whoops of drunken revellers, a strange disorderliness in the decorous West End. I am no enemy to rejoicings, but this debauchery over ten million graves seemed to me indecent. I saw nothing to rejoice about, having too many vivid recollections of endless desolation and rows upon rows of wooden crosses.

Moreover, as the camaraderie of the trenches inevitably waned, I could find no compensation in recovery of the old bohemian camaraderie. During the war I wrote D. H. Lawrence: "There are two kinds of men, those who have been to the front and those who haven't." That was true then, and after the war also. And there seemed no way at first of bridging the gap. Unluckily most of the intellectuals I met at that time had been on civilian service or at most on Cook's tours of the line. Except for Herbert Read, I don't remember one who was a pukka soldier. On the other hand, as my energies and interests were turned wholly towards intellectual aims I became unhappily aware of estrangement from my old comrades. Between the two groups I fell into a queer and painful isolation and loneliness.

Let me give an example. One evening in 1919 I was among the guests at a dinner given by May Sinclair at the Albemarle Club. Hugh Walpole was there, and annoyed me by depreciating James Joyce and Marcel Proust, who are vastly more important writers than he ever will be. But what estranged me was the sense of futility emanated by these gentle amiable people. They seemed so hopelessly out of date, so unaware that earth's foundations had trembled and that nothing would really be the same again. It was as if we were making vain gestures to each other across a river of death. No doubt this was morbid of me, but that's how it was. I felt I had nothing to say to them or they to me. Later in the evening I attended a reunion of the battalion officers. I hadn't had time to change, so that except for the Colonel I was the only one in evening dress. It was obvious that I had a job, and that most of them hadn't. We did our best to be friendly, but there was something forced and hollow about it. With the end of the war the true reason for our old feeling of union was gone, and by trying to revive it we were flogging a dead horse. We were no longer one hundred per cent soldiers, but subtly and inevitably turning back into civilians, with different aims, hopes, and antipathies.

Ezra I found still in the same small apartment in Kensington, rather overwhelmingly obstructed with one of Dolmetsch's spinets and a quantity of poor Gaudier's statues. For some reason Ezra had become violently hostile to England—perhaps those "night dogs" were biting him. At any rate he kept tapping his Adam's apple and assuring me that the English stopped short there. I thought at first he meant that he had been menaced by the returning troops as a slacker, but it eventually came out that he was implying that the English had no brains. There can be no doubt that at this time appreciation of Ezra's works had diminished to a pin-point. He told me that he was moving permanently to Paris, where he would be among intelligent people. Perhaps that was why he so soon moved on to Rapallo. In any event, this attitude did not seem a very good basis for a renewal of our old intimacy. It was impossible to disguise the fact that I was English, and therefore also stopped short at Ezra's Adam's apple. Why should I uselessly fatigue myself in a vain attempt to understand the workings of that mighty brain?

Yet there were compensations even for this calamity. One of them was T. S. Eliot, now the model for all university *Kulturmenschen,* but in 1919 almost unknown and having rather a tough time. I met him once when I was on leave during the war. He was invited to tea, and turned up an hour late, looking pale and tired. There had been an air-raid the night before and he had taken refuge in the subway, only to find himself locked in until morning. This was not a fortunate moment to meet anybody, but even at that first unpromising meeting I thought him attractive and intelligent.

Tom Eliot's career in England has been exactly the reverse of Ezra's. Ezra started out in a time of peace and prosperity with everything in his favour, and muffed his chances of becoming literary dictator of London—to which he undoubtedly aspired—by his own conceit, folly, and bad manners. Eliot started in the enormous confusion of war and post-war England, handicapped in every way. Yet by merit, tact, prudence, and pertinacity he succeeded in doing what no other American has ever done—imposing his personality, taste, and even many of his opinions on literary England. This was an interesting achievement, and since I was in close touch with him from 1919 to 1928, I know more than most people of the difficulties he had to overcome, the mistakes he had to avoid.

Eliot's early poems amused me. I thought them a skilful and legitimate adaptation of Laforgue's manner. There was more originality in them than in Ezra's poems, which are mostly a pot-pourri of paraphrases. But I believe personally that Eliot's greatest service to English literature at that time was his insistence that writers could not afford to throw over the European tradition. Just after the war, in the confusion and reaction against everything pre-war and war, there was an almost unanimous belief among artists and writers of the vanguard that all art of the past was so much dead stuff to be scrapped. They were wilfully trying to make themselves barbarians. I felt unhappy about this, for my instinct was to do just the opposite. After the long hiatus of the war I thought we should for a time at least steep ourselves in the work of the masters; but nobody would agree with me. I was delighted, therefore, when I came across a sensitive and well-written article by Eliot on Marivaux, in one of the small arty periodicals which sprang up in 1919. Evidently here was somebody who could write and who did not believe that illiteracy was a symbol of originality.

Of course, Eliot was not the only one. However much

Aldous Huxley may now laugh at his experience on the Athenæum, he and Murry also did useful work in maintaining standards. But Eliot was a particularly valuable influence. Strange as it seems now, it is a fact that in 1919 to admire his poetry was daring and revolutionary. This gave him a growing influence over rebellious youth which he used on the whole modestly and rightly. But the defenders of the *status quo* in literature—the amorphous mass of Georgians and the formidable rear-guard of Victorians—loathed him and went to unprecedented lengths in trying to discredit him.

The publication of some of Eliot's poems was met with a tremendous counter-attack by the allied opposition. One elderly gentleman, a mild authority on the English 18th century but profoundly ignorant of European literature, went so far as to describe them as the work of a "drunken helot." Under the English law of libel Eliot could have claimed damages for that aspersion on his character, but he very wisely did nothing at all. I wrote reviews of that book for every periodical to which I had the entry, with the exception of *The Times,* where I didn't dare even mention Eliot's name at that time. Even then I found plenty of opposition. Holbrook Jackson was an intelligent man, and yet when I asked him to let me do an article on Eliot, he looked amazed and said:

"But Eliot's a wild man."

An American friend of mine was then editing the *Outlook,* and asked me to write an article telling his readers about young writers and picking out those I thought would make a name. I made a choice which I modestly think wasn't bad for 1919: James Joyce, T. S. Eliot, D. H. Lawrence, Aldous Huxley, H.D., and Marcel Proust. I received a letter from the editor in these terms:

"For God's sake, Richard, can't you think of somebody who has been heard of or is ever likely to be heard of?"

I protested, and my article was submitted to the judgment

of that eminent expatriate, Mr. Logan Pearsall Smith, who decided that my writers never would be heard of; and the article was rejected. If I had chosen such mediocrities as Jack Squire, Hugh Walpole, Frank Swinnerton, and others whose names I have forgotten, I should have received a cheque and a crown of wild parsley.

In these circumstances it is not surprising that the most highbrow literary critic of his time failed then to get work into any of the English literary periodicals. Meanwhile, Eliot was quietly laying the foundations of his future influence by cultivating the right people. I believe Sydney Schiff (who wrote some very good novels as Stephen Hudson) introduced Eliot to Lady Rothermere's gang, but as I wasn't in on that particular racket I can say nothing definite. But it was Lady Rothermere who subsidised Eliot's *Criterion* in its early years.

Another valuable ally, but a pernicious influence on Eliot, was Charles Whibley. Eliot was already too much influenced by Irving Babbitt's pedantic and carping analysis of Rousseau —indeed to some extent he founded his prose style on Babbitt— and in Whibley he found a British counterpart to his old Harvard professor. Whibley was a Fellow of Jesus College, Cambridge, a good scholar, but a hopeless crank about politics. He was the very embodiment of the English Tory don, completely out of touch with the realities of his time. "Whig" and "Whiggism" were his terms of contempt and insult to everybody he disliked, and anybody can see how Eliot picked them up. But Whibley took Eliot to Cambridge, where his conversation enchanted the dons and procured him friends and allies, vastly more important and valuable than the Grub Street hacks who had rejected him.

I dined with Eliot and Whibley at the Oxford and Cambridge Club on the evening when Lord Morley died. Whibley was virulent on the subject, forgetting even the elements of the precept *de mortuis*. Eliot chimed in from time to time in his

G*

witty and scathing way. We drank a good deal of excellent wine, and the air was heavy with the horrors and misdeeds of Whigs and Whiggism. But Eliot forgot that he was an American and that Whibley was an intensely chauvinistic Briton. Finally Eliot said something derogatory about Morley which offended Whibley's patriotism. There was a slight pause, and I expected yet another broadside into the sinking hull of poor Morley's reputation. But the remark when it did come was this:

"There was one good thing about Morley—he always hated Americans."

The conversation, after a pregnant pause, then turned on the late war, and Eliot told us gravely that in the next war he intended to join the British army. He worked himself up almost to blood-heat in a fine frenzy of patriotism. The climax or anti-climax to this came as he and I left the club and walked down Pall Mall. To my horror Eliot lifted his derby hat to the sentry outside Marlborough House. You would have to be born British and serve in the army to understand the complex violations of etiquette involved in this generous and well-meant gesture. I wish I knew what the sentry thought.

Among other compensations for Ezra's cruel abandonment of England to the powers of intellectual darkness were Herbert Read and the two Sitwell brothers. Shortly after I returned to England I was in Beaumont's book shop when there entered a young man in the uniform of a staff captain, wearing the ribbons of the 1915 Star, Military Cross and bar, and the Distinguished Service Order. This was Herbert Read. At first I looked askance at his symbols of military glory, for experience had taught me to associate them with disagreeable personalities; but Read turned out to be a gentle, amiable, and intelligent fellow. Nobody could have carried more modestly his military honours—remarkable in a new army man who was only twenty-four at the armistice—and he had a genuine enthusiasm for art and literature. In company he was almost diffident and usually silent, but in private he talked well and thoughtfully. I liked him very much.

As a poet, Read lacks a something which I can only hint at by saying that while I admire the skill behind his poems I am never moved by them. They seem to me to lack the passion which gives life to even the worst splurgings of D. H. Lawrence, and the intellectual concentration which so effectively conceals Eliot's emotional sterility. I also think that much of Read's work suffers from a kind of metropolitan provincialism, addressing itself to a small group of super-æsthetes whose mental fashions change as quickly as those of *couturières*. But his pamphlet, "In Retreat," describing his heroic experiences in the last battle of the Somme, is a classic of the World War and will outlive many more pretentious books.

Osbert Sitwell attracted me by his wit and honesty, and his brother by his passion for beautiful things and a sensitive taste which amount almost to genius. Both, I think, found happier and more permanent expression of their gifts in prose than in poetry. I had a slightly romantic feeling about them, because they seemed to be carrying on the tradition of the cultivated English aristocrat. Instead of devoting themselves to sport and politics, they read, wrote, travelled widely, and were tireless investigators of Europe's known and unknown beauties. Wyndham Lewis has attacked them savagely as *dilettanti*, but then he attacks everybody, and after all Sir Philip Sidney and Shelley were *dilettanti*. It seems an exaggerated professionalism to want to bar the upper classes from practising any of the arts. But the newspapers evidently shared Lewis's views, and attacked the Sitwells bitterly for their "art nonsense," instead of going in for fox-hunting and polo-playing as befits gentlemen of leisure.

Soon after the war the Sitwells arranged a series of readings by poets to a group of friends. Sacheverell Sitwell acted as my chairman, and he was making a few remarks after I had finished reading when to everybody's consternation he suddenly burst into tears and fled from the platform. Afterwards I ventured to ask him what had happened and he said:

"Oh, I suddenly caught sight of Lady Mond's face, and it looked so awful I couldn't go on."

Poor Lady Mond seemed to be rather the goat of these parties. When Eliot was the guest he read one of his poems which is an ironical description of what he expects to do in heaven. When he got to the lines:

> ". . . I shall meet Sir Alfred Mond,
> And we shall lie together, wrapped
> In a five per cent Exchequer Bond,"

there was a rumpus in the audience, and Lady Mond sailed indignantly out of the room.

A singular tragedy happened in the literary world at this time. It concerned Gilbert Cannan, who is probably forgotten now, but who was then highly thought of as a novelist. I only met him two or three times, but heard a lot about him from the Lawrences. There was a complicated love story, into which I won't go, and a tremendous amount of gossip about it everywhere. One morning I read in *The Times* that Cannan had been certified as insane and removed to a mental hospital. Not ten days before I had talked with him, and noticed absolutely nothing to suggest such a calamity. Years later, going over old times with Lawrence, I found that he shared my silent opinion that Cannan was no more mad than anyone else. There was nothing we could do about it, for we had no evidence, merely our opinion and our unease. A highly strung man agitated by grief and exasperated by treachery might easily say and do things which a doctor could certify.

Chapter XIV

THE year 1919 was certainly an *annus mirabilis*, if you take the *"mirabilis"* ironically. In spite of the *Waffenstillstand*, the war still went on overtly and sporadically in various parts of the world, and with renewed zest in Europe by all methods short of actual fighting. He was a wise man who said that the European nations had only been in agreement on two points—to start fighting in 1914 and to stop it in 1918.

By way of contributing to the sanity of the world Sir Eric Geddes promised or threatened in a speech to hang the Kaiser and to squeeze Germany until the pips squeaked. This urbane contribution to civilisation was received with great satisfaction by an enlightened electorate.

I was a detached but not uninterested spectator of President Wilson's drive through London. I have never heard such loud and continuous cheering for any official personage. The British crowd evidently expected that quiet-looking gentleman to produce the millennium from his immaculate top-hat. He produced the Treaty of Versailles, whose motto should have been: "We have scotch'd the snake, not killed it." The snake being European wars. The treaty was not conciliatory enough to win co-operation of liberal and peace-loving German parties, and not stern enough to keep the warlike parties from further harm. It infuriated Italy and disgusted America, disappointed France, and humiliated Germany without crushing its latent belligerence and arrogance. In England the treaty was received with the apathy of incomprehension. The peace of 1815, made by selfish kings and cynical diplomats, lasted for fifty years; the united wisdom of the enlightened democracies failed to make the peace of 1919 last for twenty years. One notes the progress.

In contrast to their enthusiastic reception of Wilson, the London crowd was apathetic towards the huge military parade which celebrated the "peace." General Plumer was cheered by the ex-soldiers in the crowd, but Haig passed almost in silence. I don't know what the enemy thought of him, but so far as my experience went he was much disliked by his own troops. The only real enthusiasm was for the British sailors and the French infantry. That night, after dinner, I had to walk from Soho to Red Lion Square in Bloomsbury. The streets were still almost dark with the modified blackout, and were solid rivers of silent people tramping from the East End to witness non-existent "celebrations." There was something terrifying in this mute horde of shabby workers, who in their way had also laboured and suffered for victory, and who were not insensible to the emotions of patriotism. But there was little or nothing for them to see or do. The leaders toasting each other with sham enthusiasm in Buckingham Palace had apparently forgotten about the people.

They were soon reminded rather forcibly that the people existed. Except in pre-fascist Italy and pre-Franco Spain I have never known so many strikes as those which occurred in England during the years after the war. Personally I hold that the class war is not innate and inevitable, but this interminable series of strikes and lockouts looked remarkably like warfare. They did not conduce to the re-establishment of public and private tranquillity, and, to those who like myself belonged to neither party, became exasperating. However, I was still able to enjoy any touch of comedy provided by the troubled times. I happened to be in my club one morning when the head of the London police came in, looking rather pale and anxious, having just escaped from an infuriated mob of his own cops who were on strike. This seemed a bit thick even to a slightly disillusioned person like myself, and when my father came in for our usual pre-luncheon drink he seemed to regard it as an apex of public disorder and calamity. I had some difficulty in dissuading him from writing to *The Times* about it.

On the other hand the Russian Ballet season at the Alhambra was a great success. True, for elderly gentlemen like myself who remembered Nijinski, the ballet had lost its original splendour; and there was already an intrusion of French influence which was regrettable. But it still remained the only completely satisfying artistic spectacle of my lifetime. Karsavina was still dancing that year with incomparable grace and skill, and the new star Lopokova had great charm. I used to drop in at least once a week to see them, and remained faithful until they sank to the level of Satie and Cocteau. The final *débâcle* occurred when London cockneys added "ov," "ski," and "evna" to their names, and produced a lamentable and lifeless parody of that once imperial art.

In spite of these diversions I felt a growing distaste for London and a longing to get away to the country. London had become more than ever a city for the well-to-do, where life was for those who had two thousand pounds a year upwards. The old easy bohemian society seemed to be riddled with affectations. I dare say they were merely a continuation of the ancient ones of the Aw-cassin brand, but they had spread from the suburbs to the centre. Most people seemed to be pretending to a superiority they didn't possess and desperately afraid of admiring the wrong thing or failing to admire the right thing. At a party given by Jean de Bosschère, the Belgian poet and artist, I suddenly heard a high intellectual voice say:

"Oh, but my dear fellow, surely nowadays anybody who *is* anybody admires Dostoievski."

I don't know why that fatuous remark annoyed me, but it did. I asked myself why I was wasting the precious hours of life with such people. I thought longingly of a country cottage, with woods and fields and the quiet sky and the immortal company of great books. Out of the experience of the war I had brought an impatience with shams, and a correspondingly strong desire to be genuine myself on however humble a scale. And I didn't see why one should suffer fools either gladly or resentfully, if it were possible to get away from them.

But when I came to look for a country cottage I found to my dismay that they were, if possible, even more difficult to obtain than apartments in London. I had naïvely supposed that the slaughter of nearly a million men would have left a lot of vacancies, forgetting all the other factors which caused a housing shortage for more than a decade. In any event I could find nothing which was not either hopelessly dear or hopelessly suburban.

I had almost resigned myself to a dreary existence of rented rooms in London when unexpectedly Lawrence turned up on his way to Italy and offered to hand over his cottage. It was at a place romantically called Hermitage, in Berkshire. In my then state of mind you could have offered me nothing more attractive than a hermitage, and I accepted the offer without seeing the place. However, it was a safe bet, because Lawrence and Frieda were adepts at finding cheap places in beautiful surroundings.

During the war the Lawrences had had a tough time. Just before the war started, life seemed to be opening out for them. The scandal of Frieda's divorce had been weathered, and they were respectably married. *Sons and Lovers* had established Lorenzo's reputation, and he had a contract for the novel he was then writing which carried what was for those days a substantial advance. They had intended to pass a few weeks in England, and then return to Italy. The Lawrence I met in 1914 was a happy man, light-heartedly looking forward to an adventurous life, and with that happiest of all convictions for a writer—the belief that he had important things to say.

The Lawrences' troubles began with the publication of the new novel, *The Rainbow*. There was a police prosecution for obscenity, instigated by the self-styled Public Morality Council of London, a body of puritanical fanatics who were making themselves patriotically useful by trying to suppress anything they didn't approve. They particularly disapproved of young and gifted writers who held views different from their own. English law permits any magistrate to order the suppression of a book on his own authority, and in practice he usually does what the police ask. Appeals to higher courts, which in many cases would probably reverse the judgment, are expensive and could only be undertaken by wealthy authors, who for some reason are never involved. The passage complained of in *The Rainbow* was less than half a page in a book of over five hundred pages, and anyway after the war the book was several times reprinted without molestation. The prosecution skilfully obscured the issue by pointing to some criticisms of the Boer war, which were absurdly maintained to be hindering recruiting.

The suppression of the book was so obviously an error of justice that a question was asked in the Commons, but received the usual evasive reply. It is possible, though I won't assert it, that since the Lawrences were friends of the Asquiths, this prosecution may have been one little move in the immense intrigue which finally threw Asquith from power. Suppression of books, which was introduced by the Borgias and perfected by the Bourbons, always tends to re-appear in times of war; it is part of the general tendency to revert to lower levels of civilisation implied in the phrase, "a state of war."

A man coarse-fibred enough to write an intentionally pornographic or seditious book would have taken the suppression with a shrug. An irresponsible bohemian would have washed away his resentment in beer. Lawrence was wounded deeply. The fact that this action reduced him to penury at a stroke was far less important than the insult, the stigma. He came from a section of the working class which has the deepest respect for law and order, and Lawrence knew that all the friends of his family and the family itself would think him disgraced. Lawrence was so intensely English in all his feelings and beliefs that he felt as if his own mother had turned against him. It was obviously an exaggerated reaction, but highly sensitive people do react in an exaggerated way.

Lawrence immediately determined to leave England "for ever," and applied for passports for America. They were refused. Since Lawrence was rejected for military service (T.B.) there could be no reason for this except official red tape, and possibly the pleasure of being disagreeable to an artist. They went off to Cornwall, where they lived in a tiny cottage in great poverty. No English publisher would touch Lawrence's fiction, and his new book of poems sold about a hundred copies. But for American friends and some publication in America the Lawrences might have starved.

In 1917 they were ordered to leave Cornwall by the Competent Military Authority under suspicion of what would now be called fifth-column activities. We now know that just at that time the French had a spasm of spy fever, and made strong representations to the British about their laxity. Consequently, orders were sent out to round up all suspicious characters. The Lawrences' cottage faced the sea; a light had accidentally been left uncurtained in the next-door cottage; a submarine had sunk a freighter off the Bristol Channel; Frieda was a German; she and Lawrence sang German songs in the evening; they possessed some German books; and the local Cornish didn't like them. Hence the expulsion order.

In those days few of us realised that war cannot be conducted without trampling on all kinds of public and private liberties. Lawrence couldn't think of himself as one among a number of equally innocent people having an equally tough time because the authorities couldn't afford to take chances. Obviously Frieda's nationality was one fact that weighed with the military; and she was a Richthofen—one of the few German names known to every English soldier. For Lawrence this expulsion order was an invasion of his most sacred rights and privacies as an Englishman. He got into a cold rage, and said bitter things to the officer who searched his house and gave him the order. In the normal course of duty, the officer had to report these remarks.

The Lawrences retired to London with what Mr. Churchill would call haste and dudgeon, and there I found them a few days later when I came up on leave. The Lawrences had rooms in the same house, and when I arrived I discovered a strange man lurking on the stairway. I asked him what he was doing, and he astonished me by saying he was from Scotland Yard and engaged in sleuthing Lawrence. I took him to my room, and had a talk with him.

I flatter myself it was lucky for Lawrence that the detective met me and not him. Lawrence would certainly have got into a rage and have earned another black mark, if he hadn't been arrested. I was the one person in the house entitled to wear a military uniform, which naturally gave much greater weight to what I said. Although I knew Lawrence was innocent, I discovered how difficult it is to refute a charge which is based not on evidence but on suspicion and inferences from suspicion. Moreover, this thinly disguised policeman thought he was a literary critic and would keep bringing up his æsthetic views:

"I've been readin' this feller Lawrence's books, and I don't think much of 'em. What do you think?"

I had difficulty in holding this trained and logical investigator to the point, but, by keeping my temper and patiently going back time and again to the facts at issue, I managed to convince him that he was on a false trail. Naturally I didn't tell Lawrence what I had done—he would have been furious with Scotland Yard for carrying out a piece of routine investigation and equally furious with me for butting in on his affairs—but I believe the intervention was so effective that he was not again seriously troubled in this way for the rest of the war. But as I shall show in due course, this spy accusation cropped up again later in his life.

During the last year of the war the Lawrences were so poor that they had little to eat but oatmeal, while their fuel was wood chips from trees which were being cut down by Canadian soldiers for use in mines and trenches. Ten years later he had an international reputation.

It was no great surprise, therefore, in 1919 when I had a note from Lawrence to say that he was on his way through London to the Continent. I only wondered how he had the money to do it. Long afterwards, when I read his letters, I realised what a desperate adventure it had been, how little money he had, and how much he suffered.

I met him by appointment at the apartment of two American friends, and as was usual with him in cold weather he sat hunched up in a chair close to the fire. Unfortunately it was a gas fire, contrary to the Laurentian code of ethics, which held that any form of heating except an open fire of wood or coal is immoral. He was in a peculiar mood, which I thought at first was due to the indecency of a gas fire. But no, it went much deeper than that. He was in that state of animosity which comes to a man when he finds himself alone against the world. He was literally "satirical," really like a wild half-trapped creature, a satyr, desperately fighting to get free.

At first I was puzzled and a little hurt, for he twitted me sharply on what he was pleased to consider some of my weaknesses. He told us that Frieda had gone to visit her relatives in Germany, and seemed not to care if he never saw her again. And this was sad indeed after the passion and intensity of their relationship; so vivid and so complete whether in attraction or repulsion that the lives of other lovers seemed commonplace in comparison. But I need not have worried about that. After Lawrence met Frieda, no other woman meant anything to him, and those two were as certain to stay together as a river to run to the sea.

When Lawrence and I left, the crowds were coming out of the theatres; and as we made our way through the people there were gibes and sneers at Lawrence's red beard, a sudden little whirlpool of mob hostility. Of course, they had no idea who he was, had never heard of him; it was simply the ugly instinctive hatred of the crowd for the person who is different, which they suspect means some form of superiority. Then I saw the reason for his acrid mood and for his flight from England. There was no place for him in that rather sinister post-war world. Either he must escape from it or it would crush him. He had to go into the wilderness or perish, cease to be the unique thing he was. When I said good-bye to him that night I had a feeling I should never see him again.

It is the fashion now to sneer at the books which have been written about Lawrence. The sneerers forget that these were produced by people, most of whom were not writers, who had been so deeply impressed by his personality that they could not avoid trying to record what they remembered of him. Exactly the same thing happened with Byron and Shelley, as any good bibliography will show; but it does not happen to the Galsworthys and Kiplings, because they had no such vivid dynamic personality to impress upon those who came in contact with them. Those who belittle him, who strive to depreciate all he was and did, need not worry; they will never be disturbed by another Lawrence. No phœnix will rise from those poor wandering ashes. And in that complete violent destruction of our civilisation which Lawrence foresaw and foretold so clearly, it probably doesn't matter very much.

Chapter XV

THE Hermitage cottage, I discovered, was sublet from the Radford family. I knew one of the daughters, Margaret, very well by sight, for she had been a student at London University and had some local reputation as a poetess. She was a strange, fragile, over-sensitive creature, shrinking from realities and drifting about the college like a wisp of unhappy thistledown. Mrs. Radford was also a poetess; and Mr. Radford, who is mentioned somewhere in Yeats's *Autobiographies,* was a writer or a socialist or perhaps both—I forget. In pre-war days I was taken to see the family. Poor Mr. Radford was losing his mind, and his contribution to the talk was an occasional impressive belch, which we ignored like perfect little ladies and gentlemen. Such were my landlords, and it will surprise nobody to hear that although I paid them my rent regularly they forgot to hand any of it on to the original landlord, so that I was eventually in danger of eviction. In fact I should have been evicted if I hadn't gone to a more energetic lawyer than my father.

It is possible that in the middle ages some monkish eremite had set up his misanthropic cell in the neighbourhood and given it the name Hermitage, but no tradition of such an event existed. Apart from its remoteness, Hermitage belied its name, for it was a nondescript straggling hamlet without charm or antiquity in rather featureless country. The absence of parsonage and manor house showed it was of recent growth, and I could never imagine why it had grown at all, for there was no local industry and the farmland was poor. But the Radford cottage was secluded and silent, the meadows and coppices near it were full of wild flowers in the spring, and there was a garden.

There was still an acute food shortage in England. In the early part of 1920 butter was seven shillings and sixpence a pound (as against two shillings pre-war) and a small joint of New Zealand lamb fifteen shillings, instead of three or four shillings. I therefore went in rather heavily for the culture of vegetables, with the aid and counsel of my neighbour, Mr. Brown. I liked Mr. Brown very much. He was a genuine *terræ filius,* as close to the earth as the placid cows and elms of the landscape.

At my invitation Mr. Brown would sometimes drop in of an evening, and we would smoke our pipes and drink ale from blue earthenware mugs, and talk of essential things. Mr. Brown knew all the things about gardening which you don't learn at agricultural colleges or from beautifully illustrated books. He knew exactly which brand of seeds went with which soil, when and how to plant them, how much or how little nutritive dung should be supplied, how to treat plants as they grew, and many such practical points. He approved of most of my horticultural ambitions except in the matter of spinach, concerning which I had imbibed the townee's faith. He crushed me by saying briefly and decisively:

"Down 'ere we gives that there stuff to the pigs."

Mr. Brown knew a great deal about pigs and had interesting anecdotes about those animals, though I am bound to admit that he considered them less as a philosopher than from the point of view of their market value and edibility. He used to make me shudder by imaginatively eating pork chops and bacon from the still living inhabitants of his sty. The subject on which Mr. Brown most willingly philosophised was education. He was convinced that the solution of all social problems would be found if all working-class boys went to Oxford or Cambridge. Then, he said, they would all be able to earn the same wages as the bosses. He dismissed my objection that the utmost capacity of the two great seats of learning was less than ten thousand—that would be dealt with by guv'ment. Nor would he accept my suggestion that after a certain point education is a bar rather than an aid to money-making propensities. He challenged me to name an uneducated man who had made money. I mentioned Lord Northcliffe, and the mayor of Newbury (our market town), who had done pretty well in the nail and saucepan business. But Mr. Brown wouldn't have it. Depend upon it, they'd had education, it stood to reason. And when I asked how a knowledge of Greek and higher mathematics would aid the working class in putting up wages, he said he didn't mean Greek and higher mathematics, he meant education. I used to think Mr. Brown would have made an excellent president of a really modern university.

It was December when I moved to Hermitage, and for much of the time I was entirely alone. During the seven years or more that I lived in the country I was able to make an interesting observation which seems to have been overlooked by scientists, namely, the influence of the weather upon friendship. Each year when fine weather returned, and particularly if there was a hot spell, I was astonished to find how many persons felt so affectionately towards me that they simply had to come and spend the next week-end with me in the cool of my garden. But when winter came the warmth of their feelings appeared to decline with the temperature; and I very rarely saw them except when I went to London, where the only one who ever offered to put me up was T. S. Eliot. It is true that Voltaire noted some of the effects of climate on the English character ("never ask an Englishman to do anything for you when the wind is in the east") but he failed to notice its influence on reciprocal hospitality.

Whether so much complete solitude was altogether the best thing for somebody in my then frame of mind, I shall not try to decide. Less than a year of post-war London had so estranged me from that city and its inhabitants that I have never since lived there except for brief periods at rather rare intervals. I have a strong suspicion that what I disliked in the people I met in that city (there were of course notable exceptions) is much the same thing that much of the outside world dislikes—a baseless assumption of superiority coupled with an uneasy self-consciousness which made social intercourse a misery. For years I thought the fault was mine, that I wasn't aristocratic enough or something, although I got on well enough with Continental Europeans; but in fact it was not until I came to America that I found English-speaking people who were unaffected, straightforward, and simply themselves, and took for granted that I should be the same. It was a great relief.

So, as I truly preferred the country to the town, I came to accept with relish my modified solitude. At any rate, it afforded plenty of time for reflection and work. I have a vivid recollection of one evening in December 1919, soon after I went to Hermitage. While Mrs. Brown was clearing up after dinner I stepped into the garden for a few minutes, as I usually do at night. It was a clear moonless night of many stars, with a touch of frost, the kind of night which in the mild climate of England passes as cold. I stood listening to the silence, gradually discerning the dark bulk of the knoll behind the cottage with its jagged fringe of larches black against the stars. It was the silence and darkness I liked. There was no rumble or roar of distant or near night-firing, no shell-burst or rattle of machine-guns, no trampling and cursing of transport columns and working parties, no sinister sudden glare of Very lights showing a landscape bristling with barbed wire. Such were the nights I had known for more months than I care to count, and the contrast of silence and untroubled darkness was very healing.

In those early post-war days, after the gods had made us mad

217

in order to destroy us, we were gorgeous optimists. We actually believed the world had learned a lesson, that such scenes of violence and destruction would not occur in our lifetime, perhaps not ever again. After all, I reflected, it had been worth while—the exertion, the squalor, the degradation, the frustration, the damage to one's psyche—because the future and the children were safe, that future in which we now so precariously breathe, those children who as men are now dying in thousands. The thought gave me quite a glow in the cold air, a nice smug Victorian feeling of something attempted, something done. Perpetual or at any rate a very long peace—what a splendid achievement! I should have been angry and scornful if someone had whispered to me that recorded history is a grim desert of warfare with a few fertile and accidental oases of peace, that peace is perhaps only the dream of senile races as religious tolerance is the catchword of minorities and Laodiceans.

But it was cold outside in the silent darkness, and I hastened back with satisfaction to my bright fireside, where a large unopened parcel of books from *The Times* awaited me. Among them I found a handsome reprint of Victor Hugo's *Les Contemplations,* forming part of the complete edition of his works sponsored by the French Academy. I plunged into this with zest for two or three hours, thinking it would make an article to please Bruce Richmond, whose editorial object was "to send people back to their books"; and then, having temporarily reached the limit of absorption, I put the book aside and began thinking.

I had long since realised that writing on French literature for *The Times* was no sinecure. At a moment's notice I had to be prepared to turn out a more or less adequate article on any book or author from the *Chanson de Roland* to the latest Dadaiste freak. It was like holding a chair in French literature, with this difference, that, instead of talking to youngsters who knew less than I did, I had to put my views into print to be scanned by thousands of educated people, including a number of hawk-eyed and censorious experts. *The Times* itself was severe about the slightest inaccuracy. There was no mercy for a misquotation, an error in French or any other foreign language, still less for any actual blunder in matters of fact. There was a frightful hullabaloo once when I misquoted Milton as "Things unattempted yet in prose or verse," instead of "rhyme." When I jestingly claimed that I deserved commendation because I had given a more accurate version of the original line of Ariosto which Milton cribbed, it was held that I had merely added the crime of lèse-Milton to the misdemeanour of misquotation.

The head of the French staff at Eton took a perverse pleasure and wasted a good deal of his valuable time in trying to detect errors in *The Times* articles on French literature. He once wrote a letter pointing out that a comma was misplaced in a quotation from the memoirs of Saint-Simon. Believe it or not, the next time I was at *The Times* office I had to prove from my script that the error was not due to me but to the printer. Eventually God delivered this Etonian censor into my hands. Years later I published a little book on Voltaire, and the Eton gentleman sent me a very civil letter of commendation, but added condescendingly: "On page so-and-so for 'Marat' read 'Marot.'" With what bliss I realised that this omniscient hair-splitter did not know that before the Revolution Marat had published an incendiary work of sociology and that Voltaire had handled it severely in an important review! And with what greater bliss I wrote and told him so! Only once in a lifetime is it granted to a mere free-lance to convict the French master of Eton of gross ignorance about personages so eminent as Marat and Voltaire.

But in December 1919, these things were hidden behind the veil of the future. What troubled me at that moment was the perception of my incompetence to write with authority of

Victor Hugo or indeed of any writer of more than temporary significance. I knew enough to know how little I knew. Often before, I had realised that while it is legitimate to isolate a poem or a novel or the work of an individual author and enjoy it for its own sake, there was a wider significance in relating them accurately to the stream of European thought and creation.

I imagined myself standing, as I had so often done in childhood, on the South Foreland cliff, looking south-east across the Channel. Behind me was London: in front, Athens, Rome, Florence, and Paris. These were or had been the great creative centres. To know something of what they had created still seemed a good object in life. At that time I did not realise how profoundly ancient Egypt had influenced the world; I was prejudiced against the Hebrew prophets; and I did not give their full due to the Ionian founders of science. I did perceive that other achievements had come from areas on either side of the imaginary line I had drawn across Europe. To the east were the Low Countries, Germany, and Russia; to the west Provence, Spain, and Portugal. I felt that I should have to be content with a very superficial knowledge of these, but that I could know something of France and Italy, and the two classic cultures behind them.

Somebody sent me a crude and ill-informed little book called: *Dante and Other Waning Classics*. But, I reflected, the classics don't wane, they are always equal to themselves. What wanes and waxes is the ability of an individual or an epoch to respond to the classics, to perceive the life that is always in them whether the mere material book is in the hands of a scholar or used to prop a beer barrel in a boorish convent. And I decided, perhaps with an unconscious reminiscence of Pater, that when I failed to respond to any achievement in any of the arts I would try to blame myself and not the artist.

There is no need to tell me that I have not lived up to the

worthy sentiments expressed in the last sentence, but I claim some lapses into grace.

I am also aware that this orientation and—if I may so dignify it—ideal may be looked on as academic and reactionary. It is contrary to the accepted line of evolution in such matters. The young man is more or less hopefully subjected to what is called education—his head being held, as it were, for a stated interval under the academic pump—and then rapidly reverts to type. The docile and predestined become themselves professors, to train other young men to be professors to train . . . *ad infinitum*. Like the average man, the young intellectual is also expected to scrap the fruits of his brief acquaintance with literature, and to become rather more modern than anyone else has thought of being.

In my early twenties I had been closely enough connected with a modern—in its time—movement to have seen all that from the inside. I had later seen something of many kinds of men, not to mention ruined cities, and had some close brushes with death. If I continued the "literary life" at all, it had to be on a rather wider and more solid basis than of old. I couldn't reconcile myself to the attractive but sophomoric exultation in the latest thing which for so long satisfied my old friend Ezra. The negligent tutor in Anatole France's *Chat Maigre* never left his pupil to his own devices without urging him to "dig into Tacitus." It seemed to me that a little spade work on those lines was indicated.

Now that I have explained how and why I went to the country, it will be convenient to treat the next seven or eight years more or less *en bloc*. This period of about 1920–28 is now known as "the gay twenties," and I am supposed to have been one of the maddest and merriest of the gay-makers, *un petit Byron de nos jours*. It will be of small use for me to deny this, because people are less interested in the truth than in legends which seem picturesque. But in fact those years were for me a period of almost continuous work, during which I read widely and, between my own writing and translation, turned out about 200,000 words a year. My routine was as regular as that of any office worker, and my hours longer. Nothing could be less dramatic, more lacking in the characteristic flavour of the gay twenties.

But first I moved from the Hermitage cottage to another about fifteen miles away in the valley of the Kennet, in Berkshire. It belonged to an impoverished family of gentry, and was a tumble-down affair built against the end wall of an ancient malthouse. The strategic position of this cottage was superior to its accommodation and perhaps to its appearance. It was two hundred yards down a side lane which was a dead end; one flank was guarded by a row of tall unpolled willows and the disused Kennet and Avon canal; otherwise it looked onto a garden, meadows, and osier beds. I designed the garden myself and stuck to the cottage tradition, i.e., plots for vegetables surrounded with such old-fashioned English flowers as clove pinks, phlox, sweet william, hollyhocks, sunflowers, columbines, and poppies. It was really beautiful in the late spring and summer. On summer evenings we had dinner out of doors, and watched the light fade and the stars come out as we sipped yellow Puglian wine from tall tulip glasses. I doubt if the gay twenties with their hip flasks and hangovers enjoyed life as much.

Except for Windsor and Eton, I had never supposed that Berkshire and environs, either historically or in the matter of landscape, contained anything of interest. But as I gradually extended my walks in all directions, I found there was plenty of stimulus for the eye and the imagination.

Nothing but the foundations was left of the great Benedictine abbey of Reading, founded in 1121 by Henry I, one of the finest cathedrals in England and the burial place of kings. The abbey was destroyed during the Great Rebellion, and the thrifty inhabitants of Reading carried off the stones as building material; an unwise proceeding, for if it had been left moderately intact it would have been one of the show places of England, and a source of income from tourists. In a belated effort to cash in, the city fathers caused a small marble tablet to be carved with the text of "Sumer is i-cumen in," and set it up on the stump of one of the great piers of the nave, with the statement that it was written at Reading abbey—a daring statement, since nobody knows where the poem was written.

The poor relics of the abbey are now in a public garden, close to Reading gaol, where poor Oscar Wilde so bitterly expiated the sin of laughing at the British middle classes. (If every other male homosexual had been proceeded against at the same time with the same ferocity, not to say perjury, there would not have been enough gaols to imprison them.) That public garden was at one time a horror (it was afterwards immensely improved at their own expense by Sutton's Seed Company) of geometrical lawns and drilled begonias and geraniums, the kind of formalism which is not the result of taste and restraint, but of sterility and impotence of taste and imagination. And this on the site of what had been a great centre of mediæval art and culture. What a fall was there, my countrymen!

Instead of clustering round the vast Benedictine abbey, Reading now pivots on the Huntley and Palmer biscuit factory. *On sent le progrès.* Nobody sang "Sumer is i-cumen in" as the machines baked biscuits, or ever will. But a bronze statue of Mr. Palmer stands in the middle of the High Street—the only statue in England, as the inhabitants proudly boast, which includes an umbrella.

Reading, then, had nothing to offer but a contrast between a past one had to imagine and an only too intrusive present. Fortunately this wasn't true of much of the county. "England, thy beauties are tame and domestic." I suppose I must admit that the valley of the Kennet *is* tame and domestic, but it has the charm of pastoral poetry. If I didn't think it offensive for a man to quote his own verses, I should be tempted to cite some octosyllabic verses I wrote on this theme. In spring the water meadows were white and gold with daisies and buttercups and "Titania's pensioners," the cowslips. There were leafy screens of willows, aspens, and Lombardy poplars, so that we found nooks where, without scandal to the neighbours, we could taste the luxury of bathing without suits. Red-shanks flew by, uttering their curious fluting call, and out of sight in the sunny sky the snipe "drummed" as they nose-dived at terrific speed. Along the river brink grew gold and purple loosestrife, Queen Anne's pocket handkerchief, rosebay, king-cups, and the eglantine. Beyond the water meadows the land rose on either side, with woods and coppices, which were full of primroses and violets in early spring, and a little later everywhere lay pools and sheets of lovely blue wild hyacinths.

Three squirearchies divided most of the land for a considerable distance south of the Kennet. One of these was Ufton, which possessed a fine Elizabethan mansion, an "Italian" formal garden, and remains of fish ponds dating from the middle ages. For generations this beautiful old house belonged to the family of Perkins or Parkyns. Readers will at once recollect that Mistress Arabella Fermor, to whom Pope dedicated the *Rape of the Lock*, married Francis Perkins of Ufton. Whether the rape of the lock really happened at Ufton is not known, but I used to tell my visitors the story when I took them to see the house; and I never happened on anyone learned enough to contradict me. I looked hopefully in the parish church of Ufton for some memorial of this fair lady, but all I discovered was a Tudor monument to an unfortunate Mrs. Perkins of that epoch, who died in her thirties after having produced fifteen children, and probably on account of that fact. Effigies of all the children, in ruffs and kirtles or trunk hose, were dotted round the tomb.

Which reminds me that in the chapel of the Record Office in London, there is (or was before the bombing) an Elizabethan tomb of a gentleman carved in life-sized effigy, with two wives and three children. The name of this Tudor worthy was Sir Richard Alington. I discovered it when Bruce Richmond took me in to see the Torrigiani tomb. Richmond was interested, especially when I noticed that one of the shields on the tomb bore arms similar to my own—or rather, my grandfather's, for I never bothered to take out permission to assume them. Richmond was all for rushing off to the College of Heralds and plunging into genealogical research, until I reminded him that it would cost at least a guinea merely to destroy an illusion.

The squire of Aldermaston was a London business man, and his house a portentous specimen of Victorian Jacobean, for the old mansion had been burned down. But the park, with its huge ancient oaks and large herd of fallow deer, took one back to Tudor days, for Henry VIII, "our royal goat," often hunted there. Poking about in the parish church I came on a stained-glass window, containing the arms of the different families of squires back to the 16th century. Among them I noticed the Congreve escutcheon, and discovered that Aldermaston had belonged to a relative of the dramatist, who is alleged to have written *Love for Love* there. Thus, in two places within a couple of miles of my cottage I was able to establish contacts with the memory of Pope and Congreve. And this was not all. Three or four miles to the north I found an insignificant lane running for at least a mile through a magnificent avenue of elm trees. This, I discovered, was all that remained of a great estate and house once belonging to Lord Bolingbroke, whose daughter married an obscure Earl of Berkshire.

So far as I am aware, no literary associations were connected

H

with the Padworth estate, in whose parish I lived. Parts of the estate had that wantonly rustic look of George Morland's pictures—one always expected to see a blushing cottage maid in 18th-century costume emerge from the trees. But the park and particularly the grounds near the house had been re-designed by a landscape gardener of the early Romantick epoch. There was an enormous copper beech in just the right place, weeping willows, and a small pond surrounded with dark conifers where one could go and be romantically dismal, or even commit a romantic suicide in the sure and certain hope of being seen from the servants' hall and rescued in time by the butler. Beside another lake which had been allowed to disappear in a forest of bulrushes there was a Gothick fishing lodge.

From a distance Padworth House looked like a coloured engraving, illustrating an early 19th-century novel—the kind of place where Mr. and Mrs. Bennett might have lived. In fact, for all I know, they did live there, for the place is within Jane Austen's limited area. But the moment you entered, more spacious days were suggested by the vast entrance hall with its sweeping baroque stairway, instantly evoking the English *milors* who set forth on their travels with Mr. Addison's excerpts from the classics, and returned with new ideas for doing up the old home. The idea of putting up Italian palaces in the quiet English landscape sounds ridiculous, though not more so than the bright inspiration of a modern millionaire, who cabled from India to his architect to re-model his Florida home instantly as the Taj Mahal. *Il faut souffrir pour être beau*. Such painful experiments are necessary in the development of every art.

Padworth House was a treasury of family heirlooms, museum pieces which were in great demand for national and international exhibitions. There were even two bedrooms with 18th-century wallpaper—pretty coloured patterns like the flowered muslin gowns worn by the ladies. But the greatest museum piece was the squire himself, a genuine English eccentric. Unlike his neighbours, he was of an old county family, the kind of people who scorned a title because they were prouder of their names than of any "honour." Local tradition had it that the squire's title to his estate was a grant from William the Conqueror, which is highly improbable. But it is certain that the family were Cavaliers who came out strongly for King Charles, and suffered accordingly. Indeed old Padworth House must have been destroyed immediately after the battle of Newbury. Just behind it ran a sunken lane still called Red Lane. It was here that Rupert's dragoons caught Essex's rear-guard, as he was retiring on London; in consequence of which two hundred Roundheads lie buried in the little Padworth churchyard. But the main body would certainly have had time to rob and burn the house of such notorious malignants. Red Lane—it must have run with the blood of men and horses.

At the Restoration the heir of the family recovered his lands and married a wealthy heiress. The new house was lavishly stocked with furniture, silver, glass, lace, and *objets d'art* of the period, much of which had been preserved, while the collection was added to during the 18th century and later. Unhappily, the squire I knew had not inherited the artistic tastes of his ancestors, though he appreciated the financial value of his inheritance. Even this developed tardily. With a curious mixture of pride and regret he told me that as a youth he had used old family portraits as targets for archery practice, only to discover that he had done thousands of pounds' worth of damage to authentic Romneys, Gainsboroughs, and Reynoldses. In his library I found a complete set of Moxon's English poets, beautifully bound and inscribed with his mother's name in the fine angular writing of Victorian ladies. The squire was flattered that a literary man should be interested, but confessed that he had never read a line of them. I wish I could know the reasons for this sudden outcrop of philistinism in a family which had so obviously had excellent taste for centuries.

The squire was unmarried and the last of his long line. On his death—he eventually committed suicide, I am told—everything went to a distant cousin, a peer in the Guards. Yet he was astonishingly parsimonious. The fences of his estate were rotten and broken, the sure sign of a negligent landowner. His vast unkempt shrubberies harboured thousands of starlings, and his rookery was the biggest I have ever seen—the nests extended over nearly two miles of trees, and the cawing in March was prodigious. He was always lamenting that he lost money on the home farm, and claiming that he only kept it up as a patriotic duty. Instead of having the turf of his park grazed by fallow deer, he rented the land to a sheep farmer. Although his coverts were crowded with pheasants, at Christmas he bestowed on each family in the parish exactly one rabbit apiece. (You could buy them for sixpence.) He told me once he had bought some wonderful claret, which turned out to be vile Algerian red ink at eighteen shillings a dozen.

For some time I thought this was the result of the poverty which fell on so many old families after the First World War. One morning when I was on the station platform waiting for the London train, the squire turned up, having walked the two miles to the station to save gasoline. He was astonishingly dressed for a visit to the Empire's capital, but seemed totally unaware of his curious appearance. On his head he wore an old fishing cap with flaps and a couple of ragged trout flies still stuck in it. His suit was of shabby tweed; and over it he wore an immense rusty ulster with a set of flaps, like those worn by Dickens's coachmen. Round his neck was knotted a large white silk handkerchief which fell over his chest, and into this he frequently sneezed, for he had a bad cold—doubtless due to some ill-considered economy.

I could not avoid travelling with him, as he also had a third-

228

class ticket. In between his uninhibited sneezes, he discoursed
of the cupidity of the workin' classes and informed me that the
coal miners were bleedin' the country white. By an easy transition he then went on to say that he had just cleared forty thousand pounds by a deal in sugar. The money was on deposit in
the bank, as he couldn't discover immediately another safe and
profitable investment. He understood that I was connected
with *The Times*, and therefore presumably on the right side
and in the know. What did I suggest as a nice comfy investment? I nearly said:

"Sell all that thou hast and give it to the poor." But he was
impregnable to satire, and would merely have told me I was a
rotten socialist.

Yet once he was defeated and sorely tried, in terms which
went home to his bosom. There came to our village a rude red-
faced soldier, a retired Sergeant-Major of the Guards, who had
served under the squire in good Queen Vicky's golden days.
This old man had some instructive stories of *cette vieille calèche
qui s'obstine à s'appeler Victoria*. At Windsor the sentries had
to march up and down the battlements at night, and one of
these walks passed close to the Queen's bedroom. If the sentry
kept rigidly to a narrow line of flagstones his step was inaudible
in the Queen's room, but if he accidentally made one step to
the right or left and the echo woke her, she would put on the
light, make a note of the exact time, and the sentry would be
punished. Moreover, if she passed any troops in the neighbourhood, the officer would be reprimanded if he didn't halt his
men, fix bayonets, and give a royal salute to the empty air, for
the manœuvre took too long to be executed before she had disappeared. A lady in waiting was instructed to look back from
the receding carriage and make sure that the salute was properly forthcoming in every detail.

Well, the squire readily gave his old friend and servitor full
permission to fish for trout in the Kennet, assuming that he

would use the fly, by which method a fisherman seldom landed anything much over half a pound. But the Sergeant-Major wasn't a Sergeant-Major for nothing. In defiance of all the sporting rules he dabbled succulent worms in the dark pools of small tributaries, and yanked out four- and five-pounders, to the squire's dismay and wrath. When my old friend, General Mills, chaffed the squire about "worm-fishin' goin' on, bad as poachin', what?" the squire went so purple in the face I thought he was about to be smitten by apoplexy. Even that eccentric Achilles had his vulnerable heel. Perish the Romneys and the Restoration silver, but let it not be said, O Lord, that there was worm-fishin' on The Estate.

Reluctantly I must give no more space to the local fauna of that district. The reader, if curious, may consult a novel called *The Colonel's Daughter*, in which more appears. There are some fancy and caricature in that book, but on the whole I am prepared to go before a commissioner for oaths and have him say to me of it: "This is your name and handwriting you swear that the contents are true so help you God amen eighteenpence please you must get change I haven't got it," which according to Dickens is the true formula for swearing an affidavit in the United Kingdom.

Within walking distance to the south-east was the site of the Roman town of Silchester (Calleva Atrebatum). There you could see two or three miles of crumbling, ivy-covered town wall, a little grassy amphitheatre, and in dry weather the outline of the streets under the wheat fields. It was a lonely place, with only a church and a couple of farmhouses huddled in a corner of what had once been a populous town. Strange to think of men dressed in togas in that gentle English landscape and that provincial Latin was talked there. Nobody knows when the barbarians swept over Roman Silchester. It existed;

the legions were withdrawn; there is a gap in the recorded history of England; and when the Roman missionaries came, Silchester was no more. But its end must have been sudden and bloody. Among the numerous objects from Silchester in Reading Museum are buttons roughly cut from deer antlers, and antlers marked in sections to be cut into buttons. One day men were working at this humble job; the next they were dead or slaves or terrified fugitives.

Not very far to the east of Silchester was Strathfield Saye, the seat of the Dukes of Wellington. After the Peninsular war and Waterloo, Parliament voted the Iron Duke a hundred thousand pounds and a large estate. I walked over a good deal of that land, and to this day it is still the "bad land" William Cobbett said it was—infertile sandy heath with pine plantations, practically worthless. Alderman Beckford, the Duke's contemporary, a prosperous West Indian merchant, left his son, the eccentric "Vathek" Beckford, an income of a hundred thousand pounds. If the commander was held to be rewarded amply with a lot of useless land and one year's income of a Lord Mayor of London, how much do you suppose went to the rank and file of the squares of Waterloo? In their cheeseparing reward to the Duke, Parliament included a present which he may or may not have noticed and liked—several meadows which in late spring are full of the rare fritillary flower. By paying sixpence to the butler you could pick a bunch.

There is a deal of grumbling about the action of English farmers and landowners in forbidding access to their land. But the fact is that many city-dwellers don't know how to behave in the country. Partly from ignorance and partly from contempt, they look on the country as a No Man's Land where they can do as they like. They leave open the gates of pastures, so that sheep and cattle stray; they walk across standing crops, particularly hay fields; they litter the ground with picnic refuse

231

and leave broken bottles which may lame a horse or a cow; they utter discordant noises, rob birds' nests, and make a massacre of the wild flowers. After a holiday it is lamentable to see the roads littered with bunches and often huge sheaves of flowers, either carelessly dropped or flung away as a nuisance. In the south of France, forest fires invariably break out during the 14th of July holidays, and are equally invariably attributed by the newspapers to foreign spies or communist saboteurs. It is nothing of the kind—merely the carelessness of the French townsman, who chucks a lighted cigarette butt into an inflammable pine forest.

The efforts of protective societies and of landowners have been fairly successful in the case of wild birds, but the destruction of wild plants and flowers in England during this century has been rapid. So many of the delicate wild ferns were dug up by the roots and carted away that they have disappeared entirely. The wild daffodil has gone from many areas where it was common, and even such abundant flowers as the primrose and the wild hyacinth have been greatly diminished. The same thing is true of many other species, and chiefly for the one reason of indiscriminate picking by ignorant townspeople. As to their picnic habits, let one example stand for many. On the north Berkshire downs is a prehistoric dolmen, called Wayland Smith's Cave. When I visited it, the grave chamber of that ancient chieftain was littered with dirty paper, tin cans, egg shells, orange peel, and an empty champagne bottle. What would Sir Thomas Browne have said of such base desecration? It was a contingency of profanation he failed to vaticinate.

Among all the excursions in that district I liked the Ridgeway walk best, although, since it occupied three days, it was necessarily infrequent. Starting from the cottage with rucksacks, we crossed the railway and the Bath road, and climbed the high ground bordering the Kennet valley to the scattered and undistinguished village of Beenham. Once that was left behind, the modern world was abandoned, for most of the walk thereafter was by footpaths or tracks. On the ridge beyond Beenham we passed the Bolingbroke avenue, and then came to the deep valley of the Pang, which joins the Thames at Pangbourne. An hour or so of walking brought us to Yattendon, where rather surprisingly the choir was furnished with old church music, beautifully printed at Oxford, and presented by Robert Bridges. I once took Tom Eliot over to Yattendon, to enjoy the country and to see this evidence of ecclesiastical culture in the wilderness. We went to a cottage for tea, and with his usual charm and urbanity Eliot entered into conversation with our temporary hostess. Presently and with great politeness he asked her name. "Mrs. Pizzy," she said. Even Eliot's *sang-froid* was baffled by this; all he could do was to murmur: "Really?"

From Yattendon you could go on either to Aldworth or East Ilsley. Near Aldworth was a knoll with a deep moat round it, evidently ancient, and an old farmhouse. This was all that remained of the castle of the great de la Beche family, who fortunately extirpated themselves and a great many other feudal ruffians in the Wars of the Roses. One of the de la Beche family was tutor to the Black Prince, and in the little church of Aldworth were nine tombs of the 14th and 15th centuries, all of de la Beches, and all sadly mutilated by puritans and village louts.

But a better walk was by footpath to East Ilsley, a remote village hidden in a deep cup on the bare chalk downs. For some reason I always felt it was at East Ilsley that Matthew Arnold's scholar gipsy was seen "in some lone alehouse of the Berkshire moors." At any rate, he would have had plenty of choice there; for in that little village almost every other house was a pub, because it was the market for the Berkshire sheep farmers. It was once a prosperous place, but the sheep had dwindled, and miles of some of the finest sheep pasture in England were misused for training race horses. A racing stable is a moral disaster for any neighbourhood, for a blight of vulgarity and demoralisation spreads rapidly from the parasites of this sport. I was grieved indeed when that fate overtook East Ilsley.

The second day's walk was wholly along the Ridgeway, the Icknield Street or Icenhylt of the Saxons. But it was far older than either Saxon or Roman, being in fact the work of the mysterious prehistoric peoples who built the stone circles of Avebury and Stonehenge. The Ridgeway is now a broad track right across Berkshire on the highest line of the chalk downs. To the east it crosses the Thames near Streatley, but disappears before it reaches the coast. To the west, it runs plain and broad from a point just north of East Ilsley, a day's walk to White Horse Hill.

It is a curiously lonely walk for England, especially since it is not sixty miles from London. There is hardly a house all the way, and on the four or five times I made the walk I saw no human being—after the racing people were passed—except a lonely shepherd or a man ploughing a distant field. To the north there is a wide prospect across the plain towards Oxford. It was from somewhere on this Ridgeway, you remember, that Thomas Hardy's Jude looked out and saw the distant towers of Christminster (Oxford). I stared hard to see Oxford myself, but never saw it; but I suppose it can be seen in a novel.

Down in the misty blue valley you could see the diminished spires of village churches and sometimes a little curl of white smoke from a train, but there was no sound except the wind or the call of a stray bird or the rustle of beech leaves from the trees still left in piety over the barrow graves of the forgotten people. Twenty, twenty-five, thirty centuries dropped away, and you were back in those dim ages when most of England was bog and forest, and these bleak uplands were not only the safest but the most fertile parts of the island. The Ridgeway is the oldest trade route in England, and has seen men of the stone and bronze ages, the Roman merchant, the Saxon peasant, the Norman Knight, the mediæval chapman, Shakespeare's Autolycus, the 18th-century peddler, and finally no doubt Matthew Arnold, dreaming of Scholar gipsies and the Education Act.

The day's walk ended at Uffington Castle, the second of the tremendous defensive earthworks on the ridge. Here cut in the chalk is the famous white horse, which is certainly pre-Roman; and a hill called the Dragon, significantly, for the Celtic Pendragon means something like "king of kings"; and—anticlimax—in the village just below the hero of *Tom Brown's Schooldays* spent his childhood. A little further to the west along the Ridgeway is Wayland Smith's Cave, complete with orange peel and empty bottles, and beyond that a bare stretch of upland covered with the stone circles marking a prehistoric village.

The last day's walk was down the beautiful Lambourne valley to Newbury; but once, when I had more time, I pushed on for a day or two more along the Ridgeway. Sometimes it shrank to a mere footpath, sometimes a short section was incorporated in a modern road, but it went on and on, until finally it brought me to the sarsen hill above Avebury. These sarsens are glacial boulders, of which there are such quantities all over New England, but which have mostly been broken up and removed from old England. Superstition and their size and the barren land beneath them have protected the sarsens, which are great oblongs of stone from twenty to a hundred tons. From the hill you look down on Avebury, with its great earth circle and some of the ancient stones still standing upright. How those neolithic people managed to move and then to set up such vast stones is a mystery, for the only tools found are shovels made of the shoulder-blades of oxen, and picks of deer antlers. Even more mysterious is the problem of how the inner circle of stones at Stonehenge got there, for they came from a geological formation which exists only in Pembrokeshire, Wales. And who built the great earth pyramid near Avebury, known as Silbury Hill, and why?

Thus within a few miles of my cottage in a county I believed to be quite uninteresting when I went there, existed relics and fragments of English history, terminating in that singular human relic, the squire of Padworth. To someone with a sense of the past, it was fascinating; a great book, with many blanks and torn pages indeed, but more vivid than the written word. Dr. Johnson said that the difference between a literate and an illiterate man was the difference between the living and the dead, the manifest exaggeration of a very literate man. But there is some truth in it. I am glad that I had eyes to see these venerable remains, knowledge to understand them, and imagination to reconstruct the life from which they sprang. And in these bitter days there is even consolation in a sense of the past. Those primitive people of the Ridgeway must have thought it a terrible, an irremediable disaster when the cruel Romans slaughtered them or drove them back to the west. So too the Saxons when the Normans overran their country. Yet in time came Sir Thomas Browne—after how many drums and tramplings—to muse over ancient urn-burials; and the ford where the Saxon drove his oxen across the Thames became the city of dreaming spires and lost causes.

Among the people who came to see me, Eliot was most responsive to the history, Lawrence to the natural beauty and the flowers. Eliot was far from being insensitive to such things. For instance, he was interested in wild birds and knew a lot about them, which one mightn't suspect from his writings; but he hadn't, no man I have ever known had, that vivid awareness of nature which was one of Lawrence's gifts. Since Eliot was American, and the motor car has deprived most Americans of the use of their legs, I thought he might recoil from walking all day. But no, he stood up to it valiantly, and made no complaint when I dragged him on a fifteen-mile round trip to see a place I had "discovered," called Sherbourne St. John.

It was worth seeing. The parish church, a world too wide for its few worshippers, was the chancel of a great alien priory, suppressed by Henry V (not VIII) to raise money for his invasion of France. Not far from the altar was the effigy of a 13th-century knight, perhaps a crusader, since his legs were crossed; concerning which Eliot uttered pregnant reflections which I have unluckily forgotten. Outside, along what had once been the nave of a great monastic church, an avenue of ancient trees led to the parsonage. It was a peaceful and picturesque little scene, scarcely touched by the 18th century, let alone the 19th and 20th. Either I read in some antiquarian book or imagined that the living was in the gift of some university college. From this it was easy to imagine generations of Fellows, retiring each in turn with the customary *solatium* of college port to this remote place, to read his Vergil and Diodorus Siculus and possibly even the Fathers while ministering to the spiritual needs of the country copulatives. Apart from a love of the classics, I know nobody less qualified to be a country parson than myself, but I see the charm of such an existence, I see its point. One might become another George Herbert; though, upon the whole, probably not.

I also recollect an oddly prophetic conversation with Eliot, arising out of a visit to Padworth churchyard. Within the church Eliot read with becoming gravity a long and turgid Latin inscription on a tablet surmounted by weeping and nymph-like angels of the 18th century, which tablet recorded the marriage of one of the squire's ancestors to a "co-heiress," who had brought him I don't know how many messuages, hereditaments, and cash securities. With equal gravity Eliot contemplated my favourite rural gravestone of the loving couple.

Under the name of the wife, who died first, was inscribed: "Rock of ages cleft for me"; and under the subsequent husband was: "Let me hide myself in thee." From this we passed to the rude forefathers of the hamlet, and thence by a natural transition to Gray's *Elegy in a Country Churchyard*. I was surprised to find that Eliot admired something so popular, and then went on to say that if a contemporary poet, conscious of his limitations as Gray evidently was, would concentrate all his gifts on one such poem he might achieve a similar success. I didn't know Eliot was already contemplating, if he had not begun, *The Waste Land*. When a year or so later he read me the manuscript of the poem in London, I was profoundly affected. I had never heard anything so graveyardy and suicidal. The motto from Petronius about the sibyl who said: "I want to die," points the moral, if any pointing is necessary.

I enjoyed the company of my various summer visitors, but there was one brief episode with Harold Monro which caused me some anxiety. Harold and I were old friends, and I knew that he was one of those afflicted people who for their own sakes ought to be rigid teetotalers. He was not intemperate; indeed I have known many men who drank a good deal more with no evil results. The trouble with Harold was this: up to a certain point wine seemed to have no effect on him at all, and then at a quite indeterminate moment another half-glass or even a sip would make him hopelessly drunk.

Knowing this I carefully provided one small flask of Chianti for each meal, thinking that shared among three it could do him no possible harm. Unfortunately Harold also knew me, and knew that when I am working I usually go on the water wagon. Anticipating a drinkless evening he must have tanked up nicely before leaving London, and probably brought a brandy flask with him. He seemed perfectly sober when he came down to dinner. Now, those small Chianti flasks hold exactly six glasses. Harold sipped his first glass in the normal civilised way, and just at the end of dinner I refilled the glasses. To my consternation he seized his and drank it off with horrid avidity as if it had been water; and in a second my old friend had become a feckless and rather unpleasant lunatic.

I promptly called for coffee; but before it was ready, Harold insisted on going for a walk, and became violent when I tried to persuade him out of it. So for a walk we went, and I took him by the nearest way to the squire's park, hoping the cool evening air would sober him. Not a bit of it. He kept embracing and kissing tree trunks, and telling me how much he loved trees. Of course, I knew all Georgian poets love trees, but I thought he should not have been so ostentatious about it. Then, unfortunately while it was still light, he insisted on returning, appearing to get more instead of less drunk at every step. He stumbled about so alarmingly that I took his arm, and together we lurched back, Harold talking very loudly and incoherently, past all the cottagers sitting at their front doors in the cool of the evening. From this arose a pleasing local legend that I regularly indulged in "filthy orgies" ("g" hard as in classical Greek) with deboshed Londoners.

Finally I got Harold back to the cottage intact, and made him drink strong coffee. It seemed to have the same effect on him as brandy on other men. He kept insisting that he *must* go into the garden and "laugh at the stars," which I recognised as another disquieting Georgian symptom. While laughing at the stars he tripped over backwards, and knocked his head on the flints bordering the path. For a moment I thought he'd killed himself, and wondered how I should explain his corpse to the police. But no, he was totally unharmed; and after a lot more silly pranks eventually agreed to go to bed.

At that time I was working hard, and to get in as much work as possible before breakfast I had formed the habit of shaving overnight. My razor was a Valet auto-strap, which hung on the back of a bedroom door leading to the attic. Although I had never noticed it, this hollow space acted as a sounding board, so that the noise of stropping resounded through the cottage. I was stropping away energetically, when suddenly I heard a terrific thump from Harold's room. I went and opened his door and found him lying on his back in a strange confusion of ill-adjusted pyjamas. He stared at me without recognition, and said fiercely: "Who are you? What are you doing here?"

"I'm Richard," I said, rather crossly. "What the devil are you doing on the floor?"

He ignored this.

"Where's that motor-bicycle?" he demanded angrily. "Who are they? What are they doing here?"

After about five minutes I myself got so tangled up in razor-strops and motor-bicycles that I dumped him into bed and left him.

Next morning he appeared trim and self-possessed, as if nothing had happened. I never referred to what had occurred; neither did he. It's my belief that he had no recollection of anything that happened after he drank that second glass of Chianti; and, knowing himself, thought it better to make no enquiries.

Poor Monro. I was fond of him, and I think he was of me. After his death I was told that at one time he had appointed me his literary executor and had bequeathed me a hundred pounds and that he had altered his will on account of an ill-timed jest of mine. Somewhere in the early 1930s, when I was living abroad, he wrote a letter to a periodical about an article of mine, and with an old friend's license took some cracks at me. In replying I took the same license, and remarked that Harold had been the Marshal Joffre of contemporary English poetry—always ten minutes late and two divisions short. This was too true to be relished; and so I was disinherited.

I suppose I should round out the story of these rustic days by some mention of the work which occupied nine-tenths of my time. I read continuously in French, English, and Italian, and taught myself to read Old French of the *langue d'oïl* and of the *langue d'oc*. I also read a good deal in the classics. After my father's death, in 1921, my mother gave me many of his books, including his set of Elizabethan, Jacobean, Caroline, and Restoration dramatists. Apart from a few obscure plays, I possessed and read practically everything from *Gorboduc* and *Gammer Gurton's Needle* to Congreve. Through the kindness of May Sinclair, which I record with gratitude, I became a life member of the London Library—which possesses about three hundred thousand volumes and allows country members to take out fifteen at a time. I also bought a good many books, and eventually had about five or six thousand. In fact, I had more books than I had time to read.

In Perfect State, which, perhaps fortunately, we shall never see, the literature of the world will not be scattered about in bulky and costly editions or ignominious hacked-off impressions. Everything non-copyright and worth reading will be contained in a kind of Opera Omnia in volumes of about a thousand pages of India paper, costing no more than a new novel, like the Nonesuch poets in England and the Bibliothèque de la Pléiade in France. You will then be able to house all the literature of the world in a small apartment. All these people who don't buy books because they've nowhere to put them will be instantly defeated, and culture will reign from China to Peru. Once, during a week-end at Cambridge, I succeeded in convincing my friend, Dr. C. P. Snow, of the usefulness of this project. He was so much impressed that he took me to see one of the Syndics of the University Press; but he soon daffed us to a cabin hanged with care. Who was going to subsidise such a colossal scheme, and who would buy the books if they were printed? He evidently knew the book-hungry public better than we did. But would the whole vast series cost more than a battleship? And how do we know people wouldn't buy the books?

Soon after I joined *The Times* I was taken on to do signed reviews for the *Nation*, the opposition Liberal weekly—a pleasing, if rare, example of literary tolerance. And there was Eliot's *Criterion*, for which I wrote fairly often at one time. During Eliot's absence I acted as temporary editor, and saw something of the then publisher, Richard Cobden-Sanderson, who took a rather gloomy view of the *Criterion*. The only revolutionary change I introduced was in make-up; it seemed to me that the titles of all articles should be printed at a uniform distance from the top of the page. But I also aroused Ezra's displeasure. Eliot asked me to include one of Ezra's *Cantos,* and when I read the proof I discovered that Ezra had called the Pope a s. o. b. The law of libel in England is severe; Roman Catholics are sensitive; and anyway I didn't think it urbane to call the Pope a s. o. b. So I cut it out; whereupon Ezra promptly transferred the epithet to me by mail.

Some time in 1922 a French scholar, Frédéric Lachèvre, published an elaborate two-volume edition of the works of Cyrano de Bergerac. Oddly enough, M. Lachèvre was a pious Catholic, while Cyrano is one of the great free-thinkers of France. But the "Life" part of the book was solidly documented and contained much valuable information. Some years before, Remy de Gourmont had discovered in the Bibliothèque Nationale the original manuscript of Cyrano's *Voyages Imaginaires.* Apparently this had been the copy submitted to the censor, and about one-sixth of the whole book had been then excised. M. Lachèvre printed this MS., with the hitherto unknown passages in italics; and they made a comparatively unimportant book both daring and original.

I was so much interested in this that I persuaded Richmond to let me write a leading article on Cyrano for the *Literary*

Supplement. It was, of course, unsigned, as all contributions to that journal were until recently; but a few days after the article appeared, Richmond forwarded me a letter from the publishers, Routledge. They wanted the author of the article to write an introduction to a reprint they were planning of Lovell's (17th century) translation of Cyrano's *Voyages.* I took the Lachèvre book up to London to show them, and they promptly changed their plans, and commissioned me to do an entirely new version of the complete text.

Thus, by accident, began an association which eventually resulted in my doing ten books for them in five years. After Cyrano de Bergerac, I translated comedies by Regnard, Marivaux, Lesage, and Destouches, with critical biographies; and then followed *Les Liaisons Dangereuses* of Choderlos de Laclos, an anthology of *Characters* from Theophrastus to the English 17th century, *Les Quinze Joyes de Mariage,* Voltaire's "*Contes*," the *Letters of Voltaire and Frederick of Prussia,* a monograph on Voltaire, and a selection of Madame de Sévigné's *Letters.* I edited for them a series of other translations from 18th-century French authors and made a translation of a modern French book, Julien Benda's *La Trahison des Clercs.* During the same five years I issued with other publishers two books of poems, two volumes of literary essays, and a translation of Pierre Custot's curious book about oceanography, *Sturly.*

The *Mercure de France* was good enough to say of my version of Custot's *Sturly* that it was "*un véritable tour de force.*" If I may be permitted to agree with them, it was; especially as the whole book was translated in three weeks. I reviewed it for *The Times* when it appeared, and this may have introduced it to Lawrence of Arabia. Anyway, he was greatly interested by it, and engaged to translate it for Jonathan Cape, only to find that its technicalities baffled his knowledge of French. After trying another translator, who also failed, Cape applied to that universal provider of culture, *The Times;* and they handed him on to me. I knew that I couldn't do the translation on my head, as by that time I could do most French books. No dictionary contained many of the technical words used. But I agreed to do the job.

This is how I solved the problem. I went to the London Library and took out five or six French scientific textbooks on Mediterranean sea life (ichthyology, algæ, and what-not) and an equivalent number of English books. I hunted through the French books until I found the required word and its scientific equivalent; I then looked up the scientific name in an English book and soon discovered the English word. Very simple, of course. I have sometimes wondered why Lawrence of Arabia didn't remember that, so far as names go, Latin is still the universal language of Science.

Monsieur Custot, whom I had never met, overwhelmed me by suggesting that I should come and live in his home with him. I rather wish I had now, as he was director or assistant director of the aquarium at Monte Carlo. I refused, because I knew he believed I was a fellow-worker in science and not merely a rather ingenious literary faker.

It was also about 1922 that I conducted the most complicated piece of diplomacy I have ever undertaken. Richmond was always clamouring for new leader writers; and it seemed to me, on the strength of *The Sacred Wood*, that Tom Eliot was the man he needed most. Moreover, I knew that when it was whispered around that Eliot was writing *Times* literary leaders, it would shut up a lot of the opposition writers who were panning his work. Unfortunately, some of these people had Richmond's ear, and he was accordingly prejudiced. Very rightly Eliot stood on his dignity, and wasn't going hat in hand to any editor. After about six months of cautious work I finally talked Richmond into agreeing to have lunch with Eliot. I felt quite sure that he had only to meet Eliot and hear him talk for all the prejudice to melt away, and for him to realise that he was in the presence of an exceptionally gifted man.

Tom had been away on the Continent, but as soon as he came back I arranged that we should all meet in Richmond's office; and then proceed to a tavern for lunch. I arrived at *The Times* early, to avoid any embarrassment of their meeting without a third party to take the edge off, and sat talking a little nervously to Richmond. I had set my heart on bringing this off successfully. At last one of the messengers announced Mr. T. S. Eliot, and in came Tom—wearing, if you please, a derby hat and an Uncle Sam beard he had cultivated in Switzerland. I had always thought of him as handsome, certainly very distinguished in appearance; but with the combination of that hat and beard he looked perfectly awful, like one of those comic-strip caricatures of Southern hicks. Richmond shook his head and blinked; I shook my head and blinked; Tom smiled urbanely, and looked more awful than ever. It was very awkward, and I saw my beautiful plan shattered for ever by a derby hat and an Uncle Sam beard.

All's well that ends well. Over a steak and a pewter pot of bitter, Eliot began talking. In five minutes he had completely captivated Richmond, as he can captivate any intelligent person. Afterwards Richmond made a discreet Oxonian jest about the beard, but when we next met Tom it had vanished; and all was forgotten and forgiven.

Chapter XVI

MEANWHILE I had not forgotten that Europe existed in fact as well as in books, but for the first three years of the long armistice going abroad wasn't possible for me or even particularly desirable. For one thing, the war didn't really stop. Many European nations at once proceeded to have internal convulsions on their own; and what with strikes, a depreciated pound, and a fantastically high cost of living, even England wasn't so good. But at any rate we weren't fighting each other, and there seemed no particular happiness in pushing one's nose into a foreign revolution. The more you think of it, the more imbecile the behaviour of European governments and political fanatics appears. Everywhere the people wanted only peace and the chance to build up their little personal lives and have some fun before they died; and everywhere this humble wish was frustrated. The old rancours were kept alive, and new ones busily invented. Mussolini was said (I don't believe it, of course) to have solved the problem of the Neapolitan beggars by dumping them all far out into the sea at night. But if that draconian remedy could have been applied to him and to every other political, military, and financial schemer, intriguer, and trouble-maker, decent people might have had a chance to live more tranquilly.

But there is no point in going over all that weary ground. Just take any more or less pompous, quasi-official, putting-the-best-face-on-it history of the past thirty years of Europe. Read it carefully, and then ask yourself how creatures who call themselves intelligent can play such antics before high heaven as those of the people in power and the people trying to seize power. They have made worm's meat of the world.

In any rational scheme of happiness, there must be plenty of leeway for the unexpected. One should also cultivate the enjoyment of contrast. Man is an animal who is always condemning himself to a monotonous routine in the interest of some remote purpose; and then soon wearies of both purpose and routine.

But in the summer of 1919 I did manage to enjoy a contrast. I took two or three weeks off, and went to Corfe Castle in Dorset, close to the place where I had first been in camp—an experience of which I had few memories that were not disagreeable. Why revive them? I didn't. Or at least only to savour my present felicity by contrast. Where I had been an automaton in khaki I could walk as a free man. Lying at ease in the sunlight on Worbarrow Down, I could look over the marshes to the rows of empty army huts in the distance, and luxuriate in my freedom. I remembered how in dugouts and billets the soldiers would talk endlessly about what they would do when they got their "tickets," i.e., discharge from the army. One ingenious cockney expressed himself thus:

"Ah tell yer what ah'm goin' t'do, chums. Soon's ah get 'ome to the ole missus, ah'm goin' t'give a bloke 'arf a crahn to blow revally under me bedroom winder from five to ten evvy 'ahr. An' evvy time he wikes us up, ah'm goin' to sy to the ole missus: 'Let the bleeder blaow!'"

I didn't pay any bleeder to blow a bugle call, but I hope that cockney lived to enjoy his noise as much as I enjoyed the quiet of Worbarrow Down.

In 1920, I stayed home and worked. 1921 was the year of the drought, when no rain fell for six months, the sun shone every day, and the green fields of England were burned brown, while shrubs and even trees wilted and died. I hope this statement has not shattered all belief in my veracity, but the sceptical may consult the British weather reports for that year. It really was hot in England. I have every reason to remember it, for I spent most of July on a long walking tour through the West of England and Wales. Walking day after day under that sun was thirsty work. How one revived at the sight of a distant inn sign, how the flagging steps quickened, and how delicious it was to drop onto a bench in a cool tap-room and call for a pint of shandygaff! We consumed incredible quantities, and drank our way across the island.

This drought caused some perturbation in the popular mind, and even infected the serenity of Georgian poets. Harold Monro was staying with me in September, just before the drought broke and when the burned-up country was a truly desolate sight. We watched heavy clouds roll over, but not a drop of rain fell on the parched earth. Harold had all a Scotsman's genius for pessimism, and propounded an allegedly scientific theory that the water supply of the earth was drying up and that in a measurably short time we should all die of thirst.

By a push of diligence I finished the Cyrano book about August 1922, and duly received a cheque in payment of advance royalties. The cheque, impressively, was drawn on the Bank of England, but was not therefore a large one, unhappily. It is even possible that the publisher did rather better out of the book than I did, but not on a scale to arouse anybody's envy. The fact is that there isn't much in such books for either author or publisher; and, curiously enough, not because of a lack of demand. The average fairly successful novelist would be pleased if he got as good a press—these books are good pegs for "literary" articles, and after the reviewer has cribbed your facts the least he can do is to praise you. And if the same novelist had as many readers, he would not only be delighted, he would make money. The readers of such books are borrowers not buyers; 2500 copies will eventually serve at least 250,000 readers. In public and university libraries I have seen copies of these books of mine, rebound in stout boards because the original binding had gone, with worn and thumbed pages, and dozens of borrowers' date stamps at the end. And all for the price of one copy of the book. Such is the reward bestowed on author and publisher for producing works of "permanent value," instead of the ephemeral tosh of fiction.

For the sake of my own contentment then, I am glad now that I lacked the knowledge to make these reflections in 1922. I was pleased to have done a job of work a reputable publisher wanted; I knew I had taken pains to make it ship-shape; and I had my cheque. When I arrived at my bank—I still banked in London—and added this cheque to the fruits of many small frugalities, I saw that what I had long been talking of as a possibility was now a certainty. I could afford to go abroad for a couple of months. After nearly ten years of interruptions, I could once more pack my valise and utter the pilgrim's *"Italiam petimus."* There and then I arranged with the bank manager for a letter of credit. September and October should be spent in Rome.

I had a little time before my train left Paddington for Berkshire, and dropped in to see an old friend who was doing pretty well in business. He regarded me with that mixture of affection and envious disapproval which successful business men feel for those friends of their youth who manage to keep out of offices and to enjoy life. He seemed to dislike my project very much, possibly because he could not go away for two months unless he caught typhoid fever, until the dismal day of his retirement brought him the nemesis of an ill-spent life. Instead of wasting time and money with a pack of dagos, he said, I should do much better to take out that life-insurance policy he had so often mentioned. I considered this proposal carefully, and weighed in the balance of imagination the astonishment and joy of my heirs and executors at discovering that contrary to their well-founded suspicions I had after all insured my life —I weighed that against two months in Italy, I weighed it against merely my anticipation. And I told my friend that I feared he was not himself, but Satan in disguise, trying to lure me into evil paths and habits.

My friends, Hal and Etta Glover, rented me their small apartment in the Piazza Margana, close to but fortunately not in sight of the Victor Emmanuel monument. As Hal was joining his wife in Paris, he agreed to travel with us; and in the interests of economy we went by the night boat from Newhaven to Dieppe. It was the 29th of August, for I calculated on arriving in Italy well ahead of the flock of autumn tourists, but after the worst of the summer heat would be over. The Channel passage, I thought, ought to be the proverbial mill-pond.

Philip II of Spain or his admirals made a similar miscalculation. God blew with his breath and scattered them. Well, God blew with his breath on us, and we were all very sea-sick. Before the ship was well out of port God blew my hat—a new one—into the sea, and the ship started bucking like a frantic horse. We retired immediately to the unpalatial accommodation reserved for third-class passengers, only to find most of it occupied by lesser breeds without the law already in the preliminary agonies of Latin sea-sickness, a portentous spectacle. The Englishman not only resents sea-sickness, he is ashamed of suffering from it; the sea is his and he—well, perhaps he doesn't quite claim that he made it, but you know what I mean. Being sea-sick is letting Britannia down, and the Englishman, although suffering horrible internal sensations, will essay a smile with green chops and pallid lips, feebly croaking that he's as fit as a fiddle and enjoying a bit of a blow. Not so the uninhibited Latin, who has no maritime prestige to maintain. With glassy eyes and appalling groans he abandons himself to an ecstasy of anguish, despair, and terror, convinced that he is about to die and careless of disguising either his symptoms or their distressing results.

At any rate, that is how the Latins behaved on this very rough night. My companion and I took the count early, and collapsed ignominiously among the Latins. The whole weight of British prestige was left to Hal, and most nobly he shouldered it. Though he was repeatedly ill, he refused either to sit or to lie down; he remained erect, clutching an iron pillar in each hand to support him under the frightful lurchings of the ship. With his blue eyes and narrow rather ascetic face, he suggested to my delirious fancy a British Don Quixote. But then the two pillars waving so alarmingly, and his position between them, irresistibly suggested Samson. To encourage him I tried to murmur the great chorus from *Samson Agonistes*:

"Oh how comely it is and how reviving
To the Spirit of just men long opprest
When God . . ."

But I couldn't at the moment recollect what it was God did to revive just men. And in fact none of us revived until after we had safely landed in Dieppe, about two hours overdue. But nothing less than Milton could do justice to Hal's heroism that night. Among the faithless, faithful only he. Morally he ruled the waves, in spite of their fiendish activity.

This was an inauspicious start, strangely like that I made in 1912; but as then it was the only unpleasant episode of the whole trip. When we got to Paris, Hal (man of iron) left us his studio for the day to get some sleep, and we found that Etta had prepared a cold lunch for us. But we were too excited to sleep, and soon gave up the pretence. We ate the good French food and drank red wine, and talked excitedly about the coming journey and what we should see and do after we arrived, and felt very thrilled about life. I remember little about that studio except that it seemed free and easy and pleasant, and that on the walls were some paintings of southern ports with fishing boats, by Waroquier. But it was Paris.

When, on the next afternoon, we left Modane I was very sleepy. The train began hurtling down towards the great valley of Piedmont; and as we left the heights and the air in the crowded carriage grew hotter and more exhausted, a mist of sleep descended on me, and the more I tried to repulse it the more obstinately it descended. Exactly opposite me was a very small Frenchman. He had an unhealthily pink face and yellow eyes, and was dressed in a velvet jacket, check trousers, and a long yellow beard. If the beard had been black, instead of dirty yellow, it would have resembled exactly the enormously exaggerated brim of the hat worn by the priest in Rossini's *Barber of Seville*—a type of hat which is now worn only by the small boys in a premature naval academy at Venice.

Prejudiced no doubt by fatigue, I took a dislike to that Frenchman—he was consuming valuable air. His whole person emanated an aura I can only distantly qualify as obscene. He was like a minor character in one of Huysmans's early novels; though, I reflected, too timid and unmuscular to be either a souteneur or the keeper of a brothel. I decided that he must be a writer of those pornographic novels which used to be on sale in the Palais Royal. Perhaps James Lovebirch in person.

This reminded me of an essay on pornography by Remy de Gourmont. I lost sight of the little Frenchman in a mist of sleep and reflection. Pornography, Gourmont argued, is the expression of the sex instinct in words; and therefore literature cannot avoid it. Ingeniously he showed that the reticences and euphemisms of sentimental novels suggest the very ideas they pretend to avoid. Frankness, he suggested, might perhaps be better and healthier. Let us boldly accept pornography, but insist that we are given *"pornographie noble"* and not *"pornographie vulgaire."* (The yellow-eyed Frenchman was obviously an example of *"pornographie vulgaire."*) But then, I thought dreamily, who is to decide the question of what is vulgar and what is noble in this branch of art?

A shrill voice pierced my hearing: *"Il va tomber!"* It was only too true. I had momentarily fallen asleep; the train must have lurched heavily; and I was wakened by the Frenchman's scream of terror just in time to avoid crushing him to death with my hundred and seventy pounds. I felt glad there were no psycho-analysts present. They might have accused me of a subconscious desire to commit homicide.

I have never known Florence and Rome so pleasant, so seductive as they were that year. For the early part of September, at any rate, we seemed to be the only foreigners—the pornographic Frenchman having happily vanished at Turin. Something, perhaps a good deal, must be put down to the subjective factor. Plainly I was in a mood to enjoy foreign travel, having been deprived of it for nearly ten years; foot-slogging up and down muddy trenches with a rifle and pack is not foreign travel, even if it did happen in France.

Everything conspired in our favour. The great summer heat was over as (in this respect rightly) I had calculated it would be; but we were spared the prolonged and repeated thunder storms which are apt to disrupt an Italian autumn. (At a later date I endured one which lasted over the Val d'Elsa with almost American intensity for nearly twenty-four hours.) That autumn they seemed to arrive in the afternoon just in time to wake one from the siesta and be over in an hour, leaving a cool sweetened world for the evening. The Italians were recovering from the war and seemed amiable again. Socialists and communists were piping down, and everybody profoundly hoped the fascists would do likewise. At least all the Italians I talked with did, except for a party member in the train between Turin and Bologna, and a young man in the train between Bologna and Florence who got unreasonably irritated because the train was six hours late and then wasted another unscheduled hour at Pistoia. Other and earlier post-war tourists had written me that the Italians were resentful and apt to be violent about the topics of the exchange and British coal, so I was careful not to mention them, and nobody else brought them up. The great rule in social discourse, especially with strangers, is to start them talking about themselves; the subject is so fascinating they seldom abandon it.

True, the exchange was disgracefully in our favour, but I bore the shame bravely. It enabled us to indulge in a higher standard of living than we had planned; and surely it would have been bad political economy to forbid that? Governments have been known to depreciate their exchange deliberately to secure foreign trade. Very good. They are delighted to do so. Why then should there be resentment when retail trade is stimulated by the introduction of pounds and dollars by the purchaser himself? To be frank, the resentment does not come from the retailer, who is enchanted; it comes from the home consumer, who sees foreigners buying and eating things he can't afford himself. And to that resentment I see no adequate reply.

My intention in stopping a week in Florence was not to refresh my memory of the great obvious sights, but to concentrate on the *quattrocento;* and I bought for that purpose modern editions of Poliziano, Lorenzo de' Medici, and the carnival songs. But I was a little diverted from this purpose by the exhibition of *cinquecento* painting gathered that year in the Pitti. For some time I had suspected that Italian painting did not expire with Raphael (as Ruskinians believed) and that show convinced me I had been right. To see the merits of Caravaggio, the Caracci, and Guido Reni was a pleasure in itself and a welcome enlargement of experience; and it was flavoured by wilful defiance of those detestable pedants the art critics. Unhappily, the art critics were also converted by that exhibition. Soon even the *barocco,* which one had enjoyed in a stealthy incognito, was made fashionable; and a blitzkrieg of tourists shattered one's meditations over Bernini, Luca Giordano, and Tiepolo.

Luckily nobody plunged deep enough into the *settecento* to discover Zuccarelli, perhaps because so many of his pictures are in Windsor Castle, which it is lowbrow to visit.

More fascinating than the galleries, which after all are fatiguing, were the squares and streets of Florence. For once in my experience the Florentines had their city to themselves, and seemed to have staged a discreet spontaneous carnival, a carnival of Venus which might have been presided over by Botticelli's Venus herself if she had consented to be clad. In the evenings the streets were thronged with girls in brightly flowered thin summer dresses, their hair braided in the old Florentine style with a flower in it. A parade of young Venuses and Graces passed with talk and laughter, arm-in-arm in threes or fours, and of course never for one second perceived the many pairs of male eyes directed at them.

It was charming. Even Giotto's rather over-rated bell-tower seemed to be humming:

> *"Chi vuol esser lieto, sia;*
> *Di doman non c'è certezza."*

And it was perfectly discreet. Many a clergyman could have passed the fiery temptation unscathed, for he would not have noticed it. But the air was electric with challenge and response. The girls paraded, and the men sat silent and intent at the café tables on the pavement, watching and appraising. It was evidently the unofficial *festa* of Santa Venere. As the darkness fell and there was a general move in the direction of dinner, one suspected that many late lovers lingered and murmured: "Flower of the clove, all the Latin I construe is *'amo,'* I love." I am glad to have seen that autumn in Italy, a last fleeting visit from the gods in exile before they were banished once more to the deceptive strains of *"Giovinezza."*

If Venus reigned over Florence, Bacchus that year was triumphant in Rome. That miraculous drought of 1921 was not limited to England; and far from causing a universal dry epoch, as poor Harold had dreaded, resulted in a notable accession to the wine stocks of the world. France alone produced about 1,500,000,000 gallons, with Italy not far behind. And what was more to the point, it was the best European vintage in point of quality for a century. I arrived in Rome ignorant of this important fact and also of the fact that since much Italian wine is light, fragile, and quick in maturing, it is best drunk within the year and as close to its native vineyard as possible.

Mr. Liam O'Flaherty thinks that a man should not drink after forty—wine is for the young. I scouted this as a paradox when it was first told me, but having passed the fatal date line I am inclined to think it embodies a truth. Except in the Naples bust, Bacchus is always represented as a young man. How right those artists were in their intuitions! What could be more pathetic, more ignominious, than an old man with vine leaves in his hair? Think of Rubens's intoxicated old satyrs—how ill those scarlet noses consort with venerable grey hair. Think of the fate of the aged Anacreon, choked with a grape pip; a young man could swallow a dozen grape pips and be none the worse for it. And then one of Rabelais's sages—Panurge or Friar John of the Funnels—points out the melancholy truth that as we grow older we ask for better and better wine. *La dive bouteille* comes to hold more disappointments than enchantment, and one blushes to spend so much on mere gulosity.

In 1922 no such dismal reflections were forced upon me That year the wine of Italy was nectar. I first noticed it at Orvieto, where I bought a small flask from the station platform, more for the sake of the pretty straw-covered flask than anything. After the train moved on we tasted it and found it delicious. It flashed into my mind instantly that all the wine in Orvieto must be good, for if Italians had any bad wine to sell to strangers they would certainly and with wisdom do so. I therefore proposed that we should get out at the next station and instantly return to Orvieto—it is obviously an Etruscan site, there are the Signorellis in the Cathedral, thirty centuries of civilisation look down on you. . . .

But as so often and so irritatingly happens in life, worldly prudence prevailed. But for once prudence was right. I despair of conveying in words the quality of the white Castelli wines that year, especially to a generation that knows not Sion. The humblest wine-shop poured fragrant nectar in your glass for a few soldi. There are many years of my life I would gladly live again, but few periods so willingly as those two months of 1922, before the pure sky of Rome was darkened by clouds of blackshirts. One very hot afternoon in an excess of antiquarian zeal—it strikes me now as really excessive—I dragged my companion far out on the old Appian way, looking for somebody's unrecognisable tomb, that of Atticus perhaps—I always admired him for his contempt of political factions. Fainting with heat and exhaustion we turned into a dirty ruinous wine-shop filled with flies, to get out of the sun. To justify our presence I ordered a *quartino,* and to my surprise it was brought on a clean tray with a white napkin and glasses polished like crystal —a peasant who knew how Signoria should be honoured. Doubtfully I took a sip. *Per Bacco!* We had some more.

And then there was that lucky discovery in Piazza San Eustachio. I forgot what we were doing in that part of Rome— baroque architecture very likely. Anyway, it was hot and we were weary of well-doing, and I spotted a restaurant which had that look of being the right sort of place. The waiter suggested we should have Trebbiano with our dinner. I had never heard of Trebbiano and naturally would mistrust any wine recommended by a waiter until I had had a chance to tip him; but this man had a nose like Michelangelo's faun, so I thought he must be a good man. Trebbiano, I afterwards discovered, is a grape and not a district; but I cannot forget that flask of cellar-chilled liquid gold, scented like Cleopatra's bosom and a great deal less costly and embarrassing. We began by saying we would drink our usual half-litre from the two-and-a-half-litre flask standing so attractively in its metal swing-container. Then it was so good and cool and seductive, we said, hang it, we'd go on the bust and drink half the flask. Eventually, of course, we finished it and went home in a cab; to wake up next morning feeling like gods refreshed.

We became aware that something unusual was happening, and developed into enthusiastic collectors of Roman wines, from Frascati to Grottaferrata, from Marino to Aricia. I laid in some flasks of Trebbiano and Aleatico; the latter a sweet but delicious red wine, despised by connoisseurs who go to books instead of life for their wine-bibbing. Aleatico goes extremely well with late Renaissance poetry, particularly Tasso. It tastes almost exactly like the *Aminta*. I have a pleasant memory of reading the linked sweetness long drawn out of the *Aminta* over a glass of Aleatico, after a visit to Sant' Onofrio, where Tasso is buried and where he spent the last few months of his unhappy life as a guest of the monks. Surprisingly enough, there are still monks there, and we were taken round by one, who gave us the usual Tasso legends with a few more bred of his own hagiographical genius. But who reads Tasso now, even though Milton did so obviously crib him? Come to that, who reads Milton? "It is surprising," says Dr. Johnson, "that there is so little literature in the world," meaning by "literature," love and knowledge of literature. Evidently, the behemoth of Fleet Street knew more about books than human beings. It doesn't surprise me. What surprises me is that there should be any "literature" at all.

Enchanted days. I had the erroneous but pleasing illusion that the chasm of the World War had been bridged, at any rate for me, and that I had managed to link up my pre- and post-war lives. It really looked to me as if there might again be a civilised Europe. Pre-fascist Rome was a peculiarly comforting city in that respect. It had seen so much, had known such disasters and collapses, had so skilfully turned such very unpromising material to its own civilised purposes. The original brigands of the seven hills, so inferior in every respect but warlike outrage to the Greeks and Etruscans, were eventually transformed into the amiable people of the late Republic and the age of the Antonines. A set of absurd oriental myths of the kind most disruptive to civil existence had been most ingeniously evolved into their opposite—a means of subsidising literature, the arts, the good life, a tolerant cosmopolitanism. I had the greatest respect for the Renaissance Popes, particularly Leo X, whose views on the Reformation entirely coincided with mine—an uninteresting squabble of unlettered monks. *Anima naturaliter non-Christiana,* I felt the deepest sympathy for these admirable men who had the good sense to use an existing institution for their own lofty purpose, and to exploit the superstition of Europe for their own very different ideals.

Two days after I left Rome for England, work, and sobriety, the fascisti marched; and that brief delusive interlude was over. But I am glad I had the experience. It was one of those glimpses which make us less forlorn.

The chief labour of this book is the invisible one of rejection. More could be said about this 1922 Roman experience, and that in turn opens up vistas of later excursions and of people known. From this mass of memories I shall pick two people. One is George Gribble. He is one of those unexpected combinations of contraries which delight the ethnologist. His father was a distinguished Anglo-Indian, governor of the Deccan, in fact; and his mother a Polish-German lady. Consequently, George presents the appearance of a well-bred Eng-

259

lishman while actually feeling a supreme contempt for all his customs, beliefs, and habits. Like Norman Douglas, George grew up bi-lingual, equally at home with English and German. Then he married a very pretty French wife, with whom he invariably talks French. And his Italian is excellent. A good European, thoroughly at home in Europe.

When I first knew him he was inhabiting a tall mediæval tower in Rome, the Torre dei Capocci. It was picturesque and the view from the top was superb, but inconvenient for housekeeping. The kitchen, living-rooms, and bedrooms were on different stages of this quadrangular column, and reached by narrow stone stairs which were worn and steep. The walls were about ten feet thick, so there was not a great deal of light; and the two upper stages of the tower were in ruins. Here dwelt George with complete insouciance, in all the splendid squalor of a mediæval noble.

His insouciance was one of his many endearing qualities, the more so to me since I have never, for all my efforts, succeeded in attaining it. Such confidence in the benevolence of fate amounts to genius, especially since in George's case something always turns up. I'm sure it wouldn't for me. Once, when George was a young man living in Paris, he found himself without funds, owing to a disagreement with his family. "Heavens!" I said when he casually mentioned this. "What on earth did you do?" "Oh, it was very hot weather, so I used to go and sleep under the trees at Saint-Germain." "And then what?" "Oh, something turned up." If we read that in the pages of Diogenes Laertius or some ancient Stoic, how much we should admire it! What character, we should say, what admirable contempt for worldly goods and worldly opinion, what devotion to virtue! Instead of which, people incapable of such philosophical fortitude used to go about saying that George didn't take life seriously.

One lovely autumn day in Rome, the gun and bells announced noon; and I put away work for the day. At that moment, enter George. No, he wouldn't sit down, he was in a hurry, he merely wanted to ask . . . I forget what. I was engaged in removing the oil from the top of a wine-flask for lunch, which was being prepared over a charcoal fire. I was conceited about this wine, and insisted that George must taste it. Protesting that he must leave at once, he sat down on the edge of a chair and took a glass. Conversation started. George grew interested, and discoursed with knowledge and eloquence, gradually and unconsciously settling himself more comfortably in his chair. I re-filled his glass, in spite of his fainter clamours that he must go, and we talked on. Presently lunch was put on the table. Starting to his feet, George said he must go. This, we said, was ridiculous. He had to have lunch somewhere, and how could he get it more quickly than when it was served under his nose? Still protesting, George shared our frugal meal, and finally left about four o'clock. Only later did we discover from the reproaches of his wife that George was supposed all that time or part of it to be interviewing the Pope or the Prefect of Rome or some other bigwig for the American paper whereof George was supposed to be Rome correspondent.

But what wisdom! George was bound to lose the job, so why not lose it pleasantly and instructively? His conversation with the Pope or the Prefect couldn't possibly have been one-tenth as merry and entertaining as ours. The wine was good, the spaghetti and chicken perfectly cooked, the cheese a pungent Gorgonzola. Would the Pope—a notorious ascetic who lived on ten lire a day—have invited George to lunch? Probably not, and even if H. H. had so condescended, it would inevitably have been a dull lunch, ruined with ceremonious formality and ecclesiastical discipline. And then, what a favour George conferred on us! He not only abounded in the milk of human kindness but in the honey of wit and wisdom. When he had gone we said what a dear fellow he was, and that we'd seldom had such fun. That a section of the public was deprived of the palpitating knowledge that H. H. had corns or was going to make an allocution or something seems to me a small price to pay for such hours. If George had insisted on collecting and cabling this unimportant interview, I should never even have read it; whereas sixteen years later I still have the happiest memories of a pleasant lunch and a charming companion. Like Garrick, George added to the gaiety of nations by making us gay. And since clearly not marble nor the gilded monuments of princes shall outlive this book, those perishable moments of time are for ever preserved in the amber of my words.

Those Rome correspondents had a tough time. Their editors knew no more than the public they catered for what was or was not important in the daily panorama of Rome. Anything sensible was of course killed, and cables snowed in clamouring for "news," which the desperate correspondents were forced to invent. My old friend, Edward Storer, who represented some English newspaper, came in one day with despair written on his countenance. At last invention had failed him, and he could think of no more silly "stories." I suggested a few mild fictions, but Storer waved them away impatiently—they had all been used before. Finally we concocted a news story based on the notorious fact that the Pope had been a well-known mountaineer. H. H., it was rumoured, suffered greatly from confinement in the Vatican during the summer and especially from being deprived of mountain climbing. Passing through the colonnade of St. Peter's just at dawn Our Own Correspondent noticed with astonishment a lone figure climbing up the stately curves of the noble dome. As it reached the top a faint sound of yodelling was heard. . . .

At the last minute Storer's courage failed him, and he didn't send the story. He thought some of his friends among the Vatican officials might be annoyed. I'm certain George would have sent it. Unfortunately, by the time Storer and I thought it up, George had held every foreign correspondent's job in Rome and there were no more worlds for him to lose there. Poor Storer had a tragic life. He began well as a writer of totally unsaleable poems and eventually sank to being the head of Reuter's in Rome. But he was a good fellow, and bore up wonderfully.

Through George, I had a tantalising glimpse of an interesting character, of whom I should have liked to know more. George had innumerable friends and acquaintances—among them an Italian who had the distinction of looking exactly like one of Veronese's young Venetian nobles. But George was always insisting that I ought to meet his friend Jones, who lived in an apartment on top of a lofty palace in the Corso. Eventually I braced myself for the test of mountaineering which was involved in visiting Mr. Jones. We were climbing innumerable flights of steep stone stairs when the noon clamour of bells erupted, so what with that and panting I didn't hear very well what George told me about Mr. Jones. I gathered that he had been a successful architect in America, had come to Italy many years before on a vacation to look at old architecture, and on a sudden impulse had rejected the 20th century, sold his business, and settled down in Rome to a voluptuous enjoyment of other times and other manners.

Unfortunately I don't remember anything of our conversation with Mr. Jones. I remember he had a pleasant apartment, full of old Italian books, which I envied him. But what struck me at the time, and I have never forgotten it, was the attractive feeling of serenity and content which emanated from Mr. Jones. It is not uncommon to meet Americans who emit crackling waves of high nervous tension and restlessness. But here was an American entirely at peace with himself and his environment, and I could not help wondering what atavisms, what long-unsuspected impulses, what devious mental paths had led a successful designer of skyscrapers to find Nirvana in (fortunately) endless researches into Italy's immense and glorious past. I shall never know. I only hope the war has not invaded Mr. Jones's enviable existence. Perhaps he hasn't heard of it.

Chapter XVII

OWING to a naturally cheerful temperament and the fact that I energetically resisted my early conditioning, I am very little afflicted with what is now called a guilt complex, and used to be more mysteriously called a sense of sin. I know it is asserted that if we say we have no sin we deceive ourselves and the truth is not in us. But, in the first place, I would claim that I know my own psychology better than the man who wrote that statement, for he died long before I was born. And, in the second place, I don't claim to be without sin; I merely have no inclination to worry about being sinful. Extensive observation of those who suffer from remorse induces me to believe that they suffer less from being sinful than from being found out in what local opinion considers sinful.

But I regret one persistent sin of which I was guilty during the first ten years of the long armistice—I worked too hard. I am still infected by this vice. Try as I may to live a life of decent and rational idleness, I soon feel guilty if I don't spend at least part of the day spoiling nice white paper with black words. The only way I can escape is at sea, or on a long walking or motor tour; all of which reduce one to the state of a contemplative cabbage. True, in the early days I had the base excuse of necessity, and always that some of my "work" was voluntary and disinterested, i.e., without hope or intention of earning money. But I have to admit that I did work merely because it was paid.

Be sure your sin will find you out. I was punished in a way so comparatively mysterious that an uncritical age might easily have seen the finger of offended deity—Comus, perhaps, or Laughter holding both his sides.

This is what happened. I had expended a good deal of nervous and emotional energy in writing a long poem. Before it was finished I had undertaken to do a translation and a book on Voltaire, with rather short time limits. In addition I had my regular work for *The Times* and *Nation*. By working all day and every day for the four months allotted I could just do it. By some perversity of fate, a number of editors suddenly conceived the idea that they wanted articles from me. The London edition of *Vogue* wanted a series; the *Spectator* suggested I review regularly for them; Jack Squire wanted five thousand words on Napoleon Bonaparte; my old friend, Amy Loveman, wrote that the *Saturday Review* would like another article; Miss Cutting wrote from the *North American Review*.

How I cursed them! Two months earlier or five months later would have been welcome, but at that moment! Unluckily, I still naïvely believed in the virtuous apprentice's erroneous maxims, that to succeed in a job you should always do your best and never refuse any work that you can honestly do. I have long since perceived that this is not the way to financial success in writing. What is needed to exploit literary ability is business skill, such as I frankly envy in my old friend, Dikran Kouyumjian, known to the world as Michael Arlen. Lacking this preeminently Shakespearian gift, I foolishly accepted these kindly meant offers, toiled madly, cut down my sleep and walks, and generally lived with an asceticism I should have mocked at in somebody else.

Well, I succeeded in this imbecility, and, feeling as virtuous as a wagonload of sheep, I mailed the last typescript—the book on Voltaire—the day before it was due. I then took a deep breath and a five-mile walk. On the way back, about a mile from my cottage, I suddenly began to feel very queer. My heart behaved in the most extraordinary manner, leaping and fluttering and then apparently dying away altogether. The sunny landscape grew dim and I could hardly drag one foot past the other. At first I had that incredulous, it-can't-happen-here feeling which healthy people experience during their rare illnesses. But almost immediately I had to sit down by the roadside, with the unpleasant sensation that I was about to disgrace myself by swooning in the manner of Victorian ladies.

My companion was greatly alarmed, and so was I, for according to several army doctors—who had commented with cynical geniality on the fact—I was medically supposed to have an A 1 heart. But my father had died of heart failure, and I gloomily supposed I was about to imitate him prematurely. Somebody got me some brandy, which made me feel a little worse; and then I was taken home in a car, and with stalwart aid ignominiously carried to bed. The local G.P. looked puzzled. The heart was certainly weak, he said, but he couldn't detect anything fundamentally wrong. So he shot some digitalis into me, and went hopefully away.

I spent the next two weeks in a detestable state of inaction. As long as I remained in bed, I felt perfectly well; but the moment I got up and made any physical exertion I felt like a sick puppy somebody has just trodden on. The only consolations were that, like Charles II, I seemed to be an unconscionably long time a-dying, and that I did a lot of reading for pleasure. Among the books I read was an advance copy of an anthology of post-classical Latin, which struck me as being very meagre and uninteresting considering the enormous amount of work there is to draw on. Collecting all the texts and histories of the literature I happened to have and summoning up my recollections of what I had read, I spent a week in writing a longish article discussing the authors omitted by the anthologist. As an after-thought I sent it to an editor friend, who wrote back that it had amused him very much, and promptly published it. I too was amused when I saw the anthologist's friends rallying round

(as in a P. G. Wodehouse novel) in various periodicals to refute me with the most elaborate avoidance of mentioning my
article.

Refreshed by this bit of literary slaughter, I listened willingly
to the proposal that I should consult a specialist; and was accordingly transported to London with as many precautions as
if I had been the first batch of plovers' eggs of the season. I am
bound to say that I felt better by the time I got to London, and
very much better when the specialist showed me the graph of
my heart, saying regretfully that he had seldom seen a healthier
one. After asking a lot of leading questions he impressively di-
agnosed "rapid nervous exhaustion," which I take to be the
polite Harley Street equivalent of the rude army doctor's
"medicine and duty." At any rate I emerged from the clutches
of this savant reassured about the status of that invaluable little
pump, my heart, and more than inclined to suspect I had made
an ass of myself. The doctor ordered "absolute rest and
change," so I went and walked twenty miles a day through the
most mountainous part of Wales for three weeks. As I got wet
through every other day and sometimes had to walk all day in
that inhospitable country of teetotalers on nothing but a glass
of milk and a handful of crackers, I considered that a fair test
of physical fitness.

This psychological disturbance, simulating a real illness, was
a strong indication of inner discontents and disharmonies. I had
an obvious hint of this in writing the long poem I mentioned.
I take it that there is a genuine difference between deliberate
and impulsive writing; for in the first case we consciously set
ourselves a task, such as an essay or a biography, and in the
second case the writing seems suggested and controlled by subconscious influences. There is a sensation, which many writers
have experienced, that what is written comes from the dictation of an inner voice. It is our subconscious life getting a
chance to express itself.

268

Even if fatiguing, this experience is almost always pleasurable. But the writing of this poem had been accompanied by moods of depression which were quite alarming. I disregarded these warnings, and set them down as after-effects of the war. No doubt that was an important factor, but there were others. I failed to see that by devoting myself to literary studies to the extent of over-work I was frustrating a whole series of impulses and condemning myself to a life of unnecessary monotony. The bi-annual escape to the Continent merely underlined this condition, if I may judge by the extreme regret with which I returned. Above all I was irritated and oppressed by having to spend nearly all my time in England, where some curious incompatibility between me and most of the people I met exasperated me.

The desire to get away permanently from England became an obsession. Hal Glover delights to test his own imagination and other people's by putting hypothetical situations to them. Once, as we were returning from a walk in Berkshire, he said:

"Suppose you suddenly inherited a large sum of money, what would you do?"

To which, without the slightest hesitation, I replied emphatically:

"You wouldn't see me for dust."

In this I was not unique. One of the obvious features of the long armistice was the considerable minority of persons of many nationalities who felt a strong impulse to live out of their own country. Now people are heavily conditioned and even bullied into being nationalists, so this would seem to indicate a spontaneous impulse towards cosmopolitanism, a revolt from the patriotic pump, and a genuine desire to tear away the artificial barriers between different groups of men so sedulously cultivated by governments and militarists. It is worth noting that one of the first acts of every totalitarian government is to prevent its slaves from travelling abroad. The abolition of nationalism would not abolish war, merely its most fashionable pretext; for war is the symptom of an imperfectly understood psychological disorder which afflicts primitive as well as highly civilised communities. Of course, the desire to live outside your country of origin may also be a symptom of psychological troubles; but it is not confined, as journalists appear to think under the influence of sour grapes, to the debauched aristocracy and fetid intellectuals. I have seldom had a servant in a foreign country who did not beg to be taken on permanently, even at reduced wages, frankly for the sake of getting away from the dear old native land.

At any rate, in the spring of 1926 I pushed off once more for Italy, this time to make a carefully planned tour of Tuscan and Umbrian hill towns. Among the places we stayed at was Montepulciano, because I particularly wished to read the verses of my old favourite Angelo Poliziano in his native town. And then there was that haunting refrain from Redi's famous poem on the wines of Italy:

"Montepulciano d'ogni vino è il re."

The wine was certainly good, but too strong for my simple tastes. If the Romans drank that at their feasts they must have got as tight as owls. One day we took a picnic lunch and walked several miles to a lovely little hill town called Monticchiello, where we found the inhabitants busily preparing for a festival in honour of the venerable hermit whose bones enriched and sanctified their church. Evidently the inhabitants were materially less wealthy than they had been, for though their church was originally a fine building, it was dilapidated, and all the "decorations" for the *festa* were of coloured paper. We contributed a few lire to a chest set up for the purpose of getting the Beato made a full-fledged Saint—I believe they told us he was a repentant cobbler and that it would cost 20,000 lire—and then walked round the town. I was delighted to see them decorating their doorways with long sprays of ivy, arranged with great taste and skill in patterns similar to those on ancient pilasters. Less satisfactory in so treeless a country were the numbers of small trees cut off at the roots and planted along the route of the coming procession. But the effect was very pastoral and pagan, and would have been less surprising in honour of Romulus and Remus or the divine Augustus than for a cobbler, however repentant and beatified.

As we approached Montepulciano on our return we heard all the church bells jangling furiously and continuously, and found the streets hung with innumerable flags. Unable to believe that so much enthusiasm was aroused on behalf of the Beato of Monticchiello (there is much jealousy between the rival saints of neighbouring towns in Italy), I enquired the cause of this *festa*. The reply startled me extremely:

"*Mussolini è stato assassinato.*"

By an incredible stroke of luck, instead of giving three hearty British cheers, I asked:

"*E morto?*"

But no. It appeared that only the tip of his nose was damaged. I was wondering what there was to rejoice about in this trivial damage to despotism when a carload of blackshirts hurtled into the town and rushed up the narrow street to the infinite peril of all pedestrians, howling "*Giovinezza*" and evidently on their way to the bliss of all fascists, i.e., making a noise, in this case by discordantly ringing the church bells. That night they caroused in our hotel until a very late hour. When we came down for breakfast, a scene of strange disorder met us. The tables were covered with dirty plates, remnants of food, and overturned wine-flasks. The dining-room smelled abominably, not only from the spilled wine but from pools of urine which decorated the floor. None of the female servants was on duty, and we could get no breakfast. So, having obtained that in a café, we departed from Montepulciano on the next bus, not a little disgusted. I wondered what the Renaissance gentlemen and scholars of that beautiful old town would have thought of that spectacle.

Like everybody else I read in a newspaper that this feat of marksmanship had been performed by the Hon. Violet Gibson, who was insane and related to an Irish peer. Such is one's reluctance to connect any acquaintance in real life with the daily melodrama of the press that I have only just realised this lady must have been the same Mrs. Violet Gibson who was so civil to me in Rome in 1912. The reader will blame me for not having cultivated this interesting acquaintance. I can only plead that in 1912 neither I nor anybody else ever imagined that an ex-socialist lance-corporal would be dictator of Italy or that Mrs. Gibson would acquire temporary notoriety by shooting off the tip of his nose. My impression of her is that she was kind-hearted, fearless, and a stickler for the proprieties. Thus, although she must have been at least twenty years older than I, she never received me without a chaperon. She went out of her way to be kind to me merely on the strength of a letter from Violet Hunt. But when we were walking or driving in Rome she frequently embarrassed me by stopping to denounce in fluent Italian anyone she saw ill-treating an animal—and animals, particularly mules, were very badly treated in Italy. The only explanation of her attempted crime which seems at all reasonable is that she saw the Duce shaking hands exuberantly with a Personality, and imagined he was beating his mule.

I got back from Italy just in time to be involved in the General Strike, which was conducted by both sides with a splendid inefficiency which led to the happiest result—an early peace. But at first it looked serious, and many foreign observers hopefully prophesied the ruin and dissolution of the British Empire—a form of wishful thinking which has cropped up frequently in the last few centuries. For my part I warmly wished a plague on both their houses. The upheaval stopped dead the sales of my Voltaire, which had come out three weeks before and was going very nicely. Incidentally, it is some evidence of the troublous nature of the long armistice that I never published a book of major importance (to me) without the book trade's being convulsed by some public calamity. My first novel had a clear run in England, but within a month of its appearance in America, Wall Street staged the spectacular crash of 1929; so that the American sales, which until then had been well ahead of the English, by Christmas were far behind. Exactly the reverse happened with my next novel, which had a comparatively clear run in America, while England was sensationally pushed off the gold standard; and this time the American sales were much higher than the English. There is nothing new under the sun; the Goncourts make the same complaint in their *Journal*.

I was sufficiently disturbed by the prospect of civil confusion ahead not to be able to work with any enthusiasm; and when I got a telegram from *The Times* asking me to come and help the paper continue, I stuffed some underclothes and a book in my army pack and hitch-hiked to London, no regular transport being available. I suppose I ought really to have been on the other side, for I had no particular liking for Mr. Baldwin and his friends or what they represented. On the other hand, a dictatorship of wooden-headed trade union leaders seemed no great happiness; while contact with Labour-minded intellectuals had made them positively distasteful to me. Still, they could hardly have made a bigger mess of things than the people whose bacon was saved, if it was ever seriously threatened, in 1926. I suppose my real motive was dislike of inactivity in a crisis, and as I couldn't get on with my own job the best thing to do was to take on somebody else's.

Actually I had a variety of jobs, which included standing by, consuming sandwiches and beer at 2 a.m., loading large bundles of *The Times* onto private cars for distribution, protecting the said cars from possible attack on their departure, and wrapping up individual copies to be mailed to subscribers. I sent Mr. Lloyd George his copy, and Mr. Leon Trotsky his, and then a crowd of diplomats, ending up with British Consuls exiled in Manchurian towns I had never heard of. By the time that job was finished it was generally about 6 a.m., and I had a nice morning walk along the Embankment to my club, where I invariably quarrelled at breakfast with a philoprogenitive parson who believed in the duty of man to beget as many legitimate children as nature permitted. Obviously another Labourite.

The one sensible man I met during that fatiguing fortnight was Tommy Earp, who writes pleasant articles for London literary periodicals. I bumped into him near Charing Cross just before the strike ended, and asked him what he was doing during these days of our country's peril.

"Well," said Earp very deliberately, "as a matter of fact I'm sitting in pubs contradicting false rumours."

Tommy certainly deserves credit for having invented the sixth column long before anyone had ever heard of the fifth.

But, for me, the great event of that year was the return of the Lawrences from America to the European scene. I had not seen them since 1919, and our correspondence had been extremely irregular. At one time Lawrence took a strong dislike to European things and people, and one heard only rumours of his wanderings to Ceylon and Australia and his settling in New Mexico. And now most surprisingly he wrote from London suggesting a meeting. I promptly wrote and invited the Lawrences for a long week-end, and in accepting Lawrence sent me some of his recent books which I had not read.

I had long admired Lawrence's work and, with sundry disagreements, liked him personally very much. But on reading these books and re-reading some earlier works I had, it seemed to me that I had hitherto under-rated him. Seven years' study of literature had sharpened my perceptions or, at least, taught me the rare accomplishment of how to read a book. Seven years of experience had made me more and more discontented with the Olympian, impersonal, and supposedly objective critical attitude adopted by *The Times*. I was more and more inclining to Norman Douglas's opinion that we should take up an author with the implied question: "What has this fellow to say to *me?*" and give him the fairest chance of saying it. Lawrence seemed to have a good deal to say to me, and I liked what he had to say all the more because he went his own way so perkily.

The visit began a little inauspiciously, as Lawrence declared the cottage was "sinister." I can't imagine why, as it was sunny and full of books, with bright window curtains and a smiling head of Voltaire over the piano; and the garden was brilliant with late summer flowers. And then I had forgotten that in the Midlands you show your respect to a guest by loading the high-tea table with enough provisions to stuff a dozen policemen; so Lawrence was greatly offended by my modest and wineless meal. All this was happily settled by a bottle of whisky for him to have a hot toddy at bedtime, a habit of his which was new to me and had apparently been acquired in America. After that he was in the best of spirits and good humour for the remainder of his stay.

As I knew he was contemplating a book on the Etruscans, I had a dozen standard works on the subject sent down from the London Library; and we spent a good deal of time turning them over and discussing Etruria, which was very important at that time in Lawrence's private mythology. We went for walks, and it was fascinating to see how quick he was in noticing things and making them seem interesting. Yet he could be devastating in his judgments of human beings. A neighbour of ours, an intellectual climber, had begged to be allowed a glimpse of him, and we contrived some excuse for a brief meeting. After she had gone Lawrence merely said: "Dreary little woman." I liked him for that, for I was sick of the way the London literati would suck up to the humblest of avowed or potential admirers. It would have been just the same if she had been the most potent of salon-rulers.

In private talks Lawrence and I agreed that so far as we were concerned something had gone wrong with England, our England, so that we felt like aliens in our own home. The only thing to do, Lawrence insisted, was to get out and stay out. In Mexico he had felt he ought to make one more attempt to fit into English life, but already he saw it was impossible, and was planning to go away and never return. (He went, and never did return.) He was evidently pining for his New Mexico ranch, for he talked of it constantly and with a nostalgic regret which made me quite unhappy on his behalf. But meanwhile before everything crashed—and he was intuitively certain it would crash sooner or later—we must have just a *little* more of Italy. Soon it would be *vendemmia*. As he talked I saw so vividly the pinewoods and the olive gardens and the vineyards of the Florentine *contrada,* the great cream-white Tuscan oxen, with their wide horns and scarlet muzzle shields against flies, slowly dragging the big tubs of grapes to the press, the men and women singing and laughing and joking as they gathered the big purple clusters, the men and boys dancing on the grapes to crush out the wine, the *vino santo* heating over an open fire, and smelled the air sweet and heavy with the scent of crushed grapes as the vintagers sat down to their evening soup and bread and wine. . . . And yes, I said, I would come to Scandicci for *vendemmia.*

The English, he said, had become half-angels, half-idiots. And he made us laugh with stories of the half-angelic, half-idiotic things they had done to him in the past few days. As David Garnett truly says, Lawrence was a born copy-cat. He amused us by mimicking a dialogue between himself and a woman in the train who tried to lend him her copy of the *Daily Mirror,* and another between himself and an obsequious butcher-boy—"he thanked me for going through the gate." Curious that Lawrence, who was such a good satirist in conversation, was a comparatively poor one in writing. The reason is, I think, that in talk his satire was mostly laughter, whereas in print he scolded.

Best of all perhaps were the evenings when we sang old English and German folk songs, according to the Laurentian custom, and Lorenzo and Frieda talked of their wanderings and adventures. There was a haunted look in Frieda's eyes when she spoke of Lawrence's illness in Mexico City, and of her dreadful experiences in getting him back to the ranch. Lorenzo, it appeared, refused to have a mosquito curtain, maintaining that if you muffled yourself up in the bedclothes, the mosquitoes couldn't get you. But, as thousands of mediæval angels danced on the point of a needle, thousands of anopheles danced and fed on the tip of Lorenzo's nose; with the natural result of a smart attack of malaria, which in turn aroused his latent T.B. At the height of his illness he insisted on returning to the ranch, and was held up at the frontier by immigration officers, and but for the prompt and humane intervention of the American Consul would probably have died there. I think that was the real reason why Lawrence never went back to the ranch he loved so much; he would not have been allowed to cross the frontier again.

Apart from this unhappy episode, their wandering adventurous life sounded wholly fascinating and rewarding. Most travellers fail to interest me in their experiences, especially if I haven't been to the places they talk about. But Lawrence had the remarkable gift—in his writing and especially in his talk—

of evoking his experiences so vividly and accurately that his listeners felt as if they had been present themselves, with the supreme advantage of being gifted with Lawrence's unique perceptions. It would be useless for me to try to reproduce Lawrence's talk; first, because I can't remember his exact words and anything short of that would be a travesty; second, because he has luckily left written accounts of many of these experiences in his books and letters.

He talked of that primitive, ice-cold, remote village of Picinisco where he and Frieda almost froze to death (end of *The Lost Girl*); of their life in Sicily and the trip to Sardinia (*Poems, Letters,* Introduction to *Memoirs of M.M.,* and *Sea and Sardinia*); of Ceylon, with blood-curdling imitations of night noises from the jungle and satirical acting of an American friend burning joss-sticks to Buddha (*Letters* and *Poems*); of Australia (*The Boy in the Bush, Kangaroo*); and of the ranch (end of *St. Mawr,* last essay in *Mornings in Mexico, Letters*). Some of this was already published and I had read it; but much was either unpublished or unwritten. As he related these things, they became almost epic to his listeners. So might the Ithacans have sat enraptured by the tales of wandering Odysseus. What was remarkable, I reflected, was Lawrence's immense capacity for experience and almost uncanny power of re-living it in words afterwards. Of all human beings I have known he was by far the most continuously and vividly alive and receptive. "What man most wants is to be alive in the flesh," he wrote when almost on his death-bed; and certainly few men and women can have been so much "alive in the flesh" as he was. To say that he enjoyed life intensely would be misleading, because the phrase inevitably suggests all the luxuries and amusements and gratifications Lawrence despised. And, on the other hand, Shelley's "pard-like spirit, beautiful and swift" is too abstract and ethereal. The truth was somewhere in between those extremities.

278

Soon, too soon, the Lawrences departed; Frieda for Germany (I think) and Lorenzo for Scotland to visit two maiden ladies who misguidedly thought he might like to live in that country. In the intervals between working hours I thought of him a good deal. His talk and personality, the many glimpses of his life, gave point and concentration to the vague rebellious tendencies I have described in myself. It seemed to me that I was being rather cowardly and foolish in allowing so much of life to slip by in mere labour and by allowing my energies to be diverted from writing about what I myself felt and thought to other subjects. I didn't in the least go back on my ambition to know something of European culture, and was grateful to the editors who had given me the opportunity to study it. But in comparison with real writing, all this literary stuff was trivial drudgery. It was respectable and commendable and paid reasonably, but was on the whole parasitic and unadventurous. Lawrence made less money than I did, but he was a free man; whereas I had one leg chained to a library and the other to the London literary press.

The upshot of this was that I wrote a pamphlet about Lawrence and some of his books, in which I abandoned the hocus-pocus of "objective" criticism and the desiccated style it imposes, and wrote entirely from my own feelings and allowed my words to flow spontaneously. I know it is no recommendation to say I greatly enjoyed writing this, because the worst writers take the greatest pleasure in their worst works. The production of it was a catharsis, and it seemed to me the most lively piece of prose I had written. I was confirmed in this favourable opinion by the fact that no London editor or publisher would touch it—until 1930, when Lawrence was news and I was in a position to sell anything I cared to put my name to. As so often happened in my life when I made a step forward, America came to the rescue; and my pamphlet was issued by the University of Washington, Seattle. I think it interesting that what I should now consider my first real poem was published in Chicago, and my first real bit of prose in Seattle.

To my surprise, Lawrence was not displeased with this pamphlet, but in his letter he said: "It's more about you, my dear Richard, than about me." And I dare say he was right.

If I had been Lawrence I should undoubtedly have burned my boats at once and hurled myself into a precarious existence in foreign parts. I have burned a good many boats in my time, but only after considerable resistance to the impulse. A bourgeois strain prevents me from taking drastic steps until and unless I have good reason for supposing the new adventure will succeed. Lawrence more than once put himself in the very unpleasant situation of having to be given money. I am aware that sponging on the bourgeoisie is the *summum bonum* of the crapulous intellectual with strong political beliefs; but I happen to feel differently. I was acutely conscious that another trip to Italy that year, with *vendemmia* in Tuscany and part of the winter in Rome, was going to be difficult. Moreover, I had so energetically dug myself into the "literary" world that it was astonishingly difficult to dig myself out again. One cannot break or evade contracts, and with the idea of getting free of journalism I involved myself in others.

At this distance of time I am not certain of the dates, but I know that in 1926, in addition to other work, I had engaged to edit about twenty or thirty volumes of 18th-century French memoirs in English. This, by the way, enables me to clear up a little point in Lawrence's bibliography. How did it happen that among his posthumous works there appears a short essay on the Duc de Lauzun? Ingenious theories have been formed to explain it, but the facts are simpler. I arranged with F. S. Flint to translate the duke's memoirs, but for some reason Flint didn't want to write the introduction. I had the book with me on one of the occasions when I stayed with the Lawrences at Scandicci, and I had Lorenzo read the book to see if he cared to write about it. From his breakfast-table homilies on the subject I gathered that he thought Lauzun and the whole French aristocracy and *littérateurs* of that epoch a collection of lice, and that anything he wrote on the subject would say so. I considered this would be an improper introduction to a public which was pretty languid about the French 18th century anyhow; so I said no more about it, and wrote the essay myself. Apparently Lawrence had already written his essay, for it was among the manuscripts of his I went through in Florence in 1930. I am sorry to destroy such ingenious critical theories as those excogitated to account for the existence of this essay; but those are the unexciting facts.

Not long after, I engaged myself to produce two vast translations for my old friend, Pascal Covici. One was a two-volume selection of the best of Remy de Gourmont's fifty or sixty books; the other a complete Boccaccio. I had had these two projects in mind for years, but the English publishers were afraid of them. Mr. Covici took them up blithely, and even agreed later on to a more stupendous project of translating the whole extant Greek drama. That was a grand idea while it lasted; but, owing to that little Wall Street episode of 1929, only the *Alcestis* was actually done. At the moment I can only admire the optimism, not to say cheek, of Pat Covici and myself for actually starting out so light-heartedly on such huge and difficult undertakings. As it was, we didn't do so badly— the combined Gourmont and Boccaccio must have run to three-quarters of a million words.

And then one day I was sitting as usual at my work table, which commanded a strategic view of the little private lane leading to my cottage. To my astonishment—for no visitors were expected that day—I saw a large car coming along. I was still more astonished when it stopped and slowly disgorged Jack Squire and a well-dressed urbane-looking gentleman who was totally unknown to me. This turned out to be Mr. Crosby Gaige of New York, who had acquired the costly but laudable hobby of producing unpublished works by his favourite authors in books designed by that great printer, Mr. Bruce Rogers. I was one of the authors honoured by Mr. Gaige's notice.

I realised at once that Mr. Gaige must be a man of iron will and energy if he could persuade Jack Squire to bring him to me on such an errand, and I listened favourably to his proposals. Unluckily, owing partly to the fact that I had recently published a volume of essays and another of poems, and partly because of my absurd obsession with honest work, I had nothing original to offer him. But there was one long-cherished "literary" project of mine, so apparently uneconomical that I had never even dared mention it to a publisher—namely, a collection of Romance lyric texts with translations and comments. I mentioned this unhopefully to Mr. Gaige, and to my surprise and delight he accepted it. But for Mr. Gaige this book would never have been done, and it happens to be the one I like best of all the products of my misguided "literary" energy. I am told that when Mr. Rogers saw the script, he refused at first to tackle such a complicated typographical problem. He had to deal with texts in Provençal, mediæval and Renaissance French, mediæval and Renaissance Italian; an English prose translation *en regard;* and introductory comments ranging from a few lines to a couple of pages. He solved the problem so admirably that when the book was later set up in England by Chatto and Windus (who prided themselves on their typography) they admitted there was nothing to do but to follow exactly what Mr. Rogers had done.

I hope these arid details of publishing will be forgiven, because they alone explain how it was that I was able to spend more and more time abroad, and eventually to stay there altogether except for an occasional brief visit to London. The liberty of travelling at will and living wherever whim takes you has to be paid for with hard cash. If I had merely written that I grew restless in England and eventually decided to live abroad, the reader might well exclaim: "Yes, but hold hard; a little while ago you were holding down jobs which you said gave you at most two months in the year abroad—how did you manage it?" Such a reader would share my prejudice against the novels where people engage in all kinds of uneconomic and more or less expensive activities, without a hint of how they are paid for.

My experience of life teaches me that the active portion of mankind is also the most intelligent and interesting. The most obvious fact about people with large private means is their remarkable dullness—which leads them to prey upon any vital person who comes their way—and their equally remarkable incapacity for interesting experience. They are so frightfully busy trying to amuse themselves that nothing ever happens to them. I seldom believe the startling things novelists tell me about the leisured classes. On the other hand, if a character in a novel or other book has a job, we naturally want to know how it panned out. Unluckily, my job is the over-exploited one of writing, which notoriously excites less public interest than such avocations as those of the country doctor, the criminal, the policeman, and the pugilist.

For the time being I had had enough of Italy and its inexhaustible past, and of the past of Europe; and turned all the more eagerly to the life of my own time and its creative centre, Paris. I am glad that the pattern of my life so arranged itself that I didn't go to live in Paris until I was well over thirty. By that time I was to some extent prepared to appreciate some of the many good things French civilisation and Paris have to offer, and armed against the dangers. If Paris were free again and itself—as it will be—I should still hesitate to advise a very young man or woman with gifts and ambitions to go there. I am not thinking of the so-called corruptions of Paris, which may be picked up in any large town by anyone who has tendencies that way. But there are two very insidious dangers. One is the confusion of styles and schools resulting from the almost frantic competition for notice in an over-crowded market, with the inevitable over-valuing of spurious novelty. And the other is the café life.

The Parisian café is an admirable invention of civilised life, but it must be used with caution, as the Frenchman uses it. It is so pleasant, so easy, so attractive, so perpetually varied, that quite insensibly it comes to occupy too much of the time of the unwary. The café type is unmistakable. He sits about for much of the day and night drinking and talking, severely critical of all work except that of his own little group, which he absurdly over-estimates, and holding forth at length on what ought to be done and what he is going to do, instead of doing it.

It seemed to me that after several years of strenuous work I was entitled to take a little ease in mine inn. I was still working practically every day, and never went to the café until the day's allotted task was done. Under the heading of my name the catalogues of the British Museum Library and the Library of Congress already had a considerable list of titles, which I knew would be added to. But in the cafés I would find the same groups of people, mostly rather younger than myself, all writers in theory, but with little or no tangible evidence of their genius in the shape of printed volumes. They wrote bits for advance-guard periodicals and sometimes collected them in little arty books, took in each other's artistic washing, and felt an Everest superiority to the writers who laboured to solve the difficult problem of interesting a non-professional public without betraying ideals and standards.

Many nationalities were represented in the café groups of

chatterers, but it seemed to me there were an unconscionable number of English and Americans among them. And I think the Americans succumbed to the café influence more often than the English. For one thing they were so much further from home, much more truly aliens in Paris—however deeply they understood and loved French civilisation—and hence much more dependent on each other's company. I have been thinking of all the Americans I met in Paris between 1927 and 1932, when I ceased to go there, and I remember only three who made a reputation in letters—Ernest Hemingway, Thomas Wolfe, and Hart Crane. The work of Hemingway and Wolfe in my judgment is at least as good as any contemporary European writing; but they were not typical Montparnasse or Montmartre expatriates. Tom Wolfe's heart and mind were always in America and he spent very little time in Paris; Hemingway was a success and got out long before the café had a chance of engulfing him.

Among the multitude of young Americans who, as far as I know, never got beyond the provincialism of time and place of the Montparnasse expatriate, I think with regret of one couple who may be taken as symbolical of many, though I was fonder of them than of others. They had a small allowance from Father, lived in a tiny apartment, had a very pretty baby, and led a quiet enough life. They were good companions, witty and amusing; and Andy was an original and entertaining talker. Moreover, it seemed to me that Andy's writing had a streak of genius. It was so promising, so tantalisingly near excellence, that you felt sure the next thing he did would really ring the bell. Unhappily, this never happened. Instead of writing naturally and simply from his own gifted nature, as I implored him, Andy would write silly stuff to please the café cliques. Andy and his very nice young wife were too sensible to be café loungers; yet in some inexplicable way the café ambience got him down.

There were other gifted Americans to whom Paris did no good. One evening early in 1929 I went with Donald Friede (then in partnership with Pat Covici) to a snob cabaret, founded by Cocteau, called *Le Bœuf sur le Toit*. As we were not in evening dress they hustled us downstairs to a table, where we sat talking. Suddenly there was a terrific rumpus at the entrance, and I heard Friede say:

"Good God! Here's a drunken American, with two French sailors."

I looked over, and got a worse shock myself. It was Hart Crane.

I had not been back to Montparnasse since I lived there for cheapness' sake in 1912. When in 1927 I had fixed myself up in a small apartment on the other side of the Luxembourg, I trotted off one evening to revisit that *scène de mes jeunes ébats*. When I reached that notorious *carrefour* of the Boulevard and the Rue de Rennes, I halted in something like consternation. The humble little restaurant I remembered with its floors sprinkled with sawdust had exploded into a vast gastronomic temple with brilliant lights and awnings; and instead of a *plat du jour* at seventy-five centimes there was each day a different regional menu at forty francs or thereabouts. The humble little cafés, where genuinely poor genuine artists spent a few sous a night, had not only monstrously expanded, but had seemingly multiplied. To my dazzled eyes it looked as if acres of café and sidewalk were covered with chattering multitudes; so that in one place and in one moment of time were gathered together nearly as many specimens of the genus would-be-artist as all Europe had produced of the genuine article since the fall of Troy. Coming fresh from my rustic solitudes and long communings with the mere talent of the past, I felt abashed by these thirsty legions of contemporary genius. I was surprised that so many people could afford to come to such palatial establishments so early in life, until I realised that this was the world's Barnum show of beachcombers and remittance men. How many fathers, I wonder, worked in offices during the long armistice all unwittingly to pay for drinks in the Dôme, the Rotonde, and the Coupole?

Yet I should be doing an injustice if I gave the impression that the majority of the many foreigners, particularly Americans, in Paris at that time were of this kind. Even among the café habitués there were people who had made reputations, and still more who were working hard enough without success. But, as I have indicated, there were far too many of the other kind. By way of contrast to these I should like to mention two very different types of American I knew in Paris.

Miss Natalie Barney is the "Amazone" of Remy de Gourmont's books, a nickname he gave her because of her skill and enthusiasm as a horsewoman. I suppose Miss Barney has at some time been in a café, but she is not the kind of person you would think of inviting to such a place. Her world was that meeting place of society and literature which is better understood and organised in Paris than anywhere. She really lived in the world of Paris, not in a little bit of America imported into Paris, and knew many French women distinguished either for talent or for social graces. She belongs to that small group of Americans, which includes the Symboliste poets Stuart Merrill and Francis Vielé-Griffin, who write in French. Many women in Paris attempt to found a salon; Miss Barney succeeded. Whether she were at home in the Rue Jacob or in her villa on the Riviera, you were certain to find there what are known as *des personnalités marquantes*.

The other was a man I will call William Ernest. Mr. Ernest also belonged to an old and wealthy American family, and was the most conscientiously educated person I have ever met. He was the sort of person who, long after he is an adult, takes a university degree in some hitherto untackled branch of knowledge, just to make sure that he knows about it. For many years the *Nouvelle Revue Française* issued one hundred specially printed copies of every book on its list to a hundred privileged subscribers. Naturally, Mr. Ernest had copies of every single issue. He seemed to read everything, not only in French and English, but in German, Spanish, and Italian. Eventually he acquired so many books and friends that he built a library and a guest-house on his estate outside Paris.

Unhappily, Mr. Ernest had inherited a 24-carat, A 1 at Lloyd's, New England conscience which governed his intellectual life as well as everything else. This unlucky conscience insisted that he employ one of those European architects who are so modern they might be described as premature. The style didn't harmonise very well with the 18th-century house already in existence; and the guest-house was so sonorous that a sneeze at one end of the house sounded like a thunder storm at the other. Moreover, the central heating was so very modern that when the owner attempted to live there himself during the winter he was discovered by a friend sitting in melancholy wise beside the radiator in a hat, overcoat, and muffler, knee-deep in straw; and eventually even with his iron will was beaten back by the rigours of 20th-century improvements to the comforts of the 18th century.

Mr. Ernest occasionally wrote, of course in a highly distinguished impeccable style, and of course in French. English was a language he used only in conversation and correspondence. A young Frenchman once listened to Mr. Ernest conversing with one of the highest Parisian brows on the *N.R.F.*, and solemnly reported:

"Ils sont tous les deux pour le purisme pur."

H. G. Wells once described the style of Henry James rather rudely as that of a hippopotamus trying to pick up a pea. Well, Mr. Ernest went one better—he tried to pick up a pea which wasn't there. I did my utmost to persuade one or other

288

of the London publishers to issue Mr. Ernest's works, suitably translated by somebody else into his mother tongue; but without success, and much to my regret, for the one thing Mr. Ernest wanted was the tenuous renown of an international highbrow. He was such a nice man, I should have been very happy to have been the humble means of achieving this end. For, with all his possessions, all his staggering culture, Mr. Ernest despaired of intellectual salvation. Predestination dogged him, he committed imaginary sins against the holy canons of French prose style, gehenna yawned for him, and Melancholy claimed him as her own. In spite of his infinite gentleness and good nature, I never succeeded in penetrating his reserve and dignity, never got anywhere near the point of being able to clap him cheerfully on the shoulder and say:

"Come, my lad, and drink some beer."

Yet I did once see Mr. Ernest happy, and that was when he did me the honour of staying for two or three days with me in a little cottage on the Mediterranean. Under the influence of that sea and sky he expanded into a serene geniality, swam and basked and for a time forgot all the woes of the highbrow. If only he could have drowned that New England conscience, he might have been the happiest of men as he was certainly one of the best and kindliest.

Paris . . . but no, it is time to start another chapter.

Chapter XVIII

1928 was for me a year of activity and change, a watershed of a year which set me moving in another direction. I still kept my Berkshire cottage, and spent part of the winter there; but I rather fretted at this, for it seemed to me that I had completely recovered from the effects of temporary heroism at the front and that retirement was no longer indicated as the proper treatment. Before taking the long-meditated but grave step of quitting England "for ever," I thought I ought to try myself on London again. George Gribble's play, *The Masque of Venice*, was to be produced by Marie Tempest; which provided a sufficient excuse, if one was needed.

I can't say that I disliked my stay in London—my mood was too exuberant—but I decided against living in it. I saw so many people that I have forgotten now whom I did see. What annoyed me in the London highbrows was their tacit and self-satisfied assumption that I had at last recovered my senses, and had returned belatedly but repentantly to the one true source of wisdom, knowledge, and fame; viz., themselves. As Mehitabel the cat so wisely remarked: Wotthehell, wotthehell? I could never see the enormous benefits which one was supposed to reap from their company and conversation, which was too often a loftier version of the village tea-fight in that it consisted chiefly of local gossip. From a general point of view what is the difference between hearing that the Vicar woke up one morning to find in his bed (tee-hee) a hedgehog (ha, ha); and hearing that Betty Wondershoon, who wrote that divahn book about the Syrian brothel—my dear, you *must* read it—

also woke up one morning and instead of Bobby in her bed (tee-hee) found her long-lost and much-forgotten husband (ha, ha)? Again, what is the difference between the feverish anxiety of the village to know the people who will "lead the season" and the feverish anxiety to be a little ahead of others in throwing over last season's intellectual heroes and patronising this season's? And when it comes to putting words on paper, why not a few sprouts of one's own invention?

So, as soon as I thought the Parisians would have turned off their super-heating furnaces and have permitted a few gasps of air to enter their fusty rooms, I returned to Paris.

I ought to explain "the exuberant mood" mentioned above. It was like a second youth—second childhood, if you prefer— at thirty-five. I was twenty-two when the war started, going on for twenty-seven when I was demobilised; and the next three years were pretty much nose-to-the-grindstone. I missed most of my twenties, when most people have a lot of fun. Certainly, I didn't do so badly in the way of good times, as these pages show, but there was a repressed young man under my sedate exterior clamouring to be heard. I let him be heard. And why not? Yet that year I earned over £1000.

This was partly because of Mr. Gaige, partly because I had royalties on books already written, and largely because I was able to work much more quickly than when I was obfuscated by military barbarism in 1919. For instance, I wrote a new translation of Voltaire's *Candide* in ten days. A sloppy piece of work? Perhaps. But the ordinary English edition of that translation is still in print; it has twice been pirated in America (without my name); it was chosen by John Lane for an illustrated edition, by the Nonesuch Press for their impression, and was once held in a film by Greta Garbo—I saw the title in a close-up. If that isn't success, you tell me what is.

One result of idling in Paris that spring—by which I mean

I didn't work more than four hours a day, which, all said and done, is idling from the point of view of the real working world—was a sudden and unpremeditated access of writing poetry. One of the things I wrote pleased me. I enjoyed writing it; it was long enough to make a book by itself; it was constructed; it broke all the rules for modern poetry by having a beginning, a middle, and an end and by being comprehensible. It could not without injustice have the label of any school or clique pinned on it.

All my friends who were supposed to know about these things said it was rotten, and advised me not to publish it. If I wished to retain any slight reputation I had, they said, I ought to destroy it at once. Much abashed, I hid it away; and then a couple of years later happened to turn it up when I was in a Mehitabel the cat mood, and fired it off to Chatto's and Pat Covici. It was called *A Dream in the Luxembourg*.

That summer Lawrence published *Lady Chatterley's Lover*, a grave error from the point of view of *his* reputation, as the Huxleys, I believe, tried to tell him. But once the book was out, there was nothing to do but support it, especially as those infallible critics, the policemen of England and America, were trying to destroy it. For a series of reasons too complicated to explain I was temporarily back in my English cottage; and naturally undertook to help distribute the book to subscribers. This was very easy, since I was constantly receiving and sending off books. The fact that I rendered myself liable to a fine or even imprisonment didn't trouble me in the least. Every writer worth his salt knows that he and other writers are serving—or ought to try to serve—a higher cause than any government; human civilisation, which owes precious little to governments. Since, as I have already mentioned, censorship and suppression of books were invented by the Borgias, who doubtless had their own reasons for so behaving, it shouldn't have been allowed to go any further. The whole conception is theocratic, and has no place in the common law of a free country.

One trouble with *Lady Chatterley* is that it isn't a very good novel. And Lorenzo showed a strange lack of artistic tact in trying to revive in their primitive Anglo-Saxon sense certain words which have unhappily acquired associations of vulgarity and vice. Many writers and readers are aware of the associations of meaning which in an ancient language like ours inevitably cluster round words. Indeed, part of the fun of writing is to arrange words so that an attentive reader will enjoy suggested overtones and undertones. But no writer can present his readers with words super-charged with associations, and expect them to be ignored. It takes a thundering puritan to attempt such a fantastic and hopeless task with grave sincerity.

Still, I saw clearly what Lawrence was trying to do and approved his intention; so I had no difficulty in writing him favourably about *Lady Chatterley*. Apparently, all but five of his other friends took the opposite view, and said so with that wounding frankness one seldom experiences from one's worst enemies. Naturally Lawrence welcomed my support, and wrote me a long letter in which he urged me to tell everybody what a great book it was, "a feather in the cap of the twentieth century"; and naturally I neither did nor should use such a silly phrase. Judge of my delight when I read his *Letters* and found he had written round to other people: "Richard Aldington says *Lady C.* is a feather in the cap of the twentieth century."

The sudden blaze of notoriety and influx of money which came to Lawrence after the publication of this book remind me of a passage written by Sir Richard Burton shortly after he issued his *Arabian Nights*. I can't trace the exact words, but they ran something like this:

"For thirty years I served Her Majesty at home and abroad, without acknowledgement or reward. I publish a pornographic book, and at once earn ten thousand pounds and fame. I begin at last to understand the public and what it wants."

Those who live through an epoch necessarily have a different idea of its literary and artistic achievements from those who come after. Within half a century or less the whole output has been rigorously hand-picked, imitators and mediocrities ruthlessly cast out, and a coherent scheme imposed. These judgments in turn are subject to revision and fluctuations of taste. But such arrangements, apparently so obvious in retrospect, are by no means clear at the time, particularly in such an epoch as the long armistice which was marked by an enormous output of literary and artistic work. In my judgment the 1920s formed a brilliant but anarchic period fully deserving both in a bad and good sense its favourite adjective, "amusing." The ideals and differences of artists were largely æsthetic only. In reaction, the 1930s gave themselves up to political fanaticisms, and were consequently duller and less sincere—they all quacked what the big doctrinaire duck trumpeted. Moreover, the decade became more and more clouded with menaces and fears, so that many artists were tempted beyond the boundaries of their legitimate activities; and in some countries were forced over them.

But the mere volume of production, especially in the 1920s, was baffling. So many new books poured in on me that I could not possibly have read them if I had given my whole time to the task. As I was mostly occupied with books of earlier epochs, I could only take a lucky dip here and there; and on my shelves were many uncut books I hoped some day to read, but never did. Moreover, while I was in Paris I saw thousands and thousands of new pictures by hundreds of artists. In both cases I could only admire in silence the omniscience of the critics who knew exactly what was and was not significant in this chaos; but as they often differed among themselves, they were not very helpful, at any rate to me. So I was forced back onto personal preferences, which in turn owe a good deal to chance and friendships. Therefore, I shall not attempt any description of the art and literature of that time. For one thing it would be interminable; and then I know too much to be dogmatic, too little to be encyclopædic.

I now regret that too close an observance of *The Times* ban against reviewing personal friends led me to decline repeatedly the civilities of French authors. Bruce Richmond did not raise the slightest objection to my living much of the year in Paris, so I naturally felt all the more bound to be scrupulous. Even so I received a great many inscribed books, sometimes rather fulsome in expression. A favourite formula was: *"Au grand poète, au critique avisé."* I dare say these over-appreciative authors wondered why *The Times* so seldom reviewed their books.

Luckily this ban did not apply to James Joyce, whom I saw from time to time. Unfortunately I have little of interest to report, since we established no intimacy, and I soon limited myself to a formal visit of respect on reaching and before leaving Paris. Mr. Joyce struck me as a man of great personal dignity with a fine ascetic face, but thrown back on himself by partial or complete blindness. He was very much the vogue at the time, and surrounded by followers who, I thought, seemed rather jealous of each other. On the other hand one must recognise their devotion in reading to or otherwise amusing their incapacitated hero.

I admired *Ulysses* as a work of originality and power, though I thought it over-laboured and prolix in parts, and more uniformly filled with pessimism and disgust than is justified by the experience of life. If the last paragraph of the book may be interpreted as saying "Yes" to life in spite of everything, it is too brief and belated after so many hundreds of pages of "No." And I lost interest in Joyce when he invented a complicated and polyglot language of his own, which concealed rather than expressed what he had to say. Just as *Ulysses* suffered from an excess of disgust typical of its epoch, so the fragments of this new book showed the other defect of a wilful darkness and difficulty, a veil not of profundity but of emptiness. It was a device for concealing the fact that the author had nothing more to say.

In those days *Ulysses* was banned in America and England, so it was obligatory as soon as one arrived in Paris to buy a copy from the publisher, Miss Sylvia Beach, in the Rue de l'Odéon. It was there that I ran into Ernest Hemingway. Just opposite was the French book shop of Mlle. Adrienne Monnier, who published the French version of *Ulysses* in the admirable translation by Valéry Larbaud. It is surprising that the Paris municipality, with its passion for honouring artists by giving their names to streets, didn't change the Rue de l'Odéon to Rue James Joyce.

Among the Frenchmen I did not feel disbarred from knowing personally was Jean Paulhan, editor of the *Nouvelle Revue Française*. One morning during the summer of 1928 I received a letter from him, in which he offered to lend me for the months of October and November the *vigie* of Port Cros, which he and some friends had rented from the French government. A *vigie* is a small look-out fort with a signal station, and there are several obsolete *vigies* on the French Riviera. Port Cros is the middle one of the three islands of Hyères, and from M. Paulhan's description sounded both remote and beautiful. From the very accurate plan of accommodation he sent, I saw there was plenty of room; and eventually arranged with the Lawrences and another old friend in London that we should all meet there for the autumn.

I took a rather devious way to Marseille. First, I went to Florence and out to Vallombrosa, to stay with an old university friend who had been very ill. Then we went on, and stayed a few days at his villa in Rome. The weather was hot, and I contemplated with distaste the long railway journey, which involves a lengthy crawl along the whole of the two Rivieras and that unpleasant customs office at Ventimiglia. Therefore I decided to go to Naples and take a boat to Marseille.

I remember little of Vallombrosa except its beautiful cool woods and a baroque church containing innumerable relics of I know not how many holy hermits; and that I met an otherwise uninteresting Italian who ate living ants and said they were *molto rinfrescanti*. Either Milton never went there or the character of the woods has entirely changed since he wrote "thick as leaves in Vallombrosa," for the trees now are nearly all pines.

The sea voyage was a great success. We had perfect weather, and our ship was a large freighter carrying cargo, so that it was slow and very steady. The journey took three days, but we were seldom out of sight of some mountainous coastline or picturesque island such as Monte Cristo and Elba, and we had a fine view of part of the Corsican coast. We stopped to deliver cargo at San Maurizio, and in view of the guaranteed purity of "finest Lucca oil" I was interested to see about two hundred barrels of Greek olive oil consigned to that city. Unlike the famous orange gardens of Seville which don't exist, there are olive gardens near Lucca; but not enough, I think to provide the enormous amount of Lucca oil on the market. We also carried, loose, a great quantity of white haricot beans into the mass of which the stevedores frequently expectorated and blew their noses; since when I tend to avoid that otherwise harmless vegetable.

We duly picked up our friend at Marseille, and got on a crowded train for Toulon, in doing which I learned a subtle stroke of French policy—namely, that if you wish to reserve three seats on a train by *force majeure*, you must employ not

K*

one but two porters. Such complexities would never occur to the Anglo-Saxon mind, but they are the very essence of French liberty, which consists in a precise and minute definition of rights. Have I not heard a small Parisian boy gravely reprove a horse which was standing with its fore-hoofs on the sidewalk with the words: *"Contravention, mon vieux"*? Only the Jews, I think, have been as pertinaciously legalistic in their efforts to define what is pleasing to God as the French in their hitherto hopeless efforts to find lucid and precise definitions of all liberties.

Eventually we arrived at our jumping-off place, the Salins d'Hyères, by the five-mile-an-hour local express, long after sunset on an exceedingly dark night. As I leaned from the bedroom window of the inn which Paulhan had recommended, it seemed to me built straight out of the Mediterranean, for I could distinctly hear little waves clopping against the base of the wall. Dawn showed it was merely built on the edge of a tiny enclosed port—a *darse*, as they call it in Provence. In the distance we could see the lovely wooded islands; but very nearly never got to them at all. The very *méridional* captain of the motor boat dramatically started his engine without posting anyone at the tiller, and we started rushing full tilt at the stone quay; but with the aid of sundry explosive *"Merrrde alorrrs!"* and *"'Crrré nom d'un nom!"* the collision was reduced to a minor one. Incidentally, the same boat on the way back stalled its engine in a heavy sea with a rising mistral, and gave us some awkward moments before it responded to the usual verbal treatment.

Hitherto I had avoided the French Riviera, on the theory that it was frequented by the kind of people I most wished to avoid. But at that date the Côte des Maures was practically unspoiled, and Port Cros has virtually remained so. Moreover, since April, May, June, October, and November are the loveliest months of the year in that climate, the smarties naturally never came then. The habitations of Port Cros consist of one hotel, one chateau, thirteen fisherman's cottages, and two or three old forts converted into residences; so you may imagine how popular it is with the cocktail-bar crowd. The *vigie* was six hundred feet above the sea, a mile and a half from the nearest cottage, and looked over stupendous vistas of Mediterranean and mountainous coast. The island itself is broken into steep ridges and valleys, covered with magnificent Mediterranean pines, strawberry trees, wild lavender, rosemary, lentisk, cistus, and other aromatic plants and herbs; so that on a hot October afternoon the gentle sea air seemed scented with fresh incense. It bred all kinds of rare flowers, plants, insects, and even fungi almost extinct on the mainland. And we had it practically to ourselves.

For sheer natural beauty and climate I know nothing to equal this island; and I was not surprised in later years when the great French Hellenist, Victor Bérard, told me he spent as much time as he could there because it was like Greece before the various barbarians destroyed the country. We were able to bathe almost every day in a remote uninhabited bay, fringed on the landward side by wild canes and blocked on either flank by steep wooded cliffs. The walk down and back was under tall feathery pines and strawberry trees, thick with clusters of round fruit which pass through a whole range of colour from clear lemon through orange to a rich red. Through gaps in the branches we had glimpses of the island, the sea, and distant coastline. As there were no roads on the island there were no vehicles, and our water and provisions came up on Jasper, the donkey, who was governed by a Sicilian man-servant.

Meanwhile, what had happened to the Lawrences? Frieda, it appeared, was in Italy closing down their establishment at Scandicci; a complicated process, since it involved a journey to Trieste. Lawrence was at Lavendou, waiting for her, watching the fishermen play *boules* and finding out local gossip—a plenteous field. Eventually they turned up. It sounds ungracious to say so, but we had a better and more harmonious time before they arrived. The fact is that Lorenzo's T.B. was active and he was far too ill to take any part in our expeditions or indeed to rough it in so remote and exposed a place. I used to listen to his dreadful hollow cough at night, and wonder what on earth I should do if he got worse—how I could get him carried down a mile and a half of steep rocky path, transported across twelve miles of sea in an open boat, and thence to a sanatorium. Luckily his marvellous vitality made yet another recovery, but naturally he was not in the best of spirits and apt to be bad-tempered. His talk also was too often on a lower level than his best, too personal and satirical, sharp with the reckless hatred of those about to die.

We did our best to make him comfortable, but as somebody had always to stay with him, our long bathing expeditions were rather spoiled. Moreover, just at this moment when he needed quiet and gentleness, his publishers elected to send him an enormous wodge of English press cuttings about *Lady Chatterley*. We read them one evening sitting in front of a pine-log fire. I have never seen such an exhibition of vulgarity, spite, filth, and hatred as was contained in those innumerable diatribes. Every editor and peddling reviewer had eagerly seized the opportunity to vilify and if possible crush into ignominy and poverty a man who had done—what? Publish a book whose obvious intention was to rescue sex from prudery and nastiness. Now, we writers may be fools, but we are not such utter fools as to be taken in by such stuff. I had lived with men, I knew what their talk and lives were, I knew the cynicism and depravity of journalists, I knew some of the men who had written this malevolent twaddle; and I knew they were not worthy to black Lawrence's boots.

So far as I was concerned that was the last turn of the screw. I thought it vile that, without one protest, the whole press should unite in pouring out insults, innuendoes, and abuse on a man of Lawrence's integrity and gifts, one of the very few original English writers of his time. I wanted to dissociate myself sharply from such people.

It seems to me one up to Lawrence that he went tranquilly on with his writing although he was so ill, and was angry and bitter about the attacks on him in England. Every morning he sat up in bed, wearing an old hat as protection against an imaginary draught, and produced a short story or one of the little essays of *Assorted Articles*. I remember his writing an article on a book of Mr. Morris Ernst in the blank leaves of the copy which Mr. Ernst sent him. He must also have been working secretly on *Pansies,* for two of them were inspired by books he read on the island. One was Aldous Huxley's *Point Counter Point* and the other a book on Attila from the pile of new French books I had with me. He enjoyed the Attila book very much, as it jumped with a temporary mood of destructiveness in him.

In spite of my anxiety about Lawrence's illness and the disagreeables resulting from it, I was very happy on Port Cros and full of energy. The complete detachment of the place and almost complete leisure (I had only one article a week and the Boccaccio translation in hand) enabled me to make a real start on my long-cherished project of a novel about the war, the old war of 1914–18. Some of the main themes and emotions I had already put down in poems, but I wanted to do a prose book on a larger scale. As I have mentioned, I wrote and destroyed part of such a book in 1919; and in 1925 and 1927 I made other abortive starts. It was lucky that I didn't get it done sooner, for the book eventually came out as the boom in war books was in full swing.

I was held up by several considerations during those years 1919–28. Though I didn't realise it, time was needed for the assimilation and arrangement of these experiences. I was always occupied with other work, and did not feel justified in taking time to write a long book which I didn't think anyone would publish. Moreover, I doubted my own abilities. I knew what I wanted to do. I wanted to give free expression to the feelings and ideas of one very minor actor in that great tragedy, but I wanted to do this in terms of satire. I wanted the writing to give the effect of the different movements of a symphony. And I wanted the construction to follow the main lines of a Greek tragedy, with the catastrophe fully revealed in the prologue, to avoid any cheap effects of surprise. The plot was to be revealed in the first pages, so that if anybody read on it would not be for the trivial purpose of finding out what happened, but because they were interested in what I had to say and the way I said it.

Now, thanks to Gaige, Covici and Friede, and my own efforts, I could afford to spend time on writing a long book for its own sake; for I was convinced no publisher would want it. The project was very much in my mind on the boat going up to Marseille and during the first weeks on Port Cros. Indeed I found that unconsciously I had irritated my companions by continually humming over the old war songs. Quite suddenly one morning I discovered that what had held me up was the failure to hit the right keynote in the opening sentence—so important in every long book. A sentence came into my mind: "The casualty lists went on appearing for a long time after the Armistice—last spasms of Europe's severed arteries." The effect was like that of moving the key log in a lumber jam on a river. The moment I had that sentence down, the whole book began to flow with irresistible force; and I had nothing to do but write it down each morning until I felt tired. I wrote the prologue and part one in ten days, and then stopped dead. The mysterious sense of somebody dictating vanished, and I was prudent enough not to force the pace.

It was interesting to see the reaction of the others to this piece of writing. Lawrence was entirely against it, gave me the now familiar warning that if I published it I should lose what little reputation I had, and added the original threat that I was evidently on the way to an insane asylum. One never knows; but that was twelve years ago, and I have managed to keep at large so far. As a matter of fact I took this for what it was—the querulousness of a very sick man. The women, on the other hand, were for the book, especially Frieda. I shall always feel grateful to her for the encouragement and indeed inspiration she gave at that critical time. An author is wise to knock off about ninety-five per cent of all commendations made to his face, but it was impossible to doubt Frieda's momentary sincerity and enthusiasm.

In November the weather deteriorated. We had mistrals; and then a wet southern wind from the sea which smothered us in cloud so much that Lawrence said it was *"sciroccissimo"*; and indeed it was. For my part, I liked Port Cros so much and was in such excellent health that I should have been glad to stay the whole winter there—never before had I known the experience of living in natural surroundings of almost perfect beauty without the intrusion of any unwanted humans. The only people who bothered us were some French staff officers who came to investigate the suspicious alien character, Lawrence, and weren't allowed by me to see him. But they only came once, and evidently regarded the matter as absurd. It was a wrench for me to leave, but I saw Lawrence couldn't stand the exposure any longer and must be taken to the mainland, doctors, and central heating at once.

I said good-bye to Lawrence in the ugly little salon of the Select Hotel just opposite the station at Toulon. I never saw him again, for our paths went in different directions, and within sixteen months he was dead. Yet in the hundreds of times I have since passed the windows of that room I have never failed to think of Lawrence—a remarkable man, the most interesting human being I have known.

Chapter XIX

AFTER Port Cros everywhere else seemed dull and over-populated. I got rid of my Berkshire cottage, and rather fool-ishly sold my excellent library. But I was so determined to get free from all shackles that I was prepared for any sacrifice. Then, having done this, I remained in Paris, rather at a loose end. My recipe for that state of mind, on the rare occasions I have suffered from it, is to do a little work. Unfortunately, my daimon refused to go on with the war novel, so I thought I'd make up some of my arrears of work for *The Times,* which I had rather neglected. Presently I got a letter from Richmond saying: Go easy, in the last ten days you've sent us in more articles than we can use in two months. So there was nothing to do but trot on with Boccaccio, who fortunately is a volumi-nous author. I also wrote a little satire on Christmas greetings, which Nancy Cunard printed for me on her private press near Vernon. Sent out judiciously, it got rid of a lot of rather tire-some acquaintances.

I also went to a night club—a *boite*—a thing I had never done in Paris before, strange as it may sound. Indeed, I think the only one I had ever been to was an underground pre-war con-traption in Regent Street; and I only went there because Ezra took me; and he only knew about because it had been deco-rated by our friend, Wyndham Lewis, and was run by one of the relicts of the late Strindberg. But while cabarets charge far too much for their champagne, they are not unamusing occa-sionally, and a little section of modern life one ought to see. It is instructive, for instance, to make a mental comparison between the music and dancing they provide and that of an 18th-century salon.

One morning I emerged from my hotel, and felt on my face a light but freezing cold air. I knew from experience what that portended; another cold spell like that of 1916–17 when we nearly froze to death in the trenches and the war was practically suspended while everybody on both sides had pleurisy. I forget who had given me the misinformation that Rapallo was warm in the coldest winters—nowhere in Europe is warm in a cold winter, except possibly the northern Hebrides—but thither I departed in haste. It was less cold in Rapallo, for a time; but eventually snow lay deep on the hills behind and crept down until it touched the lapping edge of the Mediterranean.

Ezra Pound of course was there, and entertained us at his tennis club. Yeats, too, was there, drawn irresistibly, one was given to understand, into the orbit of the greater genius. Ezra expressed surprise not unmingled with scorn at learning that I sat down to work every morning, but was his usual genial and modest self. George Antheil turned up, flying from a Berlin where the temperature was about forty-five below; and for a day Ezra vanished. Meeting him after lunch next day I asked where he had been, and he answered importantly that he had been "in conference" with Antheil; adding with impressive gravity that he had been amazed to find that the two greatest minds in Europe had been thinking on the same lines. I must admit that Ezra's conversation gave me one or two useful hints for the satirical passages in the second part of my novel.

My hotel window had a fine view of the esplanade, and I sometimes saw Yeats taking his daily constitutional, so wrapped in contemplation that he ought to have been as invisible as Æneas in the golden cloud of Venus. Once I saw him emerge to consciousness of the actual world, and that was to join a small crowd watching a spirited dog fight. On another occasion, for as far as he was visible from my lofty perch, he walked with sublime unconsciousness at just about two paces behind a pretty wench, who trotted along casting come-hither glances over her shoulder, evidently in an agony of impatience for the rich Irish senator to make improper advances. Luckless female. It was evident that Yeats was entirely unaware of her existence and that, if it had been humanly possible, they might have walked round the earth in their respective positions without his ever perceiving her—"the god pursuing the maiden hid."

I have no idea how long the cold lasted in Rapallo, but it was still there when I left late in February to see Donald Friede in Paris. I somewhat loudly beshrewed him for being in Paris in such uneasy weather, but as the train rushed north the air grew warmer, and Paris was positively genial. With the characteristic frugality of the American in Paris Friede had established himself at Foyot's; though, to be just, the rooms there were inexpensive, and it was only the restaurant which took the heart out of your pocket-book for a month or so. When I dropped in to see Friede I found him in conversation with two strange ladies, one of whom was dressed with a severity of taste I can only qualify as masculine. They turned out to be Lady Trowbridge and her friend, Miss Radclyffe Hall, who was being prosecuted in England and America for publishing *The Well of Loneliness.*

Friede and I discussed various plans for books, and then he asked me if I had any other work done. This reminded me of my unfinished novel; and after I had described its plan Friede asked to see it. I hesitated, as I had only one second copy, and he was just off to London by some patent method of his own via Dunkirk and Tilbury. But it seemed a good idea to get a publisher's opinion on my reckless adventure towards the insane asylum; so I handed him the script. Two or three days later I was a little startled to receive from London a long cable such as only Americans send, in which Friede expressed the warmest interest in the book and bade me get on with it at once. How often since then have I blessed the impulse in him which dictated that warm-hearted cable, and still more the readiness with which he gave me an advance on the book out of his own pocket (having spent all the firm's money he had with him) and with no more contract than my bare word that the book should be completed as soon as possible. It is likely that if Friede hadn't been willing to take that chance (remember only about a quarter of the book was written) and given me that tangible vote of confidence, I might never have finished the book, and so should have missed my opportunity.

Friede's slap on the back was what I needed. My highly encouraged daimon again began dictating at a furious speed, and the book galloped off the typewriter. On the last day I wrote without a break for eight hours, and finished the book feeling a little dazed after its emotional tempests. I wandered about the streets for a time, feeling as if my legs would telescope at any moment, and then dropped in on a young American friend, who contemplated me with a critical eye and then silently mixed and handed me a tremendous eggnog, after which I felt very much better.

By writing *Death of a Hero* I purged my bosom of perilous stuff which had been poisoning me for a decade. When I had finished, had said my say and cussed my cusses, I felt the lightness and tranquillity of a morning after a thunder storm. In fact as I had temporarily written myself out and thought I had nothing more to say, it seemed the appropriate moment to retire to a monastery of French Benedictine Maurists and ask to be allowed to work in a humble anonymous way on their monumental history of French literature. There were a good many obstacles to this, including the insuperable one that the genuine Maurists no longer exist. So I remained in Paris waiting for my proofs.

It is a fact, I think, that the literary life has become more strenuous than it was in the mid-19th century. I recollect reading, in the life of some Victorian worthy, this impressive sentence: "The whole of this summer was spent in the active labour of correcting proofs of his new book"; the work in question being about a hundred pages. A whole summer, you observe. Now, when the delays of the French customs had operated as usual, I found I had exactly twenty-four hours to read and correct the 140,000 words of my novel, and deposit the packet in the late mail bag for the *Mauretania* at the Gare Saint-Lazare. I went to the Café Voltaire, and worked continuously from 10 a.m. to 10 p.m., drinking a good deal of coffee, and having my meals served as I worked. I chose the Café Voltaire because it was old-fashioned and not expensive, and served excellent food and wine, which caused it to be entirely neglected by everyone likely to interrupt me.

I then went to La Rochelle, because I had never seen it advertised as a resort. It proved to be a picturesque place, with the old harbour and watch towers left much as they were at the conclusion of the famous siege. Even the great chain which for so long guarded the inner harbour was still there, or rather the broken sections of it. The whole place was still dominated by memories of that epic resistance. There was one drawback to La Rochelle. I have stayed in every one of the old provinces of France, and the district of La Rochelle is the only one where the food is coarse and unpalatable. Their idea of *hors d'œuvre* for instance, was to serve raw artichokes, little green crabs, and sandy cockles. I can only account for it on the theory that the restaurant-keepers are under the impression that the siege is still in progress, and arrange their menus accordingly. But I have seldom seen a more lively and coloured scene than the old port, with brown-sailed fishing smacks moving in and out, the stone quays covered with brilliant blue nets while others were draped over the moored vessels to dry in the sun, and fishermen lounging about or working in patched trousers and blouses of brown, rusty red, and blue. These men were poor and lived a hard dangerous life, but they were healthy and gay, singing and whistling and laughing; a strange contrast to the over-fed, well-paid labourers of Switzerland, who look as glum as undertakers and as resentful as men unjustly condemned to the gallows.

We tried one or two small seaside places near La Rochelle, but they had the dreary shack look of such seasonal hangouts the world over; moreover, the weather was uncertain, and the receding tide left an enormous expanse of oozy mud. I thought longingly of Port Cros; and on an impulse took the train for Toulon.

The quai de Cronstadt at Toulon is open only to pedestrians, and it has just one little hotel where the front bedrooms have a superb view of the inner port and wooded flanks of the bay. The changing colours of the bay are a perpetual delight in themselves, and there is a bustle of little navy launches and ferry boats. The shops sell souvenirs for sailors, including boxes with shells on them and wicked-looking knives inscribed in Italian: "May my wound be mortal." You can lunch or dine in front of restaurants on the quay itself, and be constantly amused by the passing of people and the coming and going of little boats. Moreover, Toulon is a distinctly literate community, and has several very good book shops. In the tiny squares of the old town are fountains, covered with dripping moss and plants, with flower stalls in front of them. And along another street is a long open-air market, with countless stalls of brilliantly coloured fruits, vegetables, and flowers.

Unluckily, only a rather perverse ascetic who desired to mortify himself would bathe in the waters near Toulon; so we looked for an unfashionable bathing place. The Lawrences had left Bandol for the mountains, and the beach there suggested a large semi-nudist camp. Eventually I found a tiny hamlet on a large *calanque* not far from Toulon, and there I spent the rest of the summer, swimming a great deal, walking in the scented *maquis*, translating the *Alcestis* and writing short stories on war themes—a kind of hangover from *Death of a Hero*. The days went by serenely, with cloudless skies and crystal clear water and little excursions, the sort of easy idling time one would like to last for ever. And then suddenly these calm waters were ruffled by a breeze from the outer world.

One day late in September an American mail came in with two very large envelopes stuffed with press clippings. They were all either violently for or against *Death of a Hero*—just the kind of press one wants. But on counting them up I discovered to my consternation that the first two days of clippings had cost about thirty dollars. I therefore cabled Friede to stop them at once, and asked how the book was going. He replied that he had sold five thousand, had a reprint just off the press and another ordered, and that the novel was a best-seller in—I forget which cities. This was interesting news. I had decided that if this novel failed, I would have to return to the literary vomit; but that if it succeeded I would write some more, and I already had two in mind.

Before making any final decision, I wanted to know what had happened to the book in England. Friede had asked me to give first refusal to Chatto and Windus, with whom he wanted to establish good relations. I agreed, of course, but not very hopefully. Chatto and Windus had a high reputation, but as their authors were people like Marcel Proust, Aldous Huxley, David Garnett, Roger Fry, Clive Bell, I didn't think they would like my plain and simple tale. But the partners of the firm, Charles Prentice and Harold Raymond, were both ex-soldiers, and therefore rather enjoyed my invectives. At any rate, they promptly accepted the book on my terms, and Prentice wrote a very amiable letter.

For some reason the English edition was scheduled for two weeks after the American; and as the summer weather had broken, I thought I might as well trot up to Paris to be nearer the scene of operations. I arrived on a warm September evening, and after dinner sat at a table outside the Closerie des Lilas under the trees of the Petit Luxembourg. It was a pleasant scene. Here and there an electric light showed a vivid patch of autumn leaves in the dark trees. Waiters bustled about with a clatter of saucers and glasses; the buzz of talk was woven in and out with the noise of traffic on the boulevards and snatches of dance tunes from the Bal Tabarin. Some Quartier types, straight out of Anatole France's *Le Chat Maigre,* were settling the future of art. One could follow the classic argument without listening: "There's the idea behind my beer-mug and the idea in front of my beer-mug. What we've got to do is bring them together in a synthesis of genius. *Garçon! Deux demi-blonds.*"

Presently a man came up to our table and joined us. This was Tom McGreevy, an Irishman I had met once or twice at Joyce's, who had crossed from England that day. Among other news he told me that "all London"—it may have been "all England"—was talking about my book. Making the usual deductions in such cases, I assumed Tom had heard it abused over a dinner-table. Although, as our friend A. S. Frere once remarked, Tom McGreevy is five hundred per cent Irish, he had served as a gunner officer in the B.E.F. in France; and therefore was well disposed towards my little efforts at reviving common memories. Since he has more than his share of Irish wit and charm, and is highly literate, we spent a pleasant evening. He is an admirable exponent of the almost lost art of conversation, and therefore I grappled him to my soul with hoops of steel—the first and certainly one of the best beloved of the many friends made for me by *Death of a Hero*.

When I arrived at Cook's next morning for my mail, the clerk handed me such a large package of letters and telegrams I thought at first he must have given me by mistake the begging-letter mail of a visiting millionaire. But no, they were for me; and I carried them to the nearest café. With the self-centred vanity of the true artist, I first hunted through this mass for letters from Chatto and Windus, easily recognisable because they modestly use the head of Pallas Athene as their crest. The news was reassuring—a modest subscription of only 1600, but such a rapid crescendo of "repeats" that they had already decided to order a second 5000 copies. The press, as was natural and I had expected, was hostile; with the very important exception of Arnold Bennett, the only English reviewer in my experience who could induce people to read the books he praised. I read the telegrams and letters from friends, glanced through the letters of abuse or commendation from strangers, noted with pleasure a kindly letter from H. G. Wells with an invitation to come and see him; and then leaned back and lit a cigarette.

That was a pleasant moment. I am careful never to count chickens before they are hatched, but a far more resolute pessimist than I am would have been contented by that batch of mail. The figures cabled and written by Friede and Prentice showed that in less than a week my book had earned its advances and was making me about sixty dollars a day. Put into francs it sounded quite impressive, though possibly not to Mr. Ford. Exactly twenty years had elapsed since my first poem crept into print in an obscure periodical. In my life I had verified the prophecy of a pacifist Canadian soap-box orator, who in or about 1912 had exultantly informed me that in this world "potes have a helluva long furrow to hoe." True indeed, O voice of the brave new world which wants to get there quickly, but how if one takes pride in hoeing the long sterile

furrow that yields at last? I could at least say that I had flattered
no man and no party, had used no intrigue or influence, had
said my say right or wrong without fear or favour to anything
or anyone on earth, respecting only the memory of great men
and those ideals of civilisation I had learned from the masters.
I had started on my own way early in life against the wishes of
my family and the advice of older friends; I had persevered in
spite of many obstacles and interruptions; and I had never bor-
rowed or been given a cent since I was twenty-one. If I had
succeeded in interesting a portion of the very little world
which reads new books, and receiving the tangible expression
of their interest in pounds and dollars, I owed it to my own
unceasing efforts. There was a time in the world when governments and men of power in the world thought it a pleasure and
a duty to assist men of letters. From governments I had received little but demands for taxes and military service, and
various restrictions on the elementary privilege of moving
about the world at will. Like Samuel Johnson, I could say: "I
never had a patron." I was aware that there was a fortuitous
element in the success of a war book at that time, but I thought
I'd now probably be able to write some of the other novels I
had in mind.

Et zut alors—that's what happens on a fine autumn morning
in Paris when the small-town boy makes good.

There I rather naïvely supposed the matter would rest. I
made no change in my way of life, for I was already living as I
wished to live—a process one cannot begin too early. But I did
decide to take a real vacation of several months without doing
any work at all—a plan I failed to carry out in its integrity. I
went to rather better restaurants, and did a little modest ex-
ploration of vintage wines, but otherwise I remained in that
mobile and unencumbered state which befits a pilgrim. It was
just as well that I had decided not to do any writing for a time,

for, what with the number of friends who turned up and the amount of mail I received, I was kept pretty busy. Never had I imagined there were so many charitable organisations in England with such bizarre objects. I was particularly dumbfounded by one which proposed to endow the ancient civilisation of China with tin chapels.

And then there were the curiosity boxes who must know at once what the asterisks in the book meant. Those asterisks! I don't apologise for them, but I will explain them. When Chatto's sent me a list of proposed excisions, I felt very contemptuous. There wasn't a word or phrase in the book which couldn't be printed in France—and in fact the original text was printed in France both in English and French. If the English are such babies, give them asterisks, I said, and let them see how absurd this cutting and slashing is. Being comparatively uninhibited myself, I overlooked the morbid emotions of a repressed public which, to judge from my mail, worried itself sick trying to fit the same few words into the context. Alas, they were not at all what the public supposed. Thus, one sentence in the printed copy runs: "Prehistoric beasts, like the ichthyosaurus and ***** ********." When you have tried to fit all the dirty words you think you know to that, I will reveal the fact that they represent the horrible obscenity, "Queen Victoria"; it being the opinion of Chatto's office that the sentence constituted the crime of *lèse-majesté*. Except for a few soldiers' remarks (not altogether inappropriate in a book about a war) many of the cuts were made for no better reason than the one I have given. By far the longest, which I fought hard to save, was a series of cracks at a canaille of the canaille, a British journalist who had been allowed to print the vilest things about Lawrence. All I said in substance was that I would like to kick him where he kept his intelligence—in the seat of his pants. That is offensive —it was meant to be—but it cannot be called obscene, unless the object against which it is directed makes it so.

H. G. Wells, who was in Paris, was very kind and hinted at social obligations. Indeed he went so far as to invite me to dinner to meet Lady Colefax, who in some mysterious way was supposed to be important to writers. These staged meetings never work with me, and I should greatly have preferred an evening alone with H. G., listening to his talk. Unfortunately, towards the end of the evening poor Lady Colefax slipped on the polished floor, and cut her mouth badly on a piece of furniture. As the youngest man in the party I of course volunteered to call a taxi, only to find that the elevator wasn't working. The apartment was high up in a kind of skyscraper in Passy, and as I went down and down innumerable flights of stairs in a long shaft, I felt very much as if I had got into one of those uncomfortably scientific futures H. G. invents for us. It seemed to me I was about ten minutes in reaching the ground floor, but no doubt anxiety for the injured lady made it seem longer than it really was.

I have a high esteem for H. G. Wells, and I feel contemptuously annoyed when little pip-squeak communists try to belittle him. No man can be complete in every respect short of being another Leonardo da Vinci (and there's a good deal of legend about him), so that I easily forgive Wells his indifference to poetry and painting, and his philistine view of life. He has great mental energy, and a power of bringing together numbers of facts in a stimulating way. He insisted on the importance of Science during a long epoch when men of letters were heinously ignorant of it. His sense of the continuity and logical development of human destiny is very valuable, and enabled him to make shrewd guesses at future happenings which sometimes have been impressively right. Let us not forget that Wells in the imagination fought battles with tanks and planes long before the practical military men anywhere had an inkling of them.

The motto of Stendhal, *"ne pas être dupe,"* has long seemed to me an excellent one, if one interprets it as "not to deceive oneself, not to be deceived, not to deceive others." For this reason certain kinds of optimism seem to me to verge on feeble-mindedness; and I am always interested when I meet a highly intelligent and gifted man like Wells who appears to be an optimist. I thought about this a lot, and one day just as he was leaving after paying me a visit I plucked up courage to say:

"Wells, when I was a boy I read a book of yours called *Anticipations,* which made a great impression on me. I should like to know if you now feel as optimistic as you did then?"

He gave me a very queer look, and then turned and went away without saying a word. I was satisfied; I had my answer.

Maddening as the senseless optimism of morons is, there is a deal to be said for all courageous souls who see the truth but keep hope and a brave front. That look in Wells's eyes reminded me of Mac, a man I knew in barracks. As happens whenever men are gathered together, the thirty men in that barrack-room fought and wrestled for supremacy (regardless of formal rank) until only Mac and I were left. We wrestled every night for a week, and then as neither could beat the other, formed a kind of dual monarchy in the manner of Sparta, and ruled the room from either end. Mac was an Irishman, a coal miner, always laughing and whistling and joking and apparently oblivious of the fact that there was a war on and we were for it. One day I said to him:

"Look here, Mac, you and I have both been in the line for months, and we'll soon be back. Don't you ever think of how much depends on us, what a serious bloody business this is?"

He gave me a queer look, almost exactly like that in Wells's eyes those many years later, and his reply astonished me:

"Ach, because I laugh ye needn't think I haven't black despair in me heart."

Wells's kindly meant hints that I should gather together with those he so rightly calls "the nobs" bore no fruit. After all, I had seen just enough of them in early London days to know how I felt about hob-nobbing. Besides, I wanted to keep free to say my say. Wells said I ought to know Lady Cunard, adding: "It's very useful. If you want to meet the Prime Minister and the Archbishop of Canterbury at lunch, she can do it." I can't myself see the point of eating out of the same trough with the great in a milieu where protocol strictly limits all talk to the unimportant. The interest of a Prime Minister lies in the fact that he rules England, of the Archbishop that he is head of the Church. I should have liked to discuss with the Prime Minister the foreign policy of the country, which seemed to me almost imbecile; and I should have liked to go round the library at Lambeth, where repose so many unique copies of English books suppressed by ecclesiastical authority, and discuss freedom of the press with the Archbishop. But I knew I could never be intimate enough with either to take such liberties—so wotthehell?

When I think of the many real friends I made through the publication of *Death of a Hero,* I realise that more than ever I must exercise what Pater calls "the subtle tact of omission" if this book is ever to end. There is, for instance, Tom Mc-Greevy, a paradox of a man if ever there was one. He looked like a priest in civvies, and I think would have made a good one since he possessed all the necessary qualities, not excluding a certain indolence; but some niceties of conscience caused him to let that bus go by. He had served in the British army and admiralty, but the wrongs of Ireland got him out of that career. Then he held an official post in Ireland, and although a Catholic, promptly resigned when they started kicking out Protestants. He was a patriot who lived out of his own country, and though he carried chauvinism so far as to write his name in hotel registers in Irish (the extent of his knowledge of his native tongue) he invariably travelled with a British passport. When I asked him why he didn't have an Irish passport, he said:

"Ah, now, d'you think I'd be travelling with a passport from a little wee country like that?"

He was a graduate of Trinity College and, when I first knew him, Lecteur d'Anglais at the Ecole Normale Supérieure, the most highbrow establishment in France. They must have thought highly of him there, for they not only took the unprecedented step of doubling his tenure of office but allowed him to keep his room long after a successor arrived. This successor was a splendidly mad Irishman who was James Joyce's white boy and wanted to commit suicide, a fate he nearly imposed on half the faculty of the Ecole by playing the flute—an instrument of which he was far from being a master—every night in his room from midnight to dawn.

Though Tom spent so much of his time with sceptical young Frenchmen who riddled every prejudice and superstition with witty satire, and though he was as much a man of the world as one so pure in heart could be, he had some singular views. Thus he astounded me by declaring emphatically that the Gunpowder Plot never existed and was entirely invented by the Protestants—a piece of Jesuit propaganda long ago exploded by competent historians. Again, we were at the house of a French professor, looking over his books, and I lighted on a book of mediæval black magic. Turning over the leaves I discovered a spell potent enough to evoke Satan in person, and therefore at once began reciting it; but before I had gone far, Tom turned pale, exclaimed: "Holy Mother of God!" and snatched the book from my hand. He was also convinced that all Englishmen of genius were Irish. Shakespeare, he said, came from County Cork. And when I mentioned Gibbon, "Ach, sure," said Tom, "he was nothing but a playboy!"

Tom knew a tremendous lot about painting, ancient and

modern, and I would as soon take his opinion of a contemporary painter as that of any man living. After I had made more money than was good for me out of my novels, we went round Italy together; and there never was a more good-humoured fellow-traveller or one who gave more by communicating a fine appreciation. Yet even he wilted sometimes. We went separately round the Scuola di San Rocca in Venice, looking at those tremendous Tintorettos; at last I saw Tom hurrying towards me, and expected one of his penetrating critical remarks. Instead, he whispered hurriedly:

"Let's go. I feel as if I'd read all Shakespeare's plays in an hour."

As a matter of fact that is a good critical remark, for it sums up precisely the effect of trying to see all those overwhelmingly dramatic pictures at one visit. Sometimes, though, Tom carried his pictorial criticism a little far. We rowed along the French coast from Lavendou to Aiguebelle one evening, when sky, sea, and land were in the hush of a dead calm and glowing with the mellow light of a golden sunset. With the mountains and the islands and the immense stretch of blue sea and sky, the sight was so majestic that we were all silent. And then came Tom's voice:

"It's as beautiful as paint—it's like a Poussin."

Tom McGreevy had all the gifts of a writer, except the urge to write. Neither his prose nor his poetry is negligible, but he hadn't in him that aggressive daimon who after each failure to reach the imagined height drives a man back to his desk to try once again. His creative impulse was satisfied by the undoubted influence his talk had on a sympathetic audience; and that is the danger of having the gift of conversation. Moreover, Tom is the kind of man whose brains are picked by other people. He once wrote a poem about driving in a cab through Dublin, imagining the historic scenes and people called up by each street; and showed it to Joyce. Bang it went into *Finne-*

gans *Wake* in the paragraph beginning: "Mr. See-Queer-Sights was rolling in his tumbril." "The crayture," said Tom, laughing good-naturedly, when he found it out; but it seemed to confirm my theory that Joyce has nothing of his own to say in *Finnegans Wake,* since he was reduced to accepting hints from less famous friends.

The other two friends I shall mention were book publishers. Before I succumb to the accusation of fraternising with the enemy there is something to be said. Any cracks against publishers in this book are to be taken with several pinches of salt. My settled opinion is that the professional author's best friend can be and should be his publisher. Apart from the author's own family, nobody is so deeply interested in the success of a book as the publisher. I don't want to go into the complicated subject of the business side of writing, but I do want to say emphatically that few things can be as harmful to an author as the foolish belief that "the publisher is out to do" him. Of course, if an author chooses to sign disadvantageous agreements that's his look-out; and if his average sales are about 1500 he can't expect the kind of contract Mr. Sinclair Lewis can get. Publishers don't pay for literary merit—a patron would do that; they pay for actual or potential sales. They are business men, governed by business ethics and custom; and a reputable publisher would no more think of practising the absurd and petty frauds attributed to him by the smaller fry of writers than any other business man. On the other hand there are plenty of authors who look on publishers merely as men to supply them with money, and who are none too scrupulous about how they get it. Isn't it dishonest to tell a new publisher that the sales of books with other publishers were higher than they actually were? Isn't it dishonest to accept an advance for a book, and then knock off a slovenly piece of work or even not produce it at all? I have only heard of three authors who wished to repay a publisher that part of an advance a book failed to earn. They are Michael Arlen, Israel Zangwill, and Benjamin Disraeli Earl of Beaconsfield.

Fortunate is the author who is able to establish and maintain friendly relations with his publisher. That I always succeeded in doing. But in Charles Prentice of Chatto's I found what was for me the ideal publisher, a scholar whose advice in literary matters was of great value and a man of such gentle sweetness and charm that I came to feel the greatest affection for him. His early letters after the publication of my first novel were more attentive and detailed than one has a right to expect of any publisher. At least once and sometimes oftener in the week he gave me a full report of the book's progress with exact figures, and of what he was doing and planning to extend operations. I could not have been better informed if I had been a partner in the firm. During the whole long period of our association he never once failed me in this or in any other respect; and his advice was of inestimable value. If I may misquote Horace: "*Non sum qualis eram boni sub regno Prentici.*"

"An Oxford man extreamely read in Greek," Prentice might have been a Fellow of his college; but with sure instinct chose the profession of publisher, for which he possessed something like genius. He was also a good business man, for he made his firm as prosperous as he raised its literary reputation high. It is something to be able to send your publisher a translation of a Greek classic and know that he will read it with the original before him, and unerringly spot the little errors which will creep into such work. And it was delightful to realise that one's first (and most important) reader would at once grasp the purpose and structure of a book and at the same time not miss a single allusion or hidden jest.

When Prentice came over to Paris to see me, I took to him at once. A man utterly without affectations, collegiate or otherwise; of simple dignity and straightforward utterance, so considerate of others as to seem almost diffident; so generous that one was always trying to restrain him; and at the same time full of laughter and appreciation of a good thing said. His bachelor rooms in London had a fine scheme of interior decoration—books, modern pictures, bottles, and cigar boxes. Yet he was a temperate man, and though he did not disdain the last two items he mostly kept them for others. We had many happy days together in Paris and on the Riviera, in Venice, Florence, Calabria, and Sicily, and during my brief visits to London.

It was a blow indeed when Prentice, though still a young man, decided to retire and devote himself to the Greek studies which chiefly interested him. Until illness and then the war cut off such activities, he spent much of the year in Athens, where he found a crony in the American Ambassador, also a Hellenist and a publisher. Yet before I had ever met Prentice I knew as a personal friend the only man in England who for me could take his place. Frere likes to play the part of a hard-boiled man of the world, but along with many other virtues and qualities which don't fit into that picture, he has a soft spot in his heart for poets. Thus I was introduced to him in Paris by an American poet, whose unsaleable works Frere was sponsoring; for it seems to be a law of nature that America and England should take in each other's rejected poets.

Frere was in the army as a gunner at the beginning of the last war, and was on Gallipoli. He was captured by the Turks but escaped during an Australian counter-attack, having disposed of his escort with a large and jagged stone in the manner of Eugene Aram. Later he joined the Royal Flying Corps (as it was then) and eventually crashed in performing some attractively perilous stunt. You could tell at once that he was a flying man, for while he claimed he was driving a baby Austin at twenty-five miles an hour, everyone else thought it was a racing Bentley going at eighty-five.

Furnished with a slightly Wellingtonian conk, indicative of aristocratic origins, Frere has a quickness of wit and irreverence which seldom flourish above the perpetual snowline of the upper classes. He can always be relied upon to say the right thing at the right moment. A young man of property was boring several of us with a political programme of obsolete Toryism, the sole object of which was to permit the said young man to keep his money and make more. Frere listened with the utmost patience and then suddenly looked at him and said:

"Obviously the leader of your party is Kylsant."

At that moment Lord Kylsant had just received a gaol sentence for falsifying the books of a shipping company. The young man gasped and fell into a long silence, for which everyone else present felt extremely grateful to Frere.

But while he can shoot down that public enemy number one the Bore with unerring accuracy, he also has an uncanny gift of saying the acceptable thing. Once in the south of France I had to pay a courtesy call on an elderly and distinguished lady of some cosmopolitan renown; and Frere came along. During the ensuing tea-fight I was mildly astonished to hear him deliver a warm panegyric of Alfred Douglas; after which so far as our hostess was concerned Frere became the party. Long afterwards I learned from Reggie Turner (last survivor of the old Wilde group) that this lady had once nourished a hopeless passion for Lord Alfred. To this day I don't know whether Frere was cognisant of this scrap of hoary gossip or whether it was merely a lucky shot. But thereafter I was *persona gratissima* with the lady, who never failed to ask: "And how is that nice Mr. Frere? *Such* an intelligent man."

When I add that Frere is the world's (unrecognised) amateur champion in tap-dancing on café tables, you will understand how warmly such a one should be cherished. Though not so remarkable, this is a more solid achievement than the record of Charles Prentice, who is the only publisher who ever milked a Calabrian goat—in competition with the Florentine antiquary, Giuseppe Orioli. Each of them claimed the victory, and I was unable to decide the question as my attention was distracted by repairs to a flat tire on a road miles from everywhere. The only time I have ever seen Frere even mildly disconcerted was when we went to visit Aldous Huxley. There was a tremendous Mediterranean sunset on view, and Frere very naturally alluded to the spectacle; only to be met with a frigid silence which showed that sunsets were definitely taboo on that particular eminence of Mount Parnassus. We neither of us recovered our spirits for the rest of the visit; and even the prodigious lies Frere told about the speed of his Bentley didn't cheer us much.

Frere, who has many accomplishments denied to lesser men, for some occult reason knows and can sing large portions of the Mass. So I was not surprised early one morning when he and Tom began their devotions in the Bateau Ivre, a Parisian cabaret run by a melancholy White Russian. They were requested to desist, on the specious ground that it would disturb neighbours who were insensible to the sounds of a jazz band. It is a nice point of theology. Might they not perform their devotions if they chose? The hour was canonical (3 a.m.), but then there was an incongruity of place and neither was in holy orders. If they had merely said their prayers, it would be a different matter, to be defended by precedent. The 18th-century poet, Christopher Smart (who for some reason was later incarcerated in an insane asylum), used to insist on his friends' kneeling down with him to pray in Fleet Street; "And, Sir," said Dr. Johnson, relating this interesting fact, "I had as lief pray with Kit Smart as any man living." If Kit Smart could pray in Fleet Street, with the assistance and approval of Dr. Johnson, why not Frere in the Bateau Ivre, with the assistance and approval of Thomas McGreevy?

I cannot feel the same tolerance for Noel Coward and a

friend, who complained to us bitterly at Saint-Tropez that they had been asked to leave the local church merely because they were wearing only bathing clothes. What would Mr. Coward have said if a priest and a verger came into the stalls on one of his first-nights wearing only bathing trunks?

There was something about that Bateau Ivre which had a curious effect on publishers. It may have been the olives, though perhaps it was only the caviar. Charles Prentice came there with me one evening; among other things we had discussed Greek poetry, and I had lamented the destruction of so much lyric verse by Byzantine bigots. We had also talked later about my writing prospects, material and otherwise. Just as he was getting into a taxi to return to his hotel, Charles suddenly paused, stamped his foot to give emphasis to his remark, and said: "Don't you worry, Aldington, don't you worry, they'll find the lost fragments of Ibycus." The dark and empty façade of the Odéon opposite returned a hollow echo: "Ibycus?"

If I had followed Wells's advice and cultivated people who habitually fed Archbishops and Prime Ministers, I think it very probable that I should never have taken part in scenes like this and consequently should have had far less fun in life. At any rate, if I had not been so strongly attracted by Frere's many virtues, I should have been in a hole when Charles Prentice suddenly abandoned the peace of publishing for the turmoil of archæology. As it was, I merely walked over to Frere's chambers in Albany, put the matter to him, and was speedily transferred lock, stock, and barrel to Heinemann's. I knew that I could rely completely on Frere, that he would keep tab on my various works and not allow them to go out of print, that he wouldn't want me to go on writing the same book, that if I wanted to try an experiment which turned out a plug he wouldn't complain, that if I needed advice his would be shrewd and sensible, and that he wouldn't presume to try and re-write my books for me.

Chapter XX

IF we wanted to keep this a pure success story, we ought at this point to drop our hero, gloating over his bank balance and dropping innumerable press clippings into the waste basket. But life goes on, and ten years have to be accounted for. In the autumn of 1929 it seemed to me that I could accept the remainder of life with a certain amount of confidence and cheerfulness. Certain contingencies might indeed give a sombre colouring to life: if, for instance, I started buying yachts and playing the stock market, or was ill for a long time, or ceased to be able to write, or there was another European war. Barring such disasters, it looked as if there might be halcyon years ahead; and indeed there were a few.

Although so much of my life, especially in this decade, was spent in travel, I don't want to fill these pages with too many travel reminiscences. Before I left Paris for the South in the late autumn of 1929, Henry Davray gave me introductions to the Governors of Tunis, Algeria, and Morocco, in case I wished to go there. But first I went to Naples, with Norman Douglas's *Siren Land* in my pocket, and stayed for some time at Amalfi; and from there went on to Palermo and Agrigentum. But whenever I stopped for more than a few days a miserable tendency to start working asserted itself, so I decided to push on.

It was at dawn on 1 January 1930, that I first saw the coast of Africa. The ship anchored outside the three-mile limit; and there was a long pause. At last three barges stinking of sulphur were towed out, and we were informed that we could either pay to be taken ashore in them or pay to be taken back to Palermo. Why? Tunis was in quarantine for "plague," a little fact which the Italian shipping company had not mentioned when we paid our fares. All third-class passengers had to be inoculated; first-class passengers could please themselves. I would have gone back to Palermo rather than submit to mass inoculation in a north African port. Such was not the view of an American boy who was going round the world third class on rather less than fifty cents. In spite of my arguments and entreaties and offers either to back him up in refusal or to have him transferred to first class at my expense, he guessed he'd go through with it. I only hope he was not infected with some ghastly Levantine illness. Finally, we and our baggage were dumped on shore near the ruins of Carthage, and waited at the Carthage railway station for a train to take us into Tunis.

The "plague" was not bubonic, but a form of acute pulmonary and gastric influenza, often fatal to the underfed natives, though rarely to whites. Anyway, the epidemic had been slight and was nearly over; but it was played up vigorously by the press of neighbouring countries which hoped to divert tourist traffic from French north Africa to themselves. After I had presented my letters of introduction, I got a rather disquieting glimpse of how some things are done in France. The director of *tourisme* called on me, and asked me how much he would have to pay to get a paragraph denying the plague scare into *The Times*. For a moment I was positively speechless at the idea that *The Times* could be bribed. Recovering, I explained the complete impossibility of such a proposition; but he went away dissatisfied, evidently not believing me.

When the French took over Tunis they acted sensibly. Instead of "improving" that ancient den of Barbary pirates by tearing it down and putting up European houses, they left it intact and built their own town outside. Thus, you can live in all the comfort of a modern French town, and stroll into a mediæval oriental city. The souks of Tunis are very animated, with their painted pillars and open shop fronts showing bright silks and coloured leather goods. The closely veiled women, the bearded Arabs and Berbers wearing the burnous and turban, the little pattering pack donkeys, the mosques and muezzins, made a complete contrast with the European life only a few hundred yards away. It is instructive if only because of its object lessons—a civilisation so different from our own, a people who would never fit into any of our paper schemes of what we consider rational world organisation. Moreover, it is good for a citizen of opulent western Europe or America to see what a really poor country looks like.

I made excursions to the edge of the Sahara in both Tunisia and Algeria. In the *bled* (the semi-desert before you get to the real thing) you unexpectedly find yourself in the book of Genesis, as illustrated in the family Bible. From the train you see one set of patriarchs with a long caravan of camels, and others with herds of sheep speckled and ring-straked as the flocks of Laban which Jacob kept. I rode a little way into the desert on a camel. The air of the desert is so pure and energising, the silence and solitude so perfectly unbroken, the colouring so vivid, that the long trek across the Sahara to the Niger would be a perfect trip. I regret very much now that I put it off to a future which will never arrive.

As I don't speak Arabic or any of the north African dialects I am not evidence about the people. But anyone with eyes can see the fatal effect of fixed ideas, rigid conservatism, and bigoted devotion to a sacred book. The disastrous results of the belief that God will provide no matter what man destroys can still be seen in Tunisia, though in fifty years the French have done something to improve it. Under the Romans this was a wealthy, fertile, and populous province, full of gardens, orchards, and shady trees. In a little over a thousand years the Mohammedans literally made it a desert; and when the French arrived there was not a single bridge or passable road left from

L*

all that the Romans had so laboriously made. There is scarcely a tree there which has not been planted by the French or under French direction.

Another disastrous thing, from my point of view, is the too literal acceptance of the injunction: "Thou shalt not make unto thee any graven image or any likeness of any thing that is in heaven above, or that is in the earth beneath, or that is in the water under the earth." It doesn't abolish superstition, for no people are more superstitious about omens, spells, amulets, and charms; but it does destroy all representational art—and, O ye pious iconoclasts, what a dull world that makes! In a very short time one grows weary of non-representational art and longs for graven images. Looking at those eternally same designs—very beautiful in themselves—the repetitive tiles and arabesques and inlays, I longed for a Hellenistic Cupid or a Renaissance Holy Family. In north Africa I developed a wholly unexpected sympathy for Aaron and his friends when they made the golden calf, for clearly all they wanted was a little of the representational art which Moses had so pedantically taken away from them.

Yet there can be no doubt that the natural colouring of the north African scene is brilliant. When you come to Marseille from the north it seems a bright picturesque place, but when I returned to it from Alger it looked to me nearly as drab as a Scotch fishing port.

During 1930 I wrote my second novel, partly on the French Riviera and partly in Venice, where Charles and Tom came and stayed near me. When they had departed, leaving me with about the last third of my book to write, I took a boat down to Brindisi, and went and stayed at Lecce in Puglia, the extreme heel of Italy. I went there partly because Sachie Sitwell's description of the place had aroused my curiosity, and partly because I found that the farther I was from England and the more alien my surroundings, the more vividly I could picture English scenes and people.

Lecce is a most interesting town, almost entirely baroque, an architect's dream. The streets and squares and palaces group themselves into new strange harmonies at almost every step; the churches have very original structural designs and are profusely decorated with carvings, especially window frames and altar pieces of lovely children and fruits and garlands. A local industry is making religious statues, which oddly enough are very tasteful, and the streets are filled with pretty madonnas and saints drying their colours in the sun outside the workshops.

Unfortunately, Lecce has one drawback—the food is atrocious. A typical meal consisted of ditch-water and hard chickpeas pretending to be soup; a piece of corrugated leather called buffalo beefsteak with a sodden mass of green garden weeds; followed by cheese, fruit, and nuts which looked as if they had just been dug out of the ruins of Pompeii. We got so hungry that we would sit about after meals and talk of food, like shipwrecked mariners. It was getting on in December, and the thought of all the people in the world who were going to have real Christmas dinners was almost more than we could bear. Luckily, I put an end to this emaciating feast of culture by finishing my book.

Came the question: Where to go to get something to eat? I had originally intended to go on to Corfu as it was so near, but the thought of tough Greek goat and turpentine wine, which had seemed so unimportant when discussing the trip in a comfortable Venetian restaurant, now looked a sombre and formidable obstacle. After several weeks of a virtual but unpleasant fast, we unfeignedly yearned for the flesh-pots. Moreover, we had not spoken to a civilised person since leaving Venice. Sudden a thought came like a full-blown rose—Florence and Norman Douglas, food for body and mind together.

I had long before abandoned my youthful interest in merely knowing people eminent in literature. Staged meetings start out on a basis of falsity and make any genuine friendship almost impossible. It is much better to trust to the hazards of life. And I must confess that my feelings towards most of my living seniors had long settled into placid indifference. Norman Douglas was an exception. I had read most of his books, and found in them a man with a sane, intelligent view of life, wit and high spirits, an astonishing variety of interests, and a fund of valuable and unusual knowledge. Here was somebody, I thought, who had not allowed life to push him around, but had forced life to give him what he wanted and had wanted many different things. A masculine adult mind and a writer of almost classical proportion.

It is impossible for me to separate Douglas and Orioli, for they were inseparable companions during the years when I visited Florence regularly. I had known Orioli slightly before the war, when I used to drop in at his book shop to pick up any Neo-Latins which were going cheap. And during the war Orioli and Cippico tried hard to get me out of the trenches and into the Italian mission in London—on what pretext I can't imagine, but it went as far as a War Office interview.

Orioli's books, good as they are and a *tour de force* for an Italian writing in English, fail to do him justice. He is an immensely entertaining companion, always alert, witty and observant, and above all intensely alive. Without falling into extravagances, I can only say that heaven wouldn't be heaven for me without Pino. No man has ever given me more of the priceless gifts of laughter and good fellowship.

I wrote to Pino from Lecce, and he got me a large front room in the Gran Bretagna, looking over the Arno between the Ponte Vecchio and the Trinità. The ceiling of this room was painted with a large mythological scene, and in the centre was alma Venus herself with a huge cut-glass chandelier depending exactly from her navel—an awkward compromise between ancient and modern. Everything was on such a scale that the ante-room to the bathroom made a study which was almost too big. Later, in the spring, I verified a fact I had previously doubted; namely, that after the town is quiet at night you can hear the nightingales singing from San Miniato.

A few days after I arrived, Pino said to me:

"Norman think he will like you and want to meet you. Go to Bianca's in Via Porto Rosso tomorrow, and Norman will lunch at your table."

Naturally we were there, and presently a man came in whom I should have known to be Norman Douglas, even if I hadn't been familiar with his photographs. This tall, strongly built, very erect Scottish laird, with a slightly stern face, very firm mouth, and beautiful white hair, could have been no one else in Florence. (The motto of the Douglas clan, "tender and true," is not applicable to Norman—"hard as nails, my dear," is his version, though that isn't true either.) When I stood up expectantly, his expression suddenly lost all sternness as he smiled and greeted us with that urbanity which will disappear from the earth with his generation of men trained in the Diplomatic Corps.

I do remember some of the topics we discussed, though unfortunately none of Douglas's exact words. We talked of Lecce, which very strangely he had not visited. He immediately made a note of it (very characteristic this) in a small black pocket-book, which I was to see very often in the future. That naturally led to a discussion of southern Italy, which Douglas knows as well as any man living, and on which he has written the best book since the Frenchman Lenormant. It is only the fear of being influenced by the partiality of friendship which makes me refrain from saying that I think Douglas's *Old Calabria* the better book, because while he is as much a savant as Lenormant, he is also the adventurous and fearless Briton of the George Borrow kind, tramping across mountain ridges and into remote places Lenormant never visited.

What was once Magna Græcia inevitably brought up Greek literature, with remarks on the birds mentioned in the Greek Anthology—this apropos of the fact that the coast of Calabria is the main line of European bird migration. At the same time he lamented that a friend of ours, who was running a small hand-press in Paris, should waste time issuing "trash" (i.e., George Moore, Douglas, and myself) instead of an edition of Athenæus "with plenty of notes." I mentioned that Professor Gulick of Harvard had begun publishing an excellent translation of Athenæus, and down that went in the little black book. Somehow we got on to early German epic poetry, and he wrote down for me several passages in some primitive German dialect. He also touched on the deforestation of the Mediterranean, the geology of those parts of Asia Minor he had ridden through, the wines of Italy, limericks, the possibility of recovering the library of Herculaneum ("never, if it's left to Italians"), D. H. Lawrence, and the right way to make a potato salad—which he demonstrated with admirable results. All this without a trace of pedantry and affectation, thrown off lightly and generally with some amusing turn of phrase—the talk of a man intelligently interested in the world he inhabits.

During the many months I was in Florence I lunched or dined with Douglas practically every day, and we covered a great deal of ground in our talk. I regret now that I didn't make notes of what he said, but I've a prejudice in favour of being rather Dr. Johnson than Boswell, even to Norman. Norman, too, had his prejudices, as I gradually discovered. Though his knowledge of biology and geology was encyclopædic, he disliked mathematics and mathematical physicists, and I totally failed to interest him in Whitehead and Eddington. Darwin was his hero, and of course he was unanswerable when he said we had no biologist of his stature—you can't expect a theory of evolution in every generation. He had a great contempt for the young men who had grown up since the war—"blood two degrees under normal." He had a prejudice in favour of Austrian cooking (his mother was Austrian) and would eat with relish a veal cutlet smothered in paprika and those abominable white truffles which taste like acetylene. He had other prejudices, but as I shared them to some extent, they did not seem so much like prejudices. But I could never go along with him in his advocacy of the revival of slavery; there his partly German ancestry and his German training peeped out, as they did in a slightly grotesque quality in his humour.

In his youth he had been a good shot and a daring chamois-hunter in the Austrian Alps. He had ridden one of those penny-farthing bicycles over the three highest passes of Europe in a day—a prodigious feat of endurance. All his life he was a great walker, which enabled him to see so much of the remote and neglected parts of Europe. He had the steady unflagging gait of the mountaineer; and climbed mountains until his seventieth year. I think he might have made a good soldier, if he had not considered such activities absurd and tedious. The only things he feared were poverty and the malevolence of human stupidity as embodied in governments, bureaucrats, armies, and officials. But he was far indeed from conforming to the absurd conventions of the he-man. He loved flowers, and perfumes, and precious stones, and jewellery, and fine linen. But he was equally far from being a fop. Indeed, as he insisted on wearing Scottish tweeds cut by an Italian tailor, I could not admire his wardrobe.

It did not trouble me in the least that I differed very strongly from Douglas on certain points of human conduct, wherein I did not and do not approve either his theory or his practice. I liked him for being such a perfect specimen of his type. He was a complete contrast to the professional writers who live by flattering the middle classes, and to the little highbrows with their cliques and affectations and lack of a sense of proportion. Like Somerset Maugham, Douglas is a man of the world, not to be imposed on by fads and pretences. The fact is that both Maugham and Douglas have a far wider and deeper knowledge of European literature than the people who give themselves airs and try to patronise them. Douglas's knowledge is encyclopædic, and is scientific and historical as well as merely literary.

Frieda Lawrence tells me that Norman's talk is even more amusing in German than in English. I can well believe it. Unexpected opportunities of humour must lurk in the morasses of the German language for someone who is familiar with more elegant tongues and cultures. Our conversation, however, was usually directed by the exuberant and inexhaustible Pino Orioli, a kind of Boccaccio junior; and Norman limited himself to occasional pungent comments. Never before had I heard so many scandalous stories or heard them told so well. Pino is a born *raconteur,* and his gusto for living, his perpetual interest in human beings and their queer ways, made him a wonderful companion.

"Look at that man," he would say. "What is he doing? He remind me of . . ."

And then would come some utterly unexpected anecdote, told as skilfully and wittily—in English—as any story in the *Decameron.* Pino is an example of the vitality, good humour, and genius of the Italian people which are still there in spite of all the nonsense imposed on them by centuries of imbecile governors. May that genius once more be free, as it was in the Renaissance!

My amateur studies of Italian came in useful, for Norman and Pino in their talk passed unconsciously from English to Italian and back again. Their little tiffs were invariably in Italian, I suppose because Pino thought that gave him an advantage. If so, he was mistaken, for he never succeeded in scoring off the old lion. The most frequent cause of disputes was a difference of opinion about the meaning or pronunciation of some rare Italian word or phrase. Pino would dispute Norman's exact philological definition (that astounding knowledge and memory!) on the absurd grounds that Norman had learned his Italian in Naples, whereas Pino came from the Romagna, which as everybody knows—or ought to know—is the summit of all human perfection. Finally we would adjourn from our tavern to Pino's 16th-century apartment, and drag out dictionaries and reference books. Of course Norman was always right.

"Well," Pino would say disconsolately, "I did not think the Nabolidani know any Italian. In Romagna . . ."

Pino always said that the highest posts in Italy were always held by Romagnuoli—after all, the Duce himself is one. We had a striking confirmation of this fact when Charles Prentice and Pino came with me on a motor tour of Calabria and Sicily. At Reggio we had to wait for the train ferry to take the car across, and went into the station bar for a drink. Almost immediately Pino got into a long conversation with the bartender in a dialect of which Charles and I understood nothing.

"He is a Romagnuolo," said Pino aside to us in English. "What did I tell you? All the important posts in Italy . . ."

Norman refused to come on this expedition; he said it was too early in the year and that we were bound to run into bad weather in Calabria. Pino ridiculed this ("Norman think he know everything about Italy") and said I was right to choose the last week in February and the first two weeks of March for our trip. We had had such a very warm and sunny January and February that my fear was that southern Sicily might prove to be too hot.

I should have done better to listen to Douglas. The very morning we left Florence the weather changed, and a cold *tramontana* chased us all the way to Rome. It was warmer there, and we told each other we would soon be too far south for the *tramontana* to matter. Alas! There was snow in Naples, not only on Vesuvius but in the outskirts of the city. Next day we drove through Salerno in a blizzard; and two days later got hopelessly stuck in the snow at Campo Tenese, the mountain pass between Mormanno and Castrovillari, and had to be ignominiously rescued.

We got very hungry up there in the snow, and Pino encouraged us by telling us that the hotel at Castrovillari was excellent (for Calabria), and with anecdotes about the waiter there. Pino had nicknamed him Moses, because he had two large warts in exactly the same places on his head where Michelangelo's Moses has horns. "Moses know me very well," Pino kept saying. "He will see we have a good dinner and some decent wine." When we got there, Moses not only failed to recognise Pino, but jumped to the conclusion that he was our Italian courier; an opinion nothing could shake. Pino got more and more angry with him, and they had quite an altercation, Pino asserting that he was a landed proprietor and Moses uttering the Italian equivalent of "Oh, yeah?"

Next morning, just as I had finished dressing, Pino crashed into my room in his underpants, exclaiming fretfully:

"Where are my trouser? Are they in here?"

"No, of course not," I said. "What would I be doing with your trousers?"

"Well, I cannot find them anywhere, and I cannot go to Sicilia without trouser."

Charles and I joined in the hunt, and eventually I found them carefully folded under Pino's mattress. He looked greatly astonished, and said:

"I never put my trouser under the mattress. Why did I put them there?"

"Don't you remember, Pino?" Charles said quietly. "Last night you said you were going to have your trousers creased like an English gentleman's, then Moses would respect you."

In Sicily we discovered that Falstaff was right, the rogues do put lime in their sack. I noticed on the first morning when Pino and I went to get our little wine-flask filled at a wine-shop that the word *gesso* (lime) was written on the casks. I asked Pino why, and he put me off with one of his ready inventions. Next day we saw the same thing, and on enquiry discovered that in fact they did put lime in the wine and were compelled by law to announce it. Pino was seriously alarmed. "We cannot drink wine with chalk in it, we shall all have gout." So we drove at once to Palermo, and laid in a stock of Tuscan wine.

I intended to write a prose and verse account of this journey, rather in the manner of Bachaumont, for it was certainly the most amusing and adventurous I ever made. Charles knew all the history and immediately identified every ancient place. Pino was interested in everything. For some reason he developed a strong admiration for Hieron of Syracuse, and insisted on visiting his tomb in an olive garden. He came out quicker than he went in, for, while the English use unguarded ancient monuments as picnic dumps, the equally practical Italians use theirs as toilets. I meditated a poem on this event, but it never got written, for as soon as I got back to Florence I began on a long novel I had been meditating for over a year.

In my first two novels I gave a certain amount of freedom to a satirical verve, which amused me and those who shared my views and annoyed the people it was meant to annoy. Can a satirist ask for more? But the project I now had in mind called for a severe curb on that almost irresistible propensity, for I wanted to write a story about two people genuinely in love, and that wasn't very easy to stage in a Europe which had become as loose and cynical as the Court of Charles II. I wanted to create a harmony of body and mind, of desire and devotion.

I have no idea how other writers feel, but when I am engaged on a book which calls for a continuous effort of the imagination, I don't want to have that effort weakened by contact with an unfriendly or irrelevant milieu. For the time being I want to abound in my own sense; I want to be treated with the consideration one gives an expectant mother; and I don't want to argue or to be plagued by people with minds like a tabloid newspaper. When the job is finished, the variety and contradictions of the world of other people become delightful. "I dogmatise, and am contradicted; and in that conflict of opinions I take delight."

That book started off with a sentence which to my notion rang the right bell; once that was down, the book was as good as finished. All I needed was a few quiet months to live with the people I had imagined and to experience vicariously their fortunes. Just at that moment an Anglo-Parisienne turned up with a letter of introduction, and for a couple of hours distracted me with chatter about that world of pseudo-artistic fashion and trifling in which no real love affair could possibly happen. It sounds absurd and prima donna, but the effect on me was exactly like that of the screaming parrot on the lover in Aldous Huxley's story. It seemed to wither every impulse, and stopped me dead in my tracks. It annoyed me to think that I was so vulnerable. The only solution seemed to be to get out of Florence, for reviving spring threatened a horde of such unwelcome twitterers. I remembered that in 1912 I had stayed in a little restaurant at Anacapri, which had only two guest-rooms, and I wondered if my former hostess, Maria di Tommaso, were still there. Rather unhopefully I wrote her, offering to rent both rooms for the summer, and to my delight she wrote back an acceptance.

Before quitting Florence and its many happy memories, one or two things must be said. I have treated Norman Douglas briefly, because at some fitting time I hope to write a biographical and critical essay on him. Adequate treatment would demand far more space than this book can afford. Curiously enough, the most realistic (though satirical) portrait of Norman Douglas is the Argyle of Lawrence's novel, *Aaron's Rod.* This was the real cause of the breach between those two and of Norman's anti-Lawrence pamphlet, though the ostensible *casus belli* was Lawrence's superbly written introduction to the *Memoirs* of Maurice Magnus, who served in the French Foreign Legion and eventually committed suicide in Malta.

It is not for me to judge my two friends in this unhappy controversy. Lawrence was not always master of his pen when moved by resentment, and I think it very probable that Norman is right when he says Lorenzo misjudged and misrepresented the unhappy Magnus. On the other hand, Norman obviously resented the too vivid and unflattering portrait of himself in *Aaron's Rod,* and his charge that Lorenzo acted meanly is absurd. At the time Lawrence was poor and his income uncertain, and he had a wife. Magnus lived with an extravagance which to the frugal Lawrence was an outrage, and he was unmarried. Why on earth should Lorenzo have given more than half the small sum he had in the world to a comparative stranger who, he had every reason to think, was a waster and perhaps a crook? Norman had much more money than Lawrence, and Magnus was his friend, not Lawrence's. Why didn't he lend Magnus the money for lack of which the wretched man killed himself? Moreover, it is no credit to Norman that he accepted a gift of a hundred pounds to write the pamphlet, from a rich woman who had a grudge against Lawrence. And after doing that, Norman had the crust to abuse Lawrence for not being a gentleman!

It would never have done for those two rare spirits to remain estranged, and fortunately dear Pino was there to reconcile them. He talked them both over to a recognition of their sins, and staged a meeting at his book shop on the Lungarno. It was done admirably. Lawrence and Frieda were there talking to Pino, and in came Norman as arranged. There was a moment of embarrassed silence, and then Norman made a gesture which with him means he accepts you as a friend—he offered Lawrence his snuff box:

"Have a pinch of snuff, dearie."

Lawrence took it.

"Isn't it curious"—sniff—"only Norman and my father"—sniff—"ever gave me snuff?"

That was all, and they were as good friends as ever. But there is an epilogue to the story. In *Looking Back* Norman gives his version of their dispute, and then speaks of going to Lawrence's grave at Vence. "I scattered some red carnations on his grave—an inoffensive gesture."

I don't know why alleged reviewers say that Lawrence couldn't draw characters realistically. Among the many portraits in *Aaron's Rod* immediately recognisable to those who knew the people is one of Reggie Turner. Reggie was the last of the Oscar Wilde group, and he and Robbie Ross stayed with Oscar up to the end. That needed courage. I got Reggie to talk about Oscar's death, and I am happy to inform the world that Reggie gave me his word of honour that there is no truth in Frank Harris's sensational account—though I don't suppose anyone who knew Harris ever believed it. Reggie was very proud of one little episode. He and Ross went to Oscar's room every morning and spent the whole day with him. On the morning before Oscar died they found him agitated and depressed; he had dreamed, he said, that he was supping among the dead.

"Ah, my dear Oscar," said Reggie, "and you were the life and soul of the party."

According to Reggie this 1890 *mot* cheered Oscar for the rest of the day. Reggie was a wrinkled ugly little man, with a habit of batting his eyelids like an owl. When he talked he waved his hand continuously, and began nearly every sentence with "however." He wrote a lot of bad novels which nobody read, except Reggie himself, and he frequently shed tears over the affecting productions of his genius. He also collected and preserved every new book of memoirs which mentioned him. People knew of this innocent mania and, I am glad to say, went out of their way to gratify it, for he was a kindly warm-hearted creature, and his devotion to Oscar in those bitter days of persecution was a noble deed. This book won't join the collection, for poor Reggie is dead. His is the only funeral to which I have ever sent a wreath. I did that for his own sake and because of what he did for Oscar.

Chapter XXI

READING epitaphs in churches and churchyards is said by some psychologists to be a symptom of approaching mental disorder. I was a little startled when I read this, for it had been a mild hobby of mine; but I was entirely reassured when I found that for fifty years it had been an inveterate pastime of Norman Douglas, who remained obstinately in the pink of sanity. Again, I read a pseudo-psychological study of Ruskin which accused him of the mysterious crime of "perseveration," because he liked to go back to places he had visited. According to this author, that was why Ruskin wound up as a "manic depressive." I knew of course that the poor old man did go off his rocker, with the strange result that while he was writing at the top of his form everybody said he was a crank and when he was crazy he was revered as a prophet and a sage. But I didn't know till then that this was the result of re-visiting Florence and Amiens.

I have to admit suffering to some extent from this dangerous symptom, for I too like to re-visit places I have known. In my various perambulations of Europe I had returned more than once to Capri, but I had not before thought of taking the same room I had had in Anacapri in 1912. There were some changes, chiefly a decline in business. The couple who owned the place had grown old, and the chief responsibility had fallen on their daughter, whom I remembered to have seen bustling about, laughing and chattering, as she waited on the tourists at the garden tables so picturesquely hidden under tall canes and lemon and orange trees. Now at lunch we were usually alone; there was no cosmopolitan chatter of German, English, and

Italian; and Maria seldom laughed. The once beautiful garden was rank and neglected.

This was an old and respected Capri family, and it was sad to see them fallen on evil days in their old age, through no fault of their own. Their life's savings had withered away in the depreciation of money and securities; their trade had gone because the old type of traveller had given place to the tourist "having a good time"; and they were crushed by taxation. To help out, Maria was now running a little tobacco shop built onto the end of the house. Tobacco is a government monopoly, and every month much of her meagre profit went on a compulsory visit to Naples to make up the accounts with an official. This in spite of the fact that Capri swarmed with idle and insolent officials, who bullied the poor in a shameful way. It made my blood boil to see hard-working men and women, with hands and faces marked by labour and privation, cringing before the insults of officials with their incessant demands for taxes, taxes, taxes. And almost every day the village notice board contained some vexatious decree. One, I remember, ordered that foreigners in hotels must be served at least once a day with *"i nostri patate nazionali"*—our own national potatoes. That struck me as a new low in the nationalist imbecility which was blighting Europe like a disease.

But some things are still beyond official control and degradation. They couldn't bully the climate or do much to sully the purity of sea and sky, and Monte Solaro was still its old self. Indeed, it had been embellished by the growth of trees in Axel Munthe's bird sanctuary. The walk along the Migliara was still pleasant, and though the wild flowers had suffered severely to little purpose in the *battaglia del grano*, part of the walk had been planted with the bush marguerites which grow so well in Capri and with other garden flowers. I regretted the change, which seemed to me characteristic of our epoch. A costless beauty which had existed for ages had been destroyed in futile obedience to a doctrinaire political economy, and money had been spent in making an artificial display—in this case an imitation of the conventional Mediterranean watering place.

I fell into my usual routine—writing all morning, excursions in the afternoon, and talk after dinner. Hal Glover came down and stayed near us, so conversation was not lacking. Then came a long telegram from Frere to the effect that his summer holiday was due—should he come to Capri or would I meet him on the French Riviera? I try to think now as I did then that my reason for wiring back that I would meet him at Toulon was that I did not want him to waste extra days of a limited holiday in travelling so far south. But there was another reason—I wanted to get out of Italy for good and all. The patient reader of this book will realise a little of what Italy had meant to me, not only its inexhaustible pleasures of art and literature and great men of the past, but the country and the people. I was not weary of any of these things, but miserable and oppressed by the sight of so much misery and oppression in the name of a pretentious national glory and power far beyond the country's real capacity and contrary to the real interests of the people. The Italian people may rejoice in their servitude and believe the imbecilities stuffed into their heads, but that was no reason why I should enjoy seeing them exploited for the benefit of an insolent and ignorant faction.

> *"Italia, O Italia, tu che hai*
> *Il dono infelice di—camicie."*

I shall not soon forget my feelings on the first night of my return to France. We met Frere and his wife at Toulon, and, after dinner in Lavendou, drove up to the café at Bormes. A local fête was in progress, and most of the *place* was roped in for dancing. There was a scratch band on a wooden platform, and everybody in the village, including the policeman and the mayor, danced. Old people sat in chairs looking on benevolently, and children ran about and played and pretended to dance too. There were tricolour flags and a decoration of trees with a few electric lights. There was something in the simplicity and good nature and innocent enjoyment of that little country festival which moved me. It was so unpretentious and anti-pompous, so pleasantly unofficial. It hadn't been ordered by the Prefect of the Var, acting under the highest authority, in order to demonstrate to the world the glorious achievements of the new France. The mayor had left his official sash in his office, and the only uniform was that of the policeman, who was hopping around as gaily as anyone else. In fact, here were people amusing themselves as they wished to be amused. In spite of all theoretical objections and practical drawbacks there seemed to me everything to be said for the regime of *liberté, égalité, fraternité;* and nothing whatever for the lying tyrannies which plotted to overthrow them. *Et zut! et vive la France quand même et toujours!*

There was a long heat wave that year on the Riviera, and the thermometer stood around ninety for weeks. When Lavendou got too oppressive, we migrated to the Korrigane at Bormes, which had a loggia and a cellar. In the loggia I read the proofs of Lawrence's *Letters* with that excellent introduction by Aldous Huxley, which Frere was publishing. When the book came out I found that either Huxley or Frere had cut out one or two cracks at my expense—I can't imagine why. It is surely an important point in Lawrence's nature that he didn't like anybody all the time, not even himself and Frieda. But, in spite of the airy loggia, the heat grew greater; and when one evening we discovered the appalling fact that the Korrigane cellar was running low I proposed that this company do now adjourn to Brantôme, a motion at once accepted by the house.

I have often congratulated myself on the singular coincidence that places associated with authors, particularly those who are considered a little improper, are usually beautiful or at least picturesque. Driving from the Riviera to London one autumn I had already diverged on such motives as far west of the main road as Périgueux; and looking at the map I saw that I had only to go another thirty kilometres out of the way to see Brantôme, I could not resist the chance of visiting the desmesnes of the *sieur* and *abbé de Brantôme,* author of those numberless anecdotes of *dames galantes—"je cognois une très grande dame de par le monde qui,"* but you must read the book yourself.

When I saw Brantôme I was glad indeed that I had gone there. It is a village of old stone houses with carved balconies on a small island formed by a splitting of the clear little river Dronne. There is a very ancient monastery, said to have been founded by Charlemagne, and even now from a distance looking like a Knight Templar on horseback. The edges of the river are lined with elegant stone balustrades; there are magnificent avenues of old trees, a Renaissance pavilion said to have been built by our *Dames Galantes* friend, and the old monastery garden. With the running water and the trees and the carved stone houses and the relics of monastic splendour, Brantôme is the kind of place you dream of when you are sick of great modern cities.

Although it was the middle or end of August, a lucky movement of guests gave us the best rooms in the place, a 16th-century house with a large balcony overlooking the river, an annexe to the hotel. From my window there as I wrote I had a view of the sparkling river and the old bridge, down the street to the *pharmacie,* from which there emerged several times a day with *furia francese* and a horse whip the *pharmacien* driving away the numerous dogs, which, for some strange reason, persisted in mistaking his immaculately white-washed shop for a lamp-post.

Eventually, my companions departed for London, leaving me alone to finish my book, and I had some opportunity to study the character of the landlady, a strong-minded woman of about fifty who did a considerable business with an inadequate staff and would endure no contradiction. I was lunching alone one day on the balcony, when she came up, and after indicating an elderly gentleman at the other end, whispered very loudly:

"*Monsieur, vous voyez ce vieux coquin là-bas?*"

"*Oui, Madame.*"

"*C'est le duc de La Rochefoucauld, voyons!*"

Madame had set views, which nothing could alter. Among them was the belief that all English-speaking people are Americans, due possibly to the fact that the first she had known in any quantity were officers of the A.E.F. from Bordeaux. Almost every evening as she visited the tables of her guests, we were apt to fall into the following curious dialogue:

"*Monsieur, vous êtes américain. . .*"

"*Non, Madame, je vous ai déjà dit que je suis anglais.*"

"*Pour moi c'est tout comme. Vous êtes américain et vous êtes écrivain—j'ai vu votre ouvrage à la gare d'Angoulême—un de ces jours vous m'en donnerez un exemplaire—vous devez écrire à vos compatriotes qu'ils nous ont corrompus!*"

In vain I said I didn't believe it; in vain I pleaded for some evidence, some example of the corruption wrought by America in France; in vain I pointed out that coming from an Englishman such a charge would rightly be considered most offensive.

"*Non, non, Monsieur! Vous nous avez corrompus. Il faut l'écrire.*"

The old man-servant who failed to clean my room would shake his head and tell me mournfully that Madame was "*très regardante, un vrai grippe-sou, quoi!*"—a thrifty Frenchwoman. I could only suppose that she had been horrified by the recklessness of American spending, and resented this insult to her religion.

Once she asked me the title of the book I was writing, and I told her truthfully: *All Men Are Enemies.*

"Pst!" said she, making a grimace of acquiescence. *"C'est juste. Vous avez bien raison, tenez! Regardez-moi ces allemands. . . ."*

Pino and Norman frequently wrote urging me to come back to Florence, but I never went after those nationalist potatoes in Capri. Instead, I returned to a summer villa at Canadel, just opposite Port Cros, with long visits to Spain and Portugal or to Austria.

My visits to Spain all occurred in the period between the abdication of Don Alfonso and the outbreak of the civil war, another frightful episode in the long agony of confusion which has distracted Spain since Napoleon destroyed the old monarchy. Every form of government, from ruthless military dictatorship to a republic and a foreign king, was tried in Spain during the 19th century; and all failed, mostly in bloodshed. The 20th century seems merely to be repeating this now familiar pattern of disorder. In Spain almost every form of doctrinaire political theory found expression and temporary power; the only two things forgotten were the welfare of Spain as a whole and the real interests of the people.

Though I read Spanish easily (it is simple when you know Latin and French) I speak it very badly, because I am always filling up gaps with Italian words, which are sometimes right but more often wrong. So my contact with the people was very superficial, and I have no right to any opinions about them. But every man can use his eyes. On my first day in Spain, we stopped in the late afternoon at Castro-Urdiales, a small town near Santander. We walked about the streets, and were struck by the abundance and cheapness of all provisions, and by the absence of that nervous tension in the people, even then (1933) so evident in the nations which felt the destructive force of the World War. Coming to the main *plaza,* we found many of the inhabitants dancing to a military band. We sat at a café, and, being new to Spain and fresh from France, were surprised to be openly jeered at as foreigners. The priests, I noted, were big burly men who ought to have been soldiers; and the soldiers undersized, underfed men who might have been priests. I said to my companion:

"These people seem to be doubly ignorant, ignorant of the outside world in that they are astonished at the sight of foreigners and feel hostile to them, ignorant of the plenty they accidentally enjoy through having kept out of the war. What will you bet that they don't destroy themselves by some violent imbecility in the next ten years?"

The most obvious social phenomenon of those years in Spain was the enormous number of strikes, many of them apparently quite aimless except for the purpose of creating confusion. They were so numerous and so frivolous that they were hardly noticed in foreign newspapers. I very soon learned to buy a Spanish newspaper the moment I crossed the frontier and to turn up the column which listed the towns and areas affected by "general strikes." It seemed to me that a government which permitted and even appeared to encourage such senseless disorders could not long endure; and in Spain I kept a sharp lookout for signs of the reaction which I thought inevitable. What surprised me was that the republic lasted as long as it did, for while its intentions may have been of the worthiest, it was incompetent and lacked real authority.

However superficially I saw it, I am glad to have seen so much of the Spanish landscape and of the ancient glories of Spain as expressed in its ancient cities. There is something majestic in the very names of the old provinces—Castilla la Vieja, Estremadura, Andalusia. I liked Seville and Salamanca best, but I'm glad I didn't miss the Prado and the Escorial, Toledo, Compostella, Trujillo, Cáceres, Cadiz, Avila, Cordoba, Granada, Murcia, Burgos, Valladolid, Santillana, Zaragoza, Ciudad

351

Rodrigo, in all of which I stayed and many of which I re-visited more than once.

The last time I drove out of Salamanca, along a narrow street, I saw an old man hesitating on the sidewalk. He looked surprised when I jammed on the brakes, and as he crossed removed my cap. It was Unamuno. Well, the bright political lads sent him to his grave with a broken heart. They murdered Lorca. Machado died of hardship. And what happened to Azorin, the best writer of them all in my opinion? And Miró, whose works I had the greatest difficulty in finding in his native city of Alicante? I can't think of Spain without an ache in my heart.

The spirit of revenge and cruelty, traditionally ascribed to Spaniards, does not seem to be extinct; and I have seen examples of a callous cruelty to animals which was revolting. I went into the *plaza mayor* at Léon and found a large open-air market in progress. Lying on the ground were many small lambs and kids with their four legs tightly tied together, so that they could not stand or move about. They lay exposed to a fierce sun, dying of thirst and heat, some bleating faintly, others too weak to do more than pant with their tongues hanging out and glassy eyes, a few already dead. Peasants, marketers, priests, soldiers, women, passed this pitiful sight without one word or action of pity or protest. Is it not the teaching of the Catholic Church that "man has no obligations to the lower animals"?

My first indication that the republican regime was uneasy and that the reaction might be coming to a head occurred on the last time when I crossed the frontier from Spain to Portugal. We were turned back by the frontier guard and had to go to some official bureau for permission. I was annoyed by this delay, because Hal Glover, who was with the party, had only just recovered from a long and serious illness—it was in fact his convalescent trip—and I was taking every precaution to avoid fatiguing him. I was still more annoyed when we were held up for more than an hour while these zealous guards made an elaborate search of the car and our persons to see if we were taking out more money than we had declared. They were evidently certain we had it, for they practically took the car to bits.

There was a humorous aspect to the situation. Although they took the wheel-caps off, looked in the carburettor, and dragged a wire about in the gas tank, they totally failed to notice the luggage container, which was fitted with four large valises capable of holding several million paper pesetas. The key was in my pocket the whole time. Hal was very much amused when I told him. The reason for this search became obvious a few weeks later when the civil war started. Evidently money was being smuggled out of Spain to Sanjurjo and Franco, but as usually happens in such cases, the real smugglers got through, and entirely innocent people were suspected.

In some respects I preferred Portugal to Spain. True, it hasn't the grandeur and the magnificent art, but the people are gentler and more friendly, while the very beautiful country has been treated far more intelligently and not rendered a treeless desert like so much of Spain. Every year by way of the Tagus the Spaniards make the Portuguese a present of their soil, which in the annual flood enriches large areas near Lisbon. This wastage could be diminished by proper attention to the problem of erosion and tree conservation, but I never heard of its even being discussed in Spain. On the other hand, in Portugal I found a very active movement towards tree planting on the mountains (to combat floods and erosion), and saw for myself something of what was being done in the area controlled by the botany professor at Coimbra. The sand dunes all along the coast are kept in check by plantations of pine, started by the mediæval King Diniz, who had the further distinction of being a very pleasant poet.

M

This botany professor was an agreeable man, with the gentle manner characteristic of many Portuguese, and was glad to find another soil-and-tree-conservation crank. We discussed various problems of the kind, and I mentioned the misdeeds of goats in destroying young trees. It was evidently a painful topic, for he raised his hands to heaven in protest and in a voice of bitterest despair groaned rather than said:

"Ah, Monsieur, les chèvres, les chèvres!"

At my request he showed me the university botanic garden, which was small and not very interesting. I supposed he noticed my disappointment, for he said:

"Why do you bother to see a little garden like this when at Kew you have the finest collection in the world?"

I got out of it by saying—what is perfectly true—that we had nothing in England to compare with the superb collection of exotic trees planted by the monks at Bussaco from seeds and cuttings brought by the great Portuguese explorers. I might have said that because I had read Shakespeare was no reason for neglecting Camões. As a matter of fact I was reading Camões with a university student with the great name of Magalhães (Magellan). He had one of the gentlest and sweetest natures I have ever known, and spoke his language so that it sounded really sonorous and beautiful, and not the nasal squeak Borrow said it is. He was a born teacher, but though he taught me to read Portuguese, he didn't succeed in teaching me to speak more than the indispensable smattering of a tourist.

At various times I explored every province of Portugal by car, including the comparatively little visited Alemtajo and Algarve. The one possible stop-off in the wild country between Lisbon and the south coast is at Setubal, where the only inn was then run by a portly German. I was slightly acquainted with Lloyd's agent there, an Englishman of course, and he came to see me after dinner. We were joined by the landlord, and in the course of conversation he suddenly became very truculent and began threatening another war. "This time it vill be vimmin and little shildrens too," he kept repeating with great satisfaction. I thought nothing of it at the time, for he had evidently been exploring a wine-flask, but I have thought of it since.

In general it is true to say that as you go north in Portugal, the country becomes more beautiful, the people gayer and less crossed with Negro genes, and the peasant costumes brighter. The one exception is Leiria, where on Sundays the women wear a beautiful mediæval costume with a wimple, closely resembling that on the effigy of Queen Eleanor of Castile in Westminster Abbey. As they ride along on their little trotting donkeys (which are well treated in Portugal) you feel as if by some accident you had wandered into the female portion of the Canterbury pilgrimage. There are places in Portugal where I could live very happily, which I never felt would be the case in Spain. I very nearly bought the famous Cork Convent at Cintra, which was going at a ridiculously cheap price. Fortunately I remembered in time that the place owes its name to the fact that the walls were so cold and damp the monks had to cover them with cork. Cintra is spectacular, but its reputation is exaggerated. There are many more beautiful places on the side roads of Portugal. Naturally Byron could write his mother truthfully that it was the most beautiful place he had seen in Europe—it was the first place he saw after leaving the British Isles.

Forty thousand British soldiers were buried in the Peninsula during the war against Napoleon, yet in all my wanderings the only memorials to them I remember to have seen are the tomb of Sir John Moore at Coruña and a memorial in Coimbra Cathedral to a junior officer who was a friend of Byron. There are battle memorials at Torres Vedras and Bussaco, but none that I remember in Spain.

I last crossed the frontier from Spain into France late in May 1936. We left rather more hurriedly than we had intended, but you must remember that I was responsible for the safety of two women and for Hal, who could still barely walk a hundred yards and had to rest every few days. There were certain disquieting signs to be noticed. Between Cadiz and Seville and in other parts of Andalusia we passed large busloads of men in uniform with rifles. At Cordoba I saw men loaded with mediæval fetters under military escort. I was told they were "criminals," but something else seemed to tell me their crime was rightism. Beyond Cordoba we were held up by quasi-military patrols, and at Escorial I read a prominent member of the Cortes had been assassinated. When members of legislative bodies take to lethal weapons or are the victims of them, honest people should look to themselves. I had a brief conference with Hal, and said, how about stepping on the gas? And Hal said, step on it.

I have pushed on in time, to complete these brief notes on the Peninsula, and must now go back to June 1934. In the early spring of that year I turned in the completed manuscript of my fourth novel, *Women Must Work*. I had at different times received letters from my publishers in Buda-Pest, Prague, and Warsaw (where my earlier novels were then coming out), asking me to visit those cities, and be entertained and meet various people who wanted to know me. I have long disliked literary parties, and indeed offended my old friend Davray by refusing to attend a literary banquet in Paris arranged by him in my honour. But this looked like a unique opportunity of seeing something of countries whose language I didn't intend to try to learn. Moreover, I had "blocked" royalty accounts in Hungary and Poland; and even thought I might push on to Moscow and spend some of the thousands of roubles standing to my account in the U.S.S.R. When my agent annually sent me a note of these various "blocked" credits in various parts of Europe, I used to wish I had gone into the armament business, in which payment is always prompt and in cash.

I don't know if you have observed it, but whenever you ask some expert what is the best time to visit any European country, the invariable answer is: "Oh, May and June of course." This is doubtless true, but one can't be all over Europe simultaneously. By way of putting in the intervening time till June pleasantly I shipped a car from London to Lisbon, and spent the best part of two months pottering about Portugal, Spain, and France. I went through Switzerland rather more rapidly, and early in June crossed into Austria on the way to Vienna and Buda-Pest.

I never got there. On a level straight piece of road between Feldkirch and Bludenz I saw a small car coming towards me at a furious speed. At about a hundred yards' distance from my car, it skidded, and rushed towards me swaying more and more violently from side to side. I stopped dead, hoping it would either upset or sweep by me on an outward swing. But no, it smashed sideways into the front of my car. I saw two people hurled out apparently dead from the wrecked car, and of course mine got a frightful jolt which hurled us first backwards and then forwards. As I recovered from the shock I heard a dripping sound, and instantly thought of fire from the gasoline tank. I shouted to my companion to jump, and scuttled out myself, only to fall helplessly on the ground. The jolt forward had broken my knee-cap against the ignition-key, and my companion's forehead was badly cut by the mirror. Otherwise we were quite unhurt.

I felt very cross when I saw the nose of my nice American car bashed in, for I had driven tens of thousands of miles in England and on the Continent and had an absolutely clean record, except for an altercation with a cop in Munich who tried to give me a ticket for passing a tram when he had let the

German car I was following pass without comment. In discharge of my motoring record, I want to say that the Austrian who ran into me had been warned by the police before this for furious driving and only the day before for going out with dangerously worn tires. He got six weeks in gaol, and his insurance company paid me over $2000 compensation—a large sum for Austria.

I didn't realise at first that my knee was broken; I thought it was merely one of those agonising cracks one can give the knee-cap, and that I'd sit still a minute. A man in short leather trousers and white stockings (the symbol of the underground Austrian Nazi movement, though I didn't know it then) ran up and asked if we were badly hurt. We said, no, and that he should look after the others. It occurred to me I might do something, but as I tried to rise my knee-cap parted into two in the most surprising and unpleasant way, and I perceived that this trifling injury made me absolutely helpless. A pretty end to my Lisbon to Warsaw trip and to prospects of eating goulash with Hungarian poets.

A broken knee-cap is a very tedious fracture. I was six or eight weeks in the Feldkirch Spital, which was run by hardworking though not very skilled nuns. Surgeons in London and New York, who afterwards examined my knee, said the incision was about twenty years out of date; so the famed Austrian medical skill evidently hadn't penetrated to the Vorarlberg. They gave me a shot of morphia the first night, and told me to sleep. As the Spital was built on a narrow plot of land between the main railway line and the main road, that wasn't very feasible. Every time I was dropping off to sleep something woke me up, and, what with the morphia and the slight fever and shock, I became a little delirious. Opposite my bed were two lurid religious oleographs, one of Mary with seven swords in her bosom, and the other of Jesus with the sacred heart fully visible in his chest, and the letters INRI. These got into my fever dreams, and I thought I heard an Irish voice constantly saying: "I Niver Read Innything, I Niver Read Innything." A singular nightmare.

Twice a day a nun stood in the corridor and chanted a rhymed German prayer, rather pretty and touching. Twice a day I was visited by the surgeon, accompanied by two internes, who looked and indeed were extremely stupid men. (The Spital charitably harboured several *Dorftrottels,* village idiots, who wandered around harmlessly, and I used to wonder if a couple might have got on the staff by mistake.) The surgeon, whose medical genius wasn't vast, made up for it by great breeziness of manner. He came charging into the room like a man late for the office (he nearly always was late), cheerfully shouting: *"Wie gehts, Herr Aldington?"* This was followed by a number of stereotyped questions about my leg, and no matter how I varied the replies his comment was always: *"Gut, sehr gut!"* Then he would beam with smiles and charge away, shouting over his shoulder: *"Gut essen, gut trinken, gut schlaffen! Auf wiedersehen, Herr Aldington!"*

These nuns were of the Order of St. Vincent de Paul, a Frenchman, whose life I had read. He was enslaved by Tunisian pirates in the 17th century, converted his captor, and escaped to France, where he spent the rest of his life in organising charities. My nuns were uneducated peasants, very hardworked, but cheerful and kindly. The night Sister (who, by the way, was never relieved the whole time I was there) struck me as being more intelligent than the others. I soon found out why. She was an Italian from Brixen (Bressanone) in Sud-Tirol, and was quite excited when she discovered I could talk some Italian and that I had actually stayed at the famous Elephant Inn at Brixen—a very snob establishment which displays an immense wooden board with the names of kings and emperors it has harboured, painted in gold letters. Thereafter, this Sister would make a pretext every evening to come in and gossip in her native tongue, which she had not spoken for twenty years.

One evening by way of entertaining her I discussed the life and virtues of St. Vincent, and then described some of the glories of the churches in Rome, which she had never seen. The next morning I was surprised by a visit from the Mother Superior, accompanied by two nuns who stood behind her with their hands folded under their long black sleeves, and their eyes fixed on me in a gaze of expectancy which perplexed me greatly. At last the clue was revealed. Was she not right in thinking I was a Catholic? Such expectancy on those three childish faces! I felt quite sorry at having to undeceive her. Disappointed, she lingered on—how then did it happen, she asked, that I knew about their sacred founder and had visited so many churches, seen so many holy relics? That was a poser. How could I explain to her that there are some people who are intellectually and æsthetically curious about all sects and religions, without belonging to any? How could I tell her that I should have been much more interested if she had been a priestess of Isis, for she might have cleared up many perplexed points in that venerable and mysterious religion? I didn't attempt it; and we separated on this misunderstanding with expressions of mutual regard.

Towards the end of my incarceration two distinguished visitors—or rather three—came to Feldkirch. Frere and his wife, Pat Wallace, diverged from their annual trip from London to the Riviera on the frivolous pretext of seeing me, though actually they only wanted to eat wild strawberries and buy Tirolese costumes. Long after my monastic establishment was supposed to be asleep, we roused its echoes with such wild laughter that I feared we should all be thrown out, as we had been from the Bateau Ivre. No sooner had they left than Dollfuss turned up, not to see me, but to address the inhabitants of Feldkirch in the open air. I heard him yapping away into amplifiers for over an hour. I was too far off to hear what he said, but one thing struck me; the applause, which came at regular intervals, seemed strangely lacking in enthusiasm and spontaneity. Each round sounded exactly like that loud but carefully measured applause we give a tedious speaker when at last he relieves us by sitting down.

Owing to the obsolescent treatment of my friend Dr. Gutessen-Guttrinken, I emerged from the Spital with my fracture imperfectly healed and a leg as stiff as a poker. And after some weeks of trying to sleep between a railway and a main road, I yearned for silence and solitude. Accordingly I was moved to the Ardetzenburgerhof on a hill outside Feldkirch. This was a pretty place, but after two weeks I was discouraged to find that I couldn't yet walk twenty yards, and by having my sleep dispelled by nocturnal revellers. Eventually the right place was found at Fontanella, a tiny hamlet of Austrian chalets, at 6000 feet, at the end of a long valley which was a cul-de-sac except for mountaineers. It was a lovely place, and I had a magnificent view across a deep Alpine valley with a river at the bottom to the vast wooded slopes of high mountains opposite. We lodged at an annexe to the Gasthaus, and there bit by bit I progressed from crutches to walking sticks and began to hobble around with extreme caution.

I was passing the Gasthaus one day when a man rushed out in great excitement and told me Dollfuss had been murdered and that there was a Nazi uprising. This was pleasant news for a helpless crock who was not precisely *persona grata* with the swastika boys—in Germany my books had been suppressed. A little later cables began arriving, some openly telling me to get out at once, others ingeniously worded to give the same hint while apparently having another meaning. In the days of Palmerston I should have felt quite safe—*civis romanus sum*—but I didn't think Mr. Baldwin cut as much ice internationally as that insolent old Whig nobleman. For a few minutes I felt some anxiety, but I had a quite irrational feeling that nothing much was going to happen—yet. As a precaution, I had my car sent up, and waited. In a few days the word *Waffenstillstand* appeared in the newspapers, and the European war was put off.

When I was able to drive again, I filled in one of my gaps in European geography by exploring Alsace and Lorraine, and then as the northern weather deteriorated went back to some of my favourite haunts in the Pyrenees. I hadn't decided what to do for the winter. My accident had stopped all serious work, but at odd times I was writing a long poem and planning a book of essays. Somehow I drifted up to Saint-Emilion, an old wine-growing town near Bordeaux, where all the churches are empty and all the cellars are full. The top vintage of Saint-Emilion is Château Ausone, said to come from vineyards owned in the 4th century by the poet Ausonius. Alas, the available evidence does not support this pleasing story; but Ausonius certainly had a vineyard and it was somewhere near Saint-Emilion, so if the story makes the wine taste better why not believe it?

I had just made up my mind that the best thing to do would be to take a French Riviera villa for the winter, and had decided to start next day for Marseille, when the radio announced another political assassination—this time, M. Barthou and the King of Yugoslavia. I began to feel a little discouraged about Continental Europe; it seemed determined to get itself into violent muddles and disorders. The only thing to do was to return to London for a breather, and spend the winter with London Library books.

On my way up from the coast to London I stopped to lunch with Hal and Etta Glover, who were staying with a friend in Sussex. After lunch I went to get something from the car to show Hal; the path was made of small, very slippery cobbles, my feet shot out from under me, and before I hit the ground I felt the crunch of my knee-cap breaking.

That meant another operation, and more dreary weeks and months of hobbling around. But this time the job was done properly, and the surgeon soon had me out of bed with my leg in one of those steel-and-leather contraptions you see in orthopædists' shop windows. I filled in the long convalescence by writing some essays and completing my poem. It was called *Life Quest*, and I thought it rather a nice poem, about the best thing I'd done in that line. Charles Prentice and Frere thought so too; indeed, Frere liked it so much I gave him the manuscript. But in the literary football scrum it is considered a foul for anybody who writes novels which are read to write poetry as well, and the reviewing umpires blew disapproving whistles.

In its unsystematic way this poem expressed my views—I will not try to dignify them with the term "philosophy"—on the subject of life for life's sake. Far from considering this life as a painful test of worthiness for future lives, we should look on it as a short holiday from nothingness, a unique opportunity to enjoy the singular prerogative of consciousness. Freed from old superstitious terrors and from hopes which are the result of extravagant wishful thinking, we cannot do better than employ our few minutes of existence in poking about our nook of the universe and taking an intelligent interest in all its functionings and productions. If, contrary to my expectations, I find myself before the Supreme Court of the Last Judgment, required to show cause why I should not be cast into hell fire, I shall promptly put in an affidavit to the effect that I tried to make the best of this life and therefore am a fit person to be trusted with another. But I should decline an eternal heaven of do-nothingness and incuriosity. As my old friend Aucassin remarked in the pious middle ages, "Why should we want to go to heaven? Thither go the halt and the lame and the blind, but to hell go all the brave knights and the fair ladies and the jolly clerks."

It was late in the winter of 1934 that I corrected the proofs of *Life Quest;* and having completed that little task I dropped into a line of thought. Though I hadn't many friends in Germany, there were a few I should have liked to read my poem; but their unbroken silence was an only too sinister hint of their fate. It was obvious long before this that the peace had failed to be a peace; now the indications were that Europe was slipping back into barbarism. Unconsciously in boyhood, later on consciously, I had given a lot of energy to the task of trying to fit myself to be a good European—an ideal which is very much older than Nietzsche and without his absurd arrogance. And on that winter evening I perceived with dismay that there might very soon be no Europe in which one might try to be good. The whole conception was being as ruthlessly destroyed as the early Christians destroyed the cosmopolitan Græco-Roman culture. Violent minorities were betraying and murdering all that had dignified their countries. Reluctantly and ruefully I had to admit that there was no longer anywhere in Europe I wanted to live in; and that there was no place for me among intellectual fanatics who were busy labelling themselves leftists and rightists, and who constantly summoned one to stand and deliver on one silly side or the other.

Of course, I was a mugwump; for, as we all know, the mugwump is a bird which sits with its mug on one side of the fence and its wump on the other, and doesn't give a hoot for either party.

When men go sour on you, there is always nature and other men; and though the world shrinks like Balzac's *peau de chagrin,* it is still a respectably large oblate spheroid. It seemed to me that at any rate for the time being I had finished with Europe. After all, from the point of view of the schoolboy looking longingly through a telescope at Calais from the cliffs of Dover,

I hadn't done so badly. I had been in every province of Italy, France, Portugal, and Spain; I knew Paris and Rome as well as I knew London; I had seen Belgium, Switzerland, the Rhine, the Schwarzwald, Bavaria, and Austria. The whole experience, extended over many years, had been of inestimable value. If I never travelled another mile, never read another book in any language, never saw another fine building, statue, or picture, I was rich enough in memories to last the rest of my life.

But I saw no reason why I should abandon my little investigations of our planet, and drop back into the sedentary provincial life of a London *littérateur*, to escape from which I had worked so hard and taken risks. If my colleagues preferred to vegetate between the club, the country cottage, and the usual London round, that was their affair. For me, as on my first long walk, it was: "*Allons, en route!* Afoot and light-hearted we take to the open road."

Reverting instinctively to my "perseveration" (which, you will remember, my authority on Ruskin had warned me was an infallible symptom of manic depressive insanity) I revived another boyish dream. The Amazon. After all, I could speak a little Portuguese, and could learn more. But the more I looked into the matter, the less attractive it seemed. Things had changed since the days of my friend Bates. You either had to accept a conducted tour, or, if you went into the virgin forest, you had to be prepared for strenuous days. I asked nothing better, but my cracked knee still kept me rather more helpless than Falstaff when Prince Hal stole his horse.

As it was winter, North America was temporarily out for two reasons. One slip on a frozen pavement would put me back in a clinic; and, as I had been an invalid for nearly six months, I didn't feel up to meeting people. Then I remembered that I had often thought that the proper way to explore the Western Hemisphere was to come first on the Columbus route. Of course, the West Indies. After going through a number of

books, I decided that Tortola in the Virgin Islands sounded remote and interesting. There was no hotel, only a small guest-
house at the disposal of the Governor or Commissioner. With
the idea of getting an introduction to this potentate, I mentioned the matter to an acquaintance at the Colonial Office; but
as he said he didn't think there were any virgin islands and had
never heard of Tortola, I gave that up. It was odd though not
unprecedented to find a Colonial Office official so indifferent
to the geography of the Empire.

I wanted to find a place where I could stay indefinitely and
re-visit occasionally, and eventually I hit on Tobago. Little has
been written about it, but I gathered it was outside both the
tourist and the hurricane zones—a valuable advantage. I got in
touch with Sir A. Aspinall, of the West India Committee, and
he gave me practical information and letters of introduction.
Early in February I was on board a banana boat, *en route to*
Barbados and Trinidad.

Chapter XXII

ONE of the tentative titles for this book was *Farewell to Europe*, for my intention was to describe the evolution of an insular provincial schoolboy into an adult European, at home in any part of western and central Europe. In the long and diverse history of that continent the wandering student is a familiar character. From the dark ages onwards monks and students from the British Isles wandered over the great pilgrim routes, visiting monasteries, shrines, and universities. Generations of Englishmen made the grand tour in their travelling carriages, and some of them settled more or less permanently in nooks which pleased them. In another epoch and in my own way I followed in their tracks.

Reversing Johnson's dictum, I would say that "seldom any true story is wholly splendid." I did succeed in living the life of a European for a number of years; and I had the satisfaction of seeing my books translated into the languages of ten or a dozen countries, and of knowing they were read not as journalism but as possible contributions to literature. Yet scarcely had these successes been achieved when they began to crumble away under the impact of the public events which are familiar to everybody. In September 1929, when I sat in the Paris café reading the letters and telegrams about *Death of a Hero*, it seemed reasonable to think that I had achieved such ambitions as I possessed. By September 1939 nothing was left.

I feel ashamed of mentioning such personal and selfish trifles against a background of such immense calamity; but if I had allowed that sense of disproportion to weigh on me, this book could not have been written.

This little story might very well end with my departure for the Western world in 1935, for out of that came my decision to spend the rest of my life there. But it would be a little unfair to take leave of any reader who has followed me thus far, from the deck of a banana boat somewhere between Bristol and the Western Isles. I can't gratify the reader with a report of my last dying words and funeral, but I can round the story out a little.

It is a common experience for the human creature to find his emotions and intuitions running prophetically ahead of his conscious mind and what he imagines to be the exercise of free will. In the autumn of 1934, all the way up from Saint-Emilion to Calais, I had a sense of valediction, of saying farewell to France. It was useless for me to tell myself that it was absurd, that I was free to return at any moment I wanted; the feeling persisted. It returned even more persistently on the railway journey from Paddington to Bristol, where my banana *Mayflower* awaited me.

On that February day all England was held by frost and mist and looked inexpressibly dreary. Frieda Lawrence's honest and touching account of her life with Lorenzo had just been published, and all the newspapers carried violent and mendacious onslaughts on the memory of Lawrence. It saddened me to think that the journalistic canaille could still be allowed to misrepresent so vilely and without contradiction the "starry genius of our time." I didn't realise then, as I do now, that this mob hatred was an unconscious tribute to Lawrence's greatness. Both in his life and writings Lawrence had vehemently denied all the values of mechanised living, and this vilification from the robots was part of his glory.

I threw the papers contemptuously aside, and looked from

the train window at the grey cold landscape. The forty miles to Reading were entirely familiar—I had passed up and down that line hundreds of times when I lived in Berkshire. I thought of my cottage under the tall willows by the canal, and wondered who now lived in it, and how it looked without my solid walls of books. Then the train diverged towards Didcot, but through the mist I could easily imagine the summer landscape. As we rushed through Uffington, I could see through the wall of mist the sunlit downs I had so often walked, the great prehistoric earthwork, the White Horse, Wayland Smith's Cave, and the little road winding down the Lambourne valley. And at one moment my heart seemed breaking, and the next I was filled with exultation at the thought of the thousands of miles of ocean and lands to me unknown which lay ahead.

The 18th-century graces of Bath were hidden in mist; and the new docks at Avonmouth, which prolong the old port of Bristol, were cold. I limped very cautiously over the icy puddles to the ship's gangway; and went early to bed, before the ship left port.

To my dismay I discovered that, in spite of my repeated injunctions to the contrary, the shipping office had given me a cabin on a "cruise" ship. Where the passengers for "cruises" come from will always be a mystery, for luckily one never sees them on land. There ought to be a large fleet of *Flying Dutchmen* to keep them permanently at sea. But my crippled leg was a famous alibi, and after a little acrimonious back-chat I managed to evade all the imbecile "amusements"; and was left in peace to enjoy a little nook of the larboard deck I had purchased from the deck steward, and staked out with deck-chairs.

I was enchanted with my foresight in having at once established a temporary reputation for being grumpy, high-hat, and uninteresting; for I have seldom been more tranquilly happy than during the twelve days of that voyage. The Orientals, to whom we conventionally ascribe such fabulous luxury, have also invented pleasures as simple as they are profound. One of these is sometimes a theme for their painters, and is called Watching the Sky. There was a fascination in watching the slow imperceptible changing of the northern sky, seemingly muffled miles deep in grim dark clouds, into the exquisite intense blue of the tropics. As well as the day-to-day changes as we steamed south, there were almost hourly changes in sea and sky from sunrise to sunset, and the night panorama of stars. There was deep satisfaction in submitting to these vast elemental influences, which re-establish the harmony and proportion we lose in the busy fretfulness of human life. I cannot help believing that in such experiences there are a health and balance of the spirit denied to all forms of mysticism.

Tobago turned out to be a lucky dip in Fortune's bag. I managed to rent an old plantation house, six hundred feet up, with a tremendous vista over steeply sloping country to the Caribbean Sea. A wide gallery occupied the whole front of the house, and near one corner grew a vast saman tree which nourished a whole garden of curious parasitic plants and was always lively with tropical birds. Except for the car of an occasional visitor and the infrequent mails, there was no sound or contact from the human world. For days the only sounds were the calls of birds and insects, the sough of the wind, and the music of a passing shower which began like a long-drawn sigh increasing to a hiss and sudden sharp patter on the roof, and then died away distantly in another sigh.

In a screened nook of this gallery I wrote nearly all the essays contained in *Artifex,* and made an anthology of the most beautiful prose passages from Lawrence's books. There are two or three pieces about Tobago in *Artifex,* and I don't want to repeat what I said in them. I soon fell into the easy rhythm of life in the tropics, varied only by excursions about the very beautiful island and bathing picnics, where I swam in a sea as clear and warm as the Mediterranean. But the most valuable part of that three or four months' experience was the living so close to nature, in an exuberant phase which was new to me.

"Isn't it very quiet up here?" a chance tourist visitor asked.

"Beautifully quiet!" I said enthusiastically; and then, seeing the astonishment on her face, realised that for some people "quiet" is synonymous not with happiness but with dullness.

My two books were finished in a long spurt of concentration, and then I idled away some days or weeks, with no mental effort beyond reading a few modern books in English. I didn't want to write anything; I felt as if I should never want to write again. . . . And then suddenly I became aware of a danger lurking in this seductive life of the tropics. It was delightful, rapturous even, to live so natural a rhythm; but it was nature in the mood of the Lotus-Eaters. On arrival I had noticed with surprise the languor of some of the old-established whites (Negroes are seldom energetic anywhere), and I saw, or thought I saw, that I was just beginning to go the same way.

Much could be said in defence of such an abdication. Respectable philosophers had described such a condition as the highest good. The poets abounded in apposite quotations. Why should one be ever climbing up a climbing wave? Why not daff the world aside, and bid it pass? Having come unto these yellow sands, why not stay there? What was wrong with the *obliviscendus meorum et oblitus illis?* In Tobago living was cheap, pleasant, and supremely irresponsible. That word "irresponsible" brought me up with a jerk. I didn't like to think I might deserve it. Something decisive had to be done, some potent counter-influence was indicated.

That afternoon I booked passage to New York by radiogram from the radio station at Scarborough, the "capital" of Tobago. I was sorry to go, but I was far more glad to think that at last I was to see the United States.

The usual method for a foreign author to see America is to do it at the expense of his hosts by lecturing across the country. I was ambitious of holding the record as the only British author who had never made a lecture tour of America; and therefore had invariably turned down all proposals to that effect. Two rather important factors seem to be forgotten by those who so blithely accept these engagements: they themselves are usually incompetent lecturers, and the audiences they propose to address are accustomed to hear trained speakers. All I had done in that line was to read papers to university clubs and societies, which is not lecturing. Moreover, in my time I had drawn a good deal of money from America in fees and royalties, and it seemed only proper that I should pay my own way.

It seems to me that the lecture-tourist gets a very lop-sided view of America. He arrives in New York, as green as a cabbage, and is met at the dock by his agent and publisher. He is immediately plunged into a series of parties, gives one or two lectures in New York, and then sets off on his tour. He goes from one large town to another, meeting hundreds of very amiable people, swallowing more cocktails than are good for him, and growing more and more weary. He boards his return ship with a hangover and the impression that America consists of thousands of miles of railways, huge industrial towns, and one long Mad Hatter's cocktail party. He then proceeds to write a series of articles or a book, entitled *My American Tour*. All this is referred to by people who should know better as spreading the light of culture and fostering international goodwill.

I have a theory to account for the amazing appetite for lectures and the extreme tolerance of incompetent foreigners. May it not be a survival of the days when the whole nation went regularly to church, and parsons preached incessantly and at great length? However much you might sigh for the glad moment when you would hear: "And lastly, dear brethren," there was spiritual merit to be won by hanging on grimly to the end. Some of this ethical prestige has been transferred to any activity which can be labelled "educative," and a vague cultural merit is won by vainly trying to hear what the spectacled denizen of Bloomsbury is mumbling on the platform. If that explanation is rejected, I see nothing for it but to call in the psycho-analysts.

The mischief of these superficial *My Tour of America* articles and books lies in the fact that the author has no means of knowing whether what he sees is exceptional or typical, and constantly falsifies his picture by representing something accidental as general. Oddly enough, on my first day in New York I noticed three or four little scenes which could very easily have been strung together into an article of a not very flattering kind. In all the time I have since spent in New York not one of these episodes has ever been repeated. In that experience I recognize the material of many a first chapter of *My American Tour* books.

What I have just been saying should explain the reluctance I feel to tell the world about America. I think that is better left to people who really know something about the subject. On that first visit to America I followed a rough scheme which experience has made me think is sensible when living in a country for the first time. I think one should avoid trying to see too much, for that only leads to a confusion of impressions and dim memories. It is better to spend a month or so in a big town, and then stay in one country place, making excursions on foot and by car until the area becomes familiar. While such an experience is naturally limited, it is more authentic and valuable than chasing around a continent. You get some idea of what living in the community would be.

In New York I made the acquaintance of Dr. Bertrand Eskell, who appeared to have read my books, and through his kindness I was able to rent exactly the sort of house I should have chosen myself in a beautiful piece of country on the Connecticut River. In later years I have explored some of northern New England, and freely admit that it is wilder and more dramatic, with a grander beauty of mountain and forest and lake. But I liked that nook of Connecticut so well that I was very happy to return to it.

There, under the crystal-blue autumn sky, when the woods are aflame with colour and the light cold wind brings the first wild duck from Canada, I made up my mind that henceforth I would make my headquarters in America. So far from feeling alien, as I had been repeatedly warned by well-wishers, I felt very much at home, perhaps because of some experience in moving about the world. Twice the complications of life took me back to Europe for rather long periods, one of these being my second marriage and the birth of my daughter about eighteen months later; but at the third attempt I succeeded in getting permanently free from European entanglements.

The trail which in the course of many years has led me from the coast of Kent to the banks of the Connecticut River has been long and devious, with many unexpected turns and some checks and misfortunes, but it has been interesting, and, I should say, upon the whole both fortunate and happy. I have not yet succeeded in writing either a poem or a prose book which satisfied me entirely, but it is fun to go on trying. I can say truthfully that during approximately half a century of infesting this planet I have very seldom indeed been bored; and that is as good as any other definition of success in life.